Everyman News

University of Missouri Press   Columbia and London

Everyman News

By Michele Weldon

The Changing American Front Page

Library of Congress Cataloging-in-Publication Data

Weldon, Michele.
    Everyman news : the changing American front page / by Michele Weldon.
        p. cm.
    Includes bibliographical references and index.
    Summary: "Examines how newspapers have changed over the past few
years, becoming story papers. Comparing 850 stories, story approaches, and
unofficial sourcing in twenty American newspapers from 2001 and 2004,
Weldon reveals a shift toward features over hard news, along with an increase
in anecdotal or humanistic approaches to all stories"—Provided by publisher.
    ISBN 978-0-8262-1777-6 (alk. paper)
    1. Feature stories—United States—History—21st century.   2. American
newspapers—Sections, columns, etc.—Front pages.   I. Title.
    PN4888.F43W45   2007
    070.4'40973090511—dc22   2007037313

♾ This paper meets the requirements of the
American National Standard for Permanence of Paper
for Printed Library Materials, Z39.48, 1984.

Designer: Jennifer Cropp
Typesetter: BookComp, Inc.
Printer and binder: Thomson-Shore, Inc.
Typefaces: Palatino, BodoniAnt, GoudyWtc

To Weldon, Brendan, and Colin,
whose stories make me whole

Contents

We're hard-wired to understand human experience in terms of story.

—Jack Hart, *Oregonian*, 2004

Acknowledgments

You never write alone. My colleagues at Northwestern University's Medill School, including John Lavine, Michele Bitoun, Mary Nesbitt, and Loren Ghiglione, were supportive and instrumental in graciously allowing me the time and space to write and research. They also offered valuable feedback along the way. My valiant writing group comrades, Elizabeth Berg, Veronica Chapa, Nancy Drew Horan, and Pam Todd, were weekly lifelines to inspiration, sanity, and creativity. They are remarkable editors, cheerleaders, and friends. Lisa Lauren is a cherished ally who keeps me smiling.

My assistants on the project, including Jessica Young, Nicole Duarte, Brian Sabin, Natasha Rotstein, Cheryl Ricci, Shana Sager, Claire Tyree, and Treacy Weldon, were heroic with details and research. Jessica Saffold was enormously helpful during the launch of the project.

I would also like to thank the following colleagues, experts, and journalists who agreed to be interviewed and offered their insight: David Abrahamson, Rosemary Armao, Tom Callinan, Christopher Daly, Bruce deSilva, Rick Edmonds, Dawn Fallik, Doug Foster, Jon Franklin, Ken Fuson, Dan Gillmor, Walt Harrington, Jack Hart, Laurie Hertzel, Barb Iverson, Steve James, Alex Kotlowitz, Michele Lowe, Dan McAdams, David Mindich, Pamela Moreland, Mary Nesbitt, Lisa Parks, James Pennebaker, Jennifer Pozner, Hazel Reinhardt, Jack Rosenberry, Christopher Scanlan, Roland Schatz, Christine Spolar, Brian Stelter, James Upshaw, Linda Wertheimer, Keven Willey, Bruce Williams, and Barbie Zelizer.

My sisters and brothers—Mary Pat, Maureen, Bill, Madeleine, and Paul—are remarkable reminders that no matter what I attempt in my life professionally or personally, they support me unconditionally with laughter and tenderness. I consider myself blessed beyond measure to have the welcomed love, kindness, and companionship—as well as brilliant editing—of Lewis Tyree.

The energetic love of my sons Weldon, Brendan, and Colin makes me feel invincible. It is because of them and for them that I feel I can do it all.

Everyman News

Everyman and Everywoman on the Front Page

There is a simple way to package information that, under the right circumstances, can make it irresistible.

—Malcolm Gladwell, *The Tipping Point*

✳ The billboard towering above the section of I-94 East heading from Milwaukee to Chicago read, "What's Your Story?" and featured a close-up photo of a jacketed torso from chest to waist. At the top of the billboard in mid-December 2006 was the banner logo of the *Milwaukee Journal Sentinel*. A decade ago, would a newspaper billboard have posed the same question? Would a reader have cared enough to answer? And if a reporter had listened, chances are the story would not have ended up on the front page. Today it just might. Newspapers want your story. Newspapers have become story papers.

The front page is a peculiar product at once permanent and ephemeral. Nothing is as old as yesterday's news, and nothing lasts longer in a reader's memory or a reporter's portfolio than front-page news. The type of news delivered in print today is dramatically different from that available even as recently as the start of the twenty-first century. The newspaper has become a portal for a stylized slow dance of information, not for the quick bursts of digests and info-nuggets a reader can get more quickly online or from broadcast. Stories in newsprint have shifted into a more deliberate choreography of information, reaction, and participation. They are everyman stories.

"A newspaper is both a record and a reflection of its times," *Washington Post* executive editor Leonard Downie Jr. wrote in the introduction to *The Century: History as It Happened on the Front Page of the Capital's Newspaper*.[1]

In the one hundred years of front pages included in the *Post*'s commemorative book, feature stories were naturally part of the mix—such as the arrival of the Beatles in the U.S. on February 12, 1964, the 1906 wedding of Alice Roosevelt, and the 1981 wedding of Prince Charles to Lady Diana Spencer. But features were not the mainstay of print news content as they are today. In this book I examine distinct changes in content, style, and sourcing in twenty American newspapers in the brief interlude from 2001 to 2004. I explore several cultural and economic reasons why the newspaper is so sharply different than even a decade earlier. This important conversation is superficially about media and more deeply about who we are as an audience of media.

The front page not only reflects the economic climate of the newspaper industry, it mirrors the editorial instincts of newspaper ownership and staff and also attempts to meet the needs and desires of readers and ultimately society. It is difficult to separate the business of newspapers from the real-life impact of newspapers on consumers; it is all one swirling cultural mosaic of story, fact, and appetite. My goal is to spark debate and to examine more closely why and how daily print news has so drastically in recent years altered the practices of daily journalists and the expectations of readers.

"Changes in media content are the most obvious effect of changes in the media industry," David Croteau and William Hoynes wrote in their 2006 book, *The Business of Media*. "Through entertainment, arts, and public affairs programming, the media allow us to learn about the history, culture, and experiences of people different from ourselves, as well as reflecting our own interests and identity in their images and content." The content of newspapers has been transformed by a shifting sensibility of what kind of story readers want when a stupefying avalanche of information is accessible, where that information is accessed and why. "If we accept that the media influence society (and are in turn influenced by it), then we can understand how significant changes in media structure and practices can alter not only media content but also the nature of the media's influence on society," Croteau and Hoynes wrote.[2]

The changes I discuss in this book mark the heralding of what I call everyman news. The term is intended as nonsexist. I could have dubbed the genre "everyman and everywoman news," but it is not as simple to say or remember. The trend toward this brand of democratic storytelling suits well the journalists, readers, and the broader American society at the beginning of the twenty-first century in an environment that reveres the individual's contribution to media. After eighty years of nominating global influence-makers for Person of the Year, *Time* Magazine in 2006 nominated "you" "for seizing the reins of the global media, for founding and framing the new digital democracy, for working for nothing and beating the pros at their own game. . . . But look at 2006 through a different lens and you'll see another story, one that isn't about conflict or great men. It's a story about community and collaboration on a scale never seen before."[3]

Everyman stories are about inclusion and a humanistic approach to the reporting of current events, not gender. They are about a society leaning toward personal storytelling, away from a reliance on factoids and news bullets. The kind of story in abundance now is as much about our tolerance—and desire—for the nonfiltered ramblings on youtube.com, as it is the expectation that the newspaper will speak to us as friend, not as civics instructor. We want to tell the newspaper our story and tell it well. "I think that's what is going to end up happening when it all shakes down," said Rick Edmonds of the Poynter Institute. "One of the differentiated products of the print paper can be the well-crafted story."[4]

Who Cares about Newspapers?

Even with so many other competing and more urgent bearers of digital and interactive daily news, millions of us loyally scan newspaper headlines looking for a summary of where we stand in the world now. We look for insight and wisdom, photos of someone we know, stories about people we wish we knew, or details about events and people we could have never known otherwise. We seek comfort, answers, and escape within the personal stories embedded in the breaking news. Many of us baby boomers consider the tactile experience of reading the newspaper an enjoyable form of learning, of keeping up with the neighborhood and the world literally within our reach. How the stories are told and who participates in the telling affect us and influence our beliefs and attitudes.

"There is a growing lack of interest in nuts and bolts, city council meeting kinds of stories, which were the kind I wrote when I was a reporter 35 years ago," Edmonds said. "Together with local trends, more features make the front pages."[5] Newspapers have moved from a model of distributing information labeled "news" to a forum for the sharing of personal experiences, anecdotes, and responses to events considered newsworthy. It marks a change from the practice of pushing official information into the paper to the trend of pulling information up from the grass roots and placing it in prominence in the newspaper. Some view the shift as economically based. James T. Hamilton wrote in 2005, "Models that explore how the number of competitors can change the content of news focus on the trade-off of breadth versus depth, the herding instincts in coverage among journalists, the impact of ownership on program duplication, and the race to the bottom in quality sections. The likely impact of each of these effects on a given media market is an empirical question."[6]

On December 14, 2006, an email from Insidenytimes.com announced the ten most-read articles on nytimes.com. Nine of the stories were features, and all of the stories had been shoveled to the website from the print version.

A news story by Michael R. Gordon and David S. Cloud on the Donald Rumsfeld memo was the exception to the feature rule. The stories included Deborah Sontag's update on Jose Padilla, an analysis of the Iraq outlooks of James A. Baker and Condoleezza Rice, the discovery of an ancient computer, a look at gender identification for young boys and girls, the politics of homosexuality in the Arab world, heading off to college as a student with mental illness, analysis of the 2008 Democratic nomination contest, speculation on the prospects of Mel Gibson winning an Oscar, and a first-person feature on drinking alcohol during pregnancy.[7]

All of these stories were well reported and written in feature style, not played as traditional hard news. And these were the stories readers wanted most—stories distinctly different from the kinds of straight, hard-news stories offered on the front page for at least a generation.

The newspapers I grew up reading in the late '60s and throughout the '70s—the *Chicago Tribune, Chicago Daily News, Chicago Today, Chicago Sun-Times* and the Sunday *New York Times*—most often, if not exclusively, reserved the terrain of the front sections for hard news. They were the breaking stories of plane crashes and fires, presidential announcements and tax cuts. The stories on A1 were a mix of national, international, and local news, with the information flowing from the top down in Moses-from-the-mountaintop style. Like most newspapers around the country, the feature sections carried the human-interest stories. Most front pages today house just those kinds of stories—features, anecdotal beginnings to news, and a wider inclusion of citizen voices as sources.

Who Am I to Write This?

My own newspaper story is a corny one; early on I was both a news consumer and news producer. I inherited my older sister Madeleine's newspaper, the *Juvenile Journal,* when I turned ten and she turned too cool to be bothered. I wrote, edited, illustrated, and copied the monthly until I hit high school. Beginning my freshman year, I wrote teen features for twenty-five dollars each for the local Pioneer Press weekly, the *Oak Leaves.*

In the thirty years since then, for the hundreds of features I have written for newspapers and magazines, I was always hungry for the precise anecdote to personify a trend or for the proper detail to summarize a life. As I began to research this book, I instinctively believed that the kinds of feature stories I have written—trends, profiles, columns, essays, reaction stories—were being deliberately placed on front pages now more than ever.

In 1975 I was a freshman at the Medill School of Journalism at Northwestern University, where we were all told unequivocally to aspire to the *New York Times* national desk. I started writing for the *Daily Northwestern*, and two years later I was editor of the weekly features sections, Midweek and TGIF. We had a humble saying on one batch of *Daily* T-shirts we thought to be quite clever: "Yesterday's news tomorrow." It summed up how we approached the news as full-time students and how quickly we could get it out to our readers.

Today daily print newspapers are still behind their own companion websites with breaking news and developing stories. They also often trail blogs, vlogs, podcasts, television, and radio broadcasts in their delivery of updates and the latest information available. After graduate school in journalism at Northwestern in 1979, I began working in staff editing and writing positions first in consumer and trade magazines, then on a daily newspaper. Eventually I freelanced for magazines, newspapers, and online outlets as well as radio.

My first job was as managing editor at *North Shore* magazine in the suburbs of Chicago. Later I began reporting and writing business news at *ADWEEK* magazine, a testy and spirited competitor to the industry leader a few blocks away, *Advertising Age*. I later moved to Fairchild Publications as a Midwest market editor. During those three years, I freelanced regularly for the *Chicago Sun-Times* and other local and national magazines, writing features and profiles. In 1984 I was recruited as a feature writer by the *Dallas Times Herald*, then owned by Times-Mirror. The news side people called us "feature creatures." Sometimes the editor-in-chief assigned me features that ran on the front page, but mostly my stories ran in the feature sections and weekly magazine, where everyone assumed features belonged.

In 1989, after the birth of my first son, I moved with my family back to the Midwest and became a regular freelance contributor for the *Chicago Tribune*. Until 2003 I freelanced, writing essays, business columns, and opinion pieces for the features sections Style, TempoWoman, and later Womanews. I also wrote essays and op-ed pieces for newspapers such as the *Los Angeles Times* and *Newsday*. In 1995 I turned to teaching journalism as an adjunct in the graduate program at Medill in addition to freelance work. My first book was a memoir published in 1999, *I Closed My Eyes*. Two years later I wrote *Writing to Save Your Life*, a book based on writing workshops I gave in Chicago and around the country beginning in 1999. From the eager participants I learned there is a huge appetite among amateurs as well as professional writers to sharpen the editorial tools necessary to write personal stories.

In my newspaper career, I never chased the fires or covered the wars; I wrote features. Once in Dallas in 1986, I covered a plane crash as a freelance stringer for the *New York Times*. I stayed on the story for two days until a staff writer from the Houston bureau arrived to take over. The hundreds of stories I wrote for the *Chicago Tribune* were non-news. I am a writer and educator of journalism, passionate about the craft of writing and the process of reporting about news and culture. I am not a statistician, historian, sociologist, economist, or media business expert. I am intrigued personally and professionally by the changes in newspapers that had been gradual over the years but then shifted in the last handful to become quite dramatic.

Why a Book on Newspapers Now?

Newspapers may be the AMC Gremlin of the information landscape. The subcompact car seemed to dominate American highways in the 1970s, but it's not likely you will see one today parked next to a Cadillac Escalade.[8] Newspapers have been hurt by "socioeconomic trends such as decreasing penetration, increasing costs, readers' moving to the suburbs and getting the news on the radio while driving to work, less homogenized consumer tastes' challenging mass advertising, and less interest in print products among the younger segments of the population," wrote Pablo Boczkowski in his 2005 book, *Digitizing the News*.[9] The response to these economic realities has been a narratization of news told through the lens of everyman. It is this belief that prompted my look at front pages.

"No study of newspaper content is complete without an analysis of the front page," the academic Orland Kay Armstrong wrote in 1926. "By the front page a newspaper is judged, and rightly so. The tone of the front page is a fairly accurate criterion of the whole paper," Armstrong continued.[10] I agree. With the onslaught of so many distracting and seductive media options, this is a time of profound transition for newspapers struggling to make an honored, traditional form of information delivery relevant and separate from its competing media cousins.

Some say the everyman news trend may not be the best thing for newspapers. "Bottom-line pressure usually steers media content away from serious substance that challenges people, to light entertainment that is familiar and comforting," Croteau and Hoynes wrote. This creates the dynamic tension of search for profits against the service to the public interest. "Homogenization can be the unintentional outcome of companies minimizing risk and maximizing profits. . . . The frequent result is very little innovation and a great deal of imitation."[11]

In Geneva Overholser's 2006 tome, *On Behalf of Journalism: A Manifesto for Change,* she wrote that such deep change in the economic landscape of newspapers has both stymied innovation and induced sameness. "As eyeballs and advertisers stage a mass migration onto new digital territories, the addictive grip of the profits that old media have trained Wall Street to expect has kept newsrooms from anything but grudging and belated forays to the new frontier."[12]

To secure their position in a constantly disrupted media environment, newspapers have been redefined, and they continue to reshape themselves. Editors and writers are searching for ways to make the front pages as fresh and effective as possible for readers. It may be that the next step for newspapers is to transfer the concept of everyman news in print to another format completely. "There is room for newspapers in the nonmonopoly environment of the newspaper future," Philip Meyer wrote in *The Vanishing Newspaper.*[13] It is a race to be relevant, but it is a race that condones sameness.

"As newspaper circulation continues to drop, editors are desperately searching for ways to win back readers, or at least hang on to the ones they still have," Donna Shaw wrote in the June/July 2006 *American Journalism Review (AJR).* She continued, "But since page one is the first thing that readers see, it's getting everything from simple cosmetic changes in some cities to expensive, full-fledged makeovers in others."[14]

The reasoning behind these makeovers can be rooted in a variety of disciplines. Hamilton explored the economic basis for content.

> Economic theories of information suggest a list of problems that may arise in news markets: underconsumption of news about public affairs; inadequate investment in developing or reporting hard news; a bias in broadcasting against high-cost news programs or those that deliver information valued by a minority of eclectic viewers; the tilt toward satisfying the information demands of viewers or readers most valued by advertisers; the need to develop journalists into celebrities to build product brand names; the temptation of conduit owners to favor content they own over offerings of other producers; the possibility that journalist herding will cause reporters to go with the common wisdom rather than developing

their own take on stories; or the potential for conglomerate owners to view news provision solely through the lens of profit maximization.

Hamilton added, "In some cases economic reasoning alone cannot indicate whether the market for content is working well."[15]

The content shift toward everyman news does have roots in economic concerns, from the desire to sustain readership to newsroom budget cuts that disallow investigative or international reporting. But I contend the roots are also strong in the cultural leanings toward a reverence for story for a variety of eclectic and fascinating reasons.

Why Call It Everyman News?

"Everyman" was a 921-line morality play written in 1495 by Flemish writer Peter van Diest and printed in the English version in 1520 by John Scot. According to Wikipedia, the term *everyman* "has come to mean an ordinary individual, with whom the audience or the reader is supposed to be able to identify, and who is often placed in extraordinary circumstances. . . . The everyman character . . . is written so that the reader or audience can imagine themselves in the same situation without having to acquire the knowledge and abilities outside their everyday experience."[16]

Wikipedia itself is an everyman source of information, written and edited by volunteers and unofficial experts. It is a source that receives more than 14,000 hits every second.[17] "Wikipedia offers more than 1 million articles in English—compared with Britannica's 80,000 and Encarta's 4,500—fashioned by more than 20,000 contributors," Chris Anderson wrote in *The Long Tail*.[18] Wikipedia is everyman's encyclopedia, so why not allow its everyman definition to stand?

Everyman was also a 2006 novel by Philip Roth, who has written more than two dozen books commenting on the state of life of the ordinary man. A critic for *Publisher's Weekly* called *Everyman* "an artful yet surprisingly readable treatise on . . . well, on being human and struggling and aging at the beginning of the new century."[19] This could serve as the definition of everyman news on American newspaper front pages.

EveryWoman was a magazine launched in 2000, with a readership of the quarterly of more than six million. Distributed through nurses in health-care offices, the magazine touts itself as "the essential guide to healthy living." Though expert-written, this magazine is filled with anecdotal-heavy information for "a comprehensive evidence-based patient-education source."[20]

In 1999, Karen Gill and Maxine Benson launched EveryWoman in England, touting itself as "the leading network for businesswomen in the U.K."[21]

Everyman.com is the website of the World News Media, which calls itself a presenter and distributor of "news, sport, business and entertainment" with fourteen million users and forty million page views a month. According to the site, which aggregates news stories from more than three hundred media partners around the world offering global and local news, "This empowers our users by providing a wide variety of perspectives and different interpretations of breaking news events."[22] I see all this as validation that everyman is a term with currency and contemporary literary appeal, appropriate for this genre of news.

Connecting the Dots

Two trained student coders and I conducted a content analysis over a period of eight months of more than 850 front-page stories on four dates each in 2001 and 2004. We measured for the incidence of features, feature leads on all front-page stories, and the use of unofficial sources. It is not the final word but an earnest beginning and a thoughtful attempt to measure and understand how newspapers have changed so much so quickly and why.

Chapter 1 is an overview of the arguments for and against everyman journalism, showing evidence of a culture broadly connected to story in a fascinating number of ways. Not all agree it is the best direction to pursue. Chapter 2 shows the results of the study, from the undeniable rise in the number of features on the front page across all the newspapers studied, to the increase of anecdotal or feature leads on all stories, including hard news. The data reveals the rise of unofficial sources in front page stories, demonstrating a more frequent reliance on everyman voices in the newspaper, giving them a larger stake in the presentation of information and a higher news priority.

A look at the research about the newspaper reader's expressed desire for this brand of everyman feature story begins in chapter 3. A shift in reader preferences toward more homespun, accessible news has demanded a different kind of front page. Chapter 4 is a look at how citizen journalism and community-written websites have forced newspapers to alter writing styles and source selection. This "Chicken Little Journalism" and its loud presence helped spawn the rise in the use of unofficial sources. The journalism that swept in after Hurricane Katrina cemented the need for citizen journalism and also for professional journalists to vet the facts and to separate themselves as accurate storytellers from emotionally charged, personally biased citizen journalists.

Blogs also changed the way newspaper stories are written. The casual conversational tone is no longer limited to the content of blogs. The blogger's personal take on the news has changed newspaper style from formal to intimate. Chapter 5 is a look at this trend and how and why blogging cannot be dismissed from any cogent discussion of twenty-first-century journalism. In chapter 6, I examine the post–9/11 contribution to the change in tone, sourcing and story type in American newspapers. The events of that day arguably influenced a new journalistic sensibility that is eulogistic and comforting. It also confirmed journalists' hyperreliance on unofficial sources outside the traditional spheres of power, opinion, and influence.

Writers, editors, and readers have embraced and saluted the appeal of narrative journalism for decades. But more than ever, today's prize-winning newspaper stories tout the elements of everyman journalism. In chapter 7, I look at the evolution of narrative journalism and how it has become the dominating trend in newspapers to a point of near-evangelism by its proponents. A diversifying newsroom can be considered one reason for inclusion of different voices in front page newspaper stories. In Chapter 8, I examine where the industry stands on sourcing and where it needs to go to achieve true democracy of voice in news.

The missing link between journalism and narrative therapy appears to be everyman news, where the deeds and comments of individuals are heralded and sanctified in writing. In chapter 9, I look at how narrative therapy has extended its reach from psychology to the medical fields, psychotherapy, sociology, and now to journalism. In chapter 10 I examine briefly the parallel non-news culture of story marketing and reality TV to understand the context of everyman journalism in a culture that craves the details abundant in the personal stories of individuals. The cry for stories is coming from everywhere—from editors of newspapers to marketers of underwear.

I contend "journalism in emergence" is what we need to label today's era of newsgathering. In chapter 11, the discussion of newspapers and the economic challenges of the industry moves beyond talk of convergence and into the future where delivery mode is less important than content. The commodity is the story and the story is what sells.

Through hard data, interviews, and extensive research of traditional and contemporary literature on journalism, I examined the respected opinions of journalists, academics, and media experts as well as the unofficial voices of bloggers and citizen journalists to come up with some new ideas about why newspapers are the way they are and perhaps where they will go.

I am nearly a half-century old. Mine may be the last generation to regularly rely on printed daily newspapers for information, companionship and story. If my students are a clear indication of the trend, generations X, Y, and Z apparently do not look to the ritual comfort of physical newspapers as did generations earlier.

Many say the trend of sliding circulation, mergers, closings, buyouts, and layoffs seems to imply that print newspapers are headed to a day of rest. I hope not, as I prefer to get my news from the print product in addition to online, though I read several sites several times a day. I look to newspapers for a different kind of approach to current events than I can—at the moment—not always get elsewhere. I am not alone in my love of newspapers. "Nothing can match quality print journalism," said David Meeks, city editor of the *Times-Picayune* of New Orleans in a 2006 speech at Northwestern.[23]

Hear, hear.

When I travel I read the local newspapers because I like to see what and who are important to the local community, even if I am in town only one day. Reading the almost endless stream of blogs about the latest hot topic is entertaining and informative, but I want my paper. I appreciate the newspaper approach—using the time for more interviews, more background, better context. I associate the physical newspaper with a certain kind of story, but I will follow that story to a new medium, even if it is not delivered in print.

I look forward to the Sunday papers even though I watch the round-up pundit shows Sunday mornings. I listen to National Public Radio on my way to and from work and enjoy the longer stories from the field. I watch the morning "news" shows out of one eye as I get dressed and *Nightline* before I go to bed. But I really like the newspaper for a thousand different reasons.

"I think there are many of us who have the old-fashioned idea about a newspaper: that it has a moral responsibility and function to perform in playing up the right sort of thing in the right sort of way," Frank Glass wrote in "The New Journalism" in 1923, an essay excerpted in *The University of Missouri Bulletin.*[24]

Is this trend the right path for newspapers? Almost a century ago, Glass, then editorial director of the *St. Louis Star,* also wrote, "I think there is an increasing tendency to improve the first page, at any rate, in news values—to get the most notable news from the United States and other parts of the world and play it up in an attractive and readable way."[25] The quest for a front page to accurately reflect the times is not a new one. But just how and why American front pages reflect the culture is different today.

Getting It Just Right

At a time when more features are filling the front pages, it seems editors across the country are playing Goldilocks and trying to make sure the product is not too hard and not too soft in its approach, but just right. Perhaps the entire industry needs to find that balance of everyman news and four-bells, five-W's straightforward news.

In a May 5, 2006, email to the *New York Times* newsroom, Rick Berke, assistant managing editor for news, wrote in the item later posted on the blog gawker.com: "We are embarking on a newsroomwide effort to make the best-written newspaper even better written." The first observation, according to Berke, was "We have too many anecdotal leads and often don't think creatively about other approaches." The memo continued: "Stories don't get to the point soon enough, and they run on too long."[26]

Sometimes the hard news is too soft.

In the same email, Berke quoted *Times* editor Bill Keller: "One of the most salient points that people made was that we have this habit of saving the good writing for the features, whereas most of what we do is news stories, and people don't feel the same obligation to write those stories. These are the stories where we really need the writing most. I'd like a lot more unorthodox approaches to conventional news stories."[27]

Sometimes the hard news is too hard. The *New York Times* is not the only newspaper facing this challenge and looking for the formula that is just right. Following the layoffs and budget cuts of 2005, Amanda Bennett, editor and executive vice president of the *Philadelphia Inquirer,* wrote about her paper's transformation, "We agreed to blast Page One out of its decades-old format, remnants of a day when newspapers were still the prime source of yesterday's news."[28]

Downie, *Washington Post* executive editor, said his paper runs fewer stories on the front page on a wider variety of topics, carrying one story per subject on 1A. According to Donna Shaw in *AJR,* Downie said he puts "important hard news stories inside the paper, with analyses, enterprise stories or exclusives out front—part of what Downie calls 'looking for ways to tell stories that are 24 hours old in a new way.'"[29]

Bill Keller, executive editor of the *New York Times,* wrote that "stories about how we live often outweigh stories about what happened yesterday. We think it's OK to include in our front-page portfolio something that is fun, human, or just wonderfully written. It's part science, part art, with a little serendipity."[30]

Not everyone in the industry or outside it who reads the paper feels everyman news is a positive change. Some say the newspaper has gone fluffy, that there is little relevant hard news in its pages anymore, often lit-tle on the front page worth reading; rather there are vapid space-fillers, feel-good stories, and tearjerkers. Critics say the shift to personal story, a narrative approach to news and the inclusion of more unofficial sources means the end of deeper analysis, objective reporting, investigative jour-nalism, and solid digging for expert sourcing. Anyone with a decent quote can be featured on the front page, and it is not news. Newsroom layoffs and budget cuts signal an end to expensive, in-depth reporting and a recurrence of bland sameness in journalism.

"The ubiquity of newspapers is tied to their significant standardization. Despite differences in yesterday's and today's news and advertisements, two recent issues of the same paper tend to look remarkably alike," Bocz-kowski wrote in 2005. "The same happens with different newspapers, to the point that visitors from a foreign country are often able to get a basic sense of the day's news by simply glancing at the local paper's headlines."[31]

The solicitation letter in my mailbox dated July 3, 2006, was pleading and desperate. Signed by Margaret Engel, president of the Alicia Patterson Foundation, and John Hyde, executive director of the Fund for Investiga-tive Journalism, it began, "Our profession is undergoing tough times. It's not too extreme to say that serious journalism is in a crisis. With news out-lets dumbing down their content and devoting more space to features and celebrities, journalists are finding less enthusiasm and fewer resources to support hard-hitting or controversial reporting."

The letter also assured the potential donor, "Our grants keep journalists from quitting the business over frustration in not being able to complete the stories they are compelled to write."[32] Apparently the abundance of features is making the kind of journalism executed by respected journalists such as Seymour Hersh, Zana Briski, and David Burnham impossible to publish.

A similar request arrived almost six months later in my email in-box from Joyce Barnathan, president of the International Center for Journalists, defined as "promoting quality journalism around the world makes a difference—for reporters, for news organizations and for the audiences they serve."[33] I was then instructed to click here to make a tax-deductible donation to help some of the more than twenty thousand journalists who have benefited from the financial help of the center over the past twenty-two years.

I contend print still delivers the enterprising, investigative journalism that changes minds and fates. In scores of daily newspapers around the country every day solid journalism is being committed by newspaper reporters. Leslie Cauley's story in *USA Today* on May 11, 2006, about the National Secu-rity Agency collecting phone records of millions of Americans was followed up in stories for print, broadcast, and online media all over the world, but it originated with one print journalist.[34] Continued investigative coverage of the war in Iraq and the influence of lobbyist funds were stories originated in print. These stories have shifted our understanding of the workings of the Bush administration. International coverage continues to be outstanding at major, elite newspapers as well as in work done by freelancers filing from around the world. Journalists at newspapers across the country doggedly follow leads, pursue their beats, and go with their instincts to uncover wrongdoings, heroism, and injustice.

"We are proud of what The Washington Post and WashingtonPost.com can mean to our community and nationally," Post CEO Donald Graham said in the early December 2006 semiannual meeting to financial analysts and investors in New York.[35]

Everyman news does not have to mean that traditional reporting methods have been abandoned. It means they have evolved to include consideration of many different factors from readers to culture to competition. It is a challenge to combine vital information in a package that is palatable to the reader who may already have received the news online a day earlier. It is a balancing act to judiciously use anecdote and personal story in front-page news. It is every writer's and editor's challenge to make necessary daily information a palatable package for the audience.

Even a key aggregator of news, MSN.com, nods to the power of the decision-making process at print news outlets and attempts to mimic its featurized packaging of stories. In a December 7, 2006, post, Inside MSN editor Jody Brannon wrote: "News writing textbooks help journalists hone their nose for news by listing basic factors. Among them: timeliness, prominence, proximity, impact, conflict, emotions, usefulness, unusualness, human interest, etc. We strive for such a blend on MSN."[36]

It is one of many signs that online content and print newsrooms may no longer be at war but eyeing the same prizes. In early November 2006, another aggregator and search engine king, Google, signed a deal with 50 traditional U.S. newspaper companies to sell advertising space for papers including the Boston Globe, Chicago Tribune, New York Times, Philadelphia Inquirer, and Washington Post. Following an earlier 2006 agreement to archive content from select major newspapers, this signaled "Google has been making moves to embrace the print medium," according to the blog, RedHerring.[37]

Just weeks later on November 20, 2006, Yahoo announced a "strategic partnership"[38] between a consortium of 150 newspapers owned by media companies Belo. Corp, Cox Newspapers Inc., Hearst Newspapers, Journal Register Co., Lee Enterprises, MediaNews Group, and E. W. Scripps Co. According to the webcast available following the conference call announcement, the move enables "newspapers to power Yahoo with deep local, original news, information and advertising" and allow newspaper companies to engage new readers and "drive new and larger audiences to newspaper online sites."[39]

"The bottom line is that these newspaper companies have decided to answer the 'friend or foe' question that all traditional media companies face regarding online players," Reuters quoted analyst Brain Schacter as saying.[40]

Some media consumers and observers say this expanded anecdotal approach to news is nothing new, that in part news has been told through narrative for more than a century. Stephen Crane[41] was doing this brand of journalism at the end of the nineteenth century, and Ernest Hemingway fifty years after that.[42] But both Crane and Hemingway were exceptions in their eras.

Does everyman news fit perfectly into this time and place in history? Or is it just a cheaper way to do the news a day late? Whatever the verdict, everyman news is a phenomenon firmly established at American newspapers and one likely to influence the content of new media forms not yet imagined.

Chapter 1

Should the Personal Become Universal?

The next few years should see the discovery of many other techniques for bringing the public under journalism's rubric. Just how far this people's journalism will extend is anybody's guess, but there is little doubt that it will extend well into the future.

—John C. Merrill, Peter J. Gade and Frederick R. Blevens,
Twilight of Press Freedom: The Rise of People's Journalism

Human interest is a valid and traditional reason for writing any newspaper story—from a feature on suburban children packing for summer camp to a series on AIDS orphans in South Africa. People like to read stories about people and have since newspapers began. Call it curiosity, call it voyeurism, call it empathy—but human interest as a classic justification of what is news has driven sales of tabloids and broadsheets for more than a century, defined reporters' instincts for generations, and underlined core journalism school curricula for many years. But only recently has human interest become the dominant measure of a print newspaper story's newsworthiness. News has become at once personal and universal. Smaller stories are magnified in importance and used as illustrations of larger issues, attempting to expose a fuller truth. In many more cases than ever before, personal stories of ordinary citizens are vehicles to explain national and global news in a way that is immediate, accessible, and understandable.

"The human interest stories show us once again how the eternal stories of humankind can be told and retold in the pages of the news," Jack Lule

16

wrote in *Daily News, Eternal Stories*. "News will be in crisis to the extent that we ignore the roots of journalists as storyteller."[1]

The approach is not new, but its dominance of the front page is a recent development. Charles Dickens intended to rouse human interest with his dire descriptions of the Ragged School behind the "odds and ends of fever-stricken courts and alleys" in *The Daily News* journal in March 1852.[2] New York Sun editor Charles Dana in his initial editorial in 1868 promised his readers full coverage "of the whole world's doings" as well as "life of the people of New York."[3]

In 1898, Stephen Crane wrote of the sinking of the *Commodore* before the start of the Spanish-American War in this newspaper article:

> John Kitchell of Daytona came running down the beach, and as he ran the air was filled with clothes. If he had pulled a single lever and undressed, even as the fire horses harness, he could not seem to me to have stripped with more speed. He dashed into the water and dragged the cook. Then he went after the captain, but the captain sent him to me, and then it was that he saw Billy Higgins lying with his forehead on sand that was clear of the water, and he was dead.[4]

The late author Graham Greene once said the human factor is the part that never dies.[5] Karen Magnuson, editor and vice president of the news at the *Rochester Democrat and Chronicle*, said front-page stories today often contain some form of "human drama."[6] In the infancy of the twenty-first century, more than ever before, the news of everyman has become big news on the front pages of newspapers in this country.

On the front page of the *Miami Herald* on March 1, 2004, was a feature story by Sara Olkron with the headline, "Buildings Redeemed by Faith." It read

"At the Sunrise Musical Theater, where Frank Sinatra sang 'My Way.' A massive congregation is now singing it . . . His way.

"When the debauched citizens of the XChange sex club on North Federal Highway took their mattresses and moved out, the Church of Hollywood Downtown moved in."[7]

Even hard news stories are more likely to have narrative or anecdotal approaches. Take, for example, one by Lyndsey Layton that ran on A-1 of the *Washington Post* on September 28, 2004:

> Sakinah Aaron was walking into the bus area at the Wheaton Metro station several weeks ago, talking loudly on her Motorola cell phone. A little too loudly for Officer George Saoutis of the Metro Transit Police.

The police officer told Aaron, who is five months pregnant, to lower her voice. She told the officer he had no right to tell her how to speak into her cell phone.

Their verbal dispute quickly escalated, and Saoutis grabbed Aaron by the arm and pushed her to the ground. He handcuffed the 23-year-old woman, called for backup and took her to a cell where she was held for three hours before being released to her aunt. She was charged with two misdemeanors: "disorderly manner that disturbed the public peace" and resisting arrest.[8]

Had this story been reported and written in the late '90s, it would have been a simple arrest story with a summary lead in the local metro section. It might not have made the newspaper at all. But chances are, in most newspapers today, the narrative, anecdotal approach to the story is the one that would take hold. And the story would likely make the front page. Why and why now?

"I would say the narrow hard news form of news isn't particularly satisfying," said Barbie Zelizer, professor at the University of Pennsylvania's Annenberg School for Communication and author of several books. "If it has a summary lead, then that is scientific and has a pattern feel to it; it hides the perspective of the person writing it."[9]

It is important to consider why readers of newspapers demand, expect, and respond more favorably to an increased dosage of everyman narrative about real folks, less critical analysis of larger issues, and fewer official sources delivering "top-down" news. It is also important to look at how editors, writers, and reporters say they satisfy that preference by delivering more narrative packages for news. A page-one news story in the *New York Times* on June 15, 2004, about bombings in Iraq highlighted this anecdote several paragraphs into the story: "Hussein Atiha was selling watermelon up the street when his stand was nearly knocked over by the bomb. Like many Iraqis, he seemed divided in his thoughts on the occupation, the future and the rising tide of violence. At one moment, as he watched the mob pound and kick the destroyed vehicles, Mr. Atiha shook his head, 'That is wrong,' he said.' 'That is disrespectful.'"[10]

Some say investigative reporting suffers when featurized stories dominate. But the realities of newspaper management and the high cost of hiring experienced staff are that investigative journalism is expensive and difficult to execute. "Journalists themselves are quite concerned by the subtle—and not so subtle—changes that have taken place at media outlets where turning profits for the corporate parent has become more important than ever," Croteau and Hoynes wrote.[13]

Usually only elite newspapers attempt the kind of journalism that changes the operating systems of the world as we know it. This brand of journalism is not dead, nor is it likely ever to be. But the kind of accessible, humanistic everyday story that is everyman news is predominant in American newspapers. This democratic approach to news is what author E. L. Doctorow referred to as the drive to "affix" our attention "to our ground level lives." Newspapers serve as the "aroused witness," he said, "with the reportage that will restore us to ourselves."[12]

Pick up a newspaper in most any city in America today. Read the front page and the jumps. Turn to the obituaries page. The extended profiles of real people, lengthy obituaries, features, news features, and reaction stories likely outnumber the hard, straightforward news stories. "The news moves from being mostly journalist-centered, communicated as monologue, and primarily local, to also being increasingly audience-centered, part of multiple conversations, and micro-local," Boczkowski wrote.[13]

A front-page story in the Monday, March 15, 2004, *Cincinnati Enquirer* under the headline "Sprawl Squeezes Parkland" had this lead: "Billy Kingsolver has been playing baseball for 10 years, and the 14-year-old Knothole Leaguer says each year it gets tougher to find a place to play and practice."[14]

"Anecdotal leads have become so popular that some journalists see them as overused," David Craig wrote in the 2006 book, *The Ethics of the Story*. When used efficiently and judiciously, he wrote, "Anecdotes, then, can do ethical good by showing readers why they should invest the time to gain truth of any kind from a story and can help to clarify that truth for readers. . . . To provide truth that takes the story forward, an anecdote must do more than read in an interesting way." But when used indiscriminately, he continued, "Anecdotes can skew the truth that readers take away from stories. They can fail to represent a broader issue well by focusing on a person whose situation is not typical or does not fit the facts of the rest of the story. They may oversimplify a situation. They may even convey an extreme case."[15]

Democracy in News

"The media landscape is far more democratic than it has ever been," said documentarian Steve James.[16] Some critics claim that *Hoop Dreams*, his 1995 Oscar-nominated film about street basketball, jump-started the growth of reality TV. The 2006 documentary *The War Tapes*, which James produced, received the Tribeca Film Festival award for best documentary.

Add to the current media soup highly stylized narrative journalism in magazines, public radio reports, and special newspaper sections, the personal commentary in blogs and community-written websites and story-driven marketing, and you see a culture with an intense reverence for personal story.

A February 2006 promotion on National Public Radio claimed listeners "strive for connection" through the stories they hear on the radio.[17] Newspaper readers apparently strive for the same thing. American Public Media, which offers programming on NPR, in January 2007 launched the daily program *The Story*, which host Dick Gordon described as a vehicle that "brings the news home through passionate points of view and personal experiences. Ordinary and extraordinary people provide perspective on the issues that affect us all. The goal is to inspire conversation, thought and understanding."[18] The site solicited listeners and visitors to log on to "Your Story" and write about personal experiences with six prompts for storytelling from "Surprised by Kindness" to "Oddest Coincidence."

Every day you can see and hear evidence that everyman journalism has dethroned the celebrity infotainment madness that prompted the tail-chasing of O. J. Simpson and Princess Diana, which dominated journalism in the '80s and early '90s. People are now tuned into the rowdy kids next door on "Brat Camp."[19] The bizarre twists in the tale of Anna Nicole Smith's death and the courtship and parenting dramas of Brad Pitt and Angelina Jolie aside, profile journalism is no longer celebrity-driven. Even the Michael Jackson trial and acquittal in June 2005 seemed less a media feeding frenzy than had the Simpson trial and verdict a decade earlier. Celebrity-following has moved mostly online to become the purview of clever blogs, snarky sites, tabloids, and entertainment magazines.

What gripped our attention in early 2004 was the trial and conviction of Scott Peterson, a noncelebrity from the San Francisco suburbs whose fictional fishing trip and double homicide brought him infamy. Jennifer Wilbanks, the runaway cold-footed bride in the spring of 2005, and the murder in March 2006 of Matthew Winkler, a Tennessee pastor, by his wife, Mary, garnered as much attention as—if not more than—the antics of movie idols.[20]

Print celebrity journalism is relegated to inside gossip columns, tabloids, and the celebrity magazines. Front pages are about real people. The celebration of the unofficial source and the everyday lives of the general public demonstrate more than coincidental symptoms of a change. As you can see in the appendix, the shift in newspaper sensibility and content is palpable growth that can be measured in the number of features, the prominence of unofficial sources, and the narrative approaches to news stories in twenty American newspapers from 2001 to 2004.

The revived journalistic reverence for the individual can be seen across the media landscape in newspaper, magazine, broadcast, and digital journalism—from the April 30, 2004, reading by Ted Koppel of the names of

"The Fallen" on ABC's *Nightline*[21] to the Citizen Journalist section on MSNBC.com of the July 7, 2005, terrorist bombings in London. Amateur eyewitness observers filed the reports that day, and the top-rated story of the day was "Saira's Dairy."[22]

The August 1, 2005, issue of *Time* featured "Eyewitnesses to Hiroshima," an anniversary special that told the personal stories of the men who dropped the bombs from the *Enola Gay*, as well as portraits of seven Japanese survivors called the *hibakusha*.[23] In early 2005, the Associated Press began delivering alternate leads to every story—the feature or the straight news approach.[24] It is in the newspaper that the drive to expose the individual's stake in the news is so prevalent.

On Monday, November 29, 2004, the *Chicago Tribune* ran five front-page stories, all of them were with anecdotal, or feature, leads. A story by Mike Dorning on returning troops began this way: "Holly Frierichsen was hoping for a tear—or a smile at least—when she held aloft her 5-month-old daughter to give her husband his first glimpse of their child."[25]

A story from Yuma, Arizona, on DNA testing of death row inmates began this way: "Thelma Youngkin used an oxygen tube to help her breathe. Her killer used it as a weapon."[26]

A feature on college freshmen by Bonnie Miller Rubin began, "As Zach Rudin tore open the fat envelope from Washington University, his pulse quickened with nervousness until he locked on the word 'Congratulations!'"[27]

A story from San Gabriel, California, by Michael Martinez read "For 39 years, Helen Nelson has stood jealous watch over the San Gabriel Mission, the longest tenure of any preservation activist at the 21 historic Spanish church compounds that run the length of California like a chain of colonial outposts frozen in time."[28]

The last story on the *Tribune's* front page about the Irish language from Dublin by Tom Hundley read "From George Bernard Shaw to Samuel Beckett, from William Butler Yeats to James Joyce, the Irish have long been masters of the English language. It's the Irish language that has them stammering."[29]

One hundred percent of the stories on the front page in a major metropolitan newspaper that day had feature leads. And it was not a fluke.

So? Who cares? What does it mean?

Journalism through the Everyman Filter

As a culture in the early twenty-first century, American journalism presents unfolding daily history through a humanistic lens. It must be reflective of American society and an indication of what we value as journalists and as consumers of journalism that front-page newspaper journalism has grown more personal, more diverse, and more grassroots-based.

French sociologist Pierre Bourdieu wrote in the 2005 translation of his book *Bourdieu and the Journalistic Field* that journalism has "to impose the legitimate vision of the social world."[30] American journalism appears to be operating on the assumption that for today the personal human story is the best way to deliver the news, that it is through the story of the individual that we can most clearly understand the events of our world. Through empathy and humanity, daily print journalism delivers life's unfolding history.

"Facts are meaningless without story; it's just noise," said Jack Hart, managing editor and writing coach at the *Oregonian*. "We cannot understand things without that framework."[31] Other journalists agreed. "We're not going back to just straight news, it's old and boring," said award-winning columnist and feature writer Ken Fuson of the *Des Moines Register*. "We're not just competing with TV and the Internet, we have got to be sharper and more real if people want to continue to make sense of their lives."[32] Laurie Hertzel of the *Minneapolis Star Tribune* agreed. "We had been smothered by this seriousness since Watergate, so newspapers are loosening up a bit," said Hertzel, the paper's enterprise editor and writing coach.[33]

If the personal story provides a more understandable framework for news, is the framework universally appropriate? Some editors and observers complain it has gone too far—that the narrative approach is used too often. Roy Peter Clark, senior scholar at the Poynter Institute, said, "Journalists use the word 'story' with romantic promiscuity."[34] Some newspaper writers have attempted to manipulate every news story into a softer overcoat by reporting it anecdotally with what I refer to as "the little Jimmy lead" and Jack Hart of the *Oregonian* calls the "bait-and-switch lead."[35]

All Anecdotal All the Time

Again on Tuesday, July 26, 2005, all five stories on the front page of the *Chicago Tribune* were features or news features with anecdotal leads. Above the fold, "Tallest Tower to Twist Rivals" was a story by Blair Kamin and Thomas A. Corfman on a new project for the Chicago lakefront. It began with a romantic, descriptive lead: "It would twist into the sky over Chicago's lakefront like an oversized birthday candle. . . ."[36] To the right, a story on the AFL-CIO's warring factions by Barbara Rose and Stephen Frankline began with an anecdotal lead from an unofficial source, "Watching Kim Bobo leap to her feet Monday to cheer at the AFL-CIO convention at Navy Pier—a meeting where some of the federations's biggest unions were notably absent—you'd have thought her loyalties were clear."[37]

Below the fold, a feature on Mormons by Margaret Ramirez began with a description and an anecdote from an unofficial source, "As sunlight flooded the church from a window above, Brad Hunter brought his 2-week-old baby girl, Leah, in front of the congregation for her first blessing."[38] A fourth story below the fold, this one about the Chicago Children's Choir written by Ofelia Casillas, began with the unofficial source anecdote, "Since he was young, Lawrice Flowers had preferred classical music to rap, singing to playing basketball."[39] On the far right of the front page, a wire story about a Gallup poll on alcohol began this way: "Beaujolais has beaten the Busch."[40]

The inside pages of the paper held stories about the Iraqi constitution, the space shuttle, suspects in the British bombings, and the Chicago Historical Society. But the front page accorded the highest priorities to Kim Bobo, Brad Hunter, and Lawrice Flowers—not household names. According to Jack Fuller, former president of Tribune Company, this is a deliberate presentation of news. "People come to a newspaper craving a unifying human presence—the narrator in a piece of fiction, the guide who knows the way, or the colleague whose view one values," Fuller wrote in *News Values: Ideas for an Information Age*. He continued, "Readers don't just want random snatches of information flying at them from out of the ether. They want information that hangs together, makes sense, has some degree of order to it. They want knowledge rather than facts, perhaps even a little wisdom."[41]

The Front Page Tells the Story of Change

Academics have similarly noted the shift in front-page sensibility. "Now the American newspaper is under siege because we get our news from radio, TV, the Internet. So newspapers are not in the news business, they offer judgment, interpretation and a second crack at what's happening. They have to become more atmospheric, interpretative and featurized," said Christopher B. Daly, associate professor of journalism at Boston University.[42]

Research supports the observation. "There's a general trend toward more narrative writing in newspapers as they're trying to engage readers," said Jack Rosenberry, associate professor at St. John Fisher College. Rosenberry compared hundreds of articles in the *Rochester Democrat Gazette* from February 1990 and the same week in February 2005. He presented the results of his study at the 2005 Association for Educators in Journalism and

Mass Communications conference, where he said that "first-day leads are significantly less prevalent."[43]

Rosenberry contended the main pressure altering newspaper writing is the Internet. "There's less need for breaking news in newspapers because of the Internet," he said in an interview. "Even if it happens at 6 p.m., it has been on your Internet site for 12 hours before readers can get it from the newspaper." Rosenberry said the idea for his research study "dawned on" him when he was hunting for different types of leads to bring in to his students for examples. "In one news story, I had to go the fifth paragraph to find out a garbage truck had backed over a woman."[44]

I assert that the revolution in American newspapers had many causes: reader appetites, citizen journalism, blogging, a post-9/11 reverence for the individual story, the proliferation of narrative journalism, diversifying newsrooms, the field of narrative therapy and the concurrent explosion in marketing of the stories of ordinary people.

Where's the News?

Even when we understand how frequently news is told in the genre of everyman journalism, it is necessary to examine the obvious caveats. For proper tone and balance, the newspaper trend toward anecdotal, personal approaches to news must be tailored for each story, considered carefully as one possible avenue, not a mandatory approach. Sometimes an anecdotal lead feels like a cheap way to write a news story; other times it works best. Whether to use the narrative feature approach is left to the discretion of the journalist or editor.

"This new journalism is based on what people think and feel and do, rather than what officials say," said Rosemary Armao, former president of Investigative Reporters and Editors, Inc., and former state and investigations editor at the *South Florida Sun Sentinel* in Fort Lauderdale. "The whole narrative movement of 'now we have to tell stories' sometimes feels too much like making it up. An anecdote is easier than nailing down the hard stuff that makes up good journalism."[45] Armao is a Knight International Fellow who worked in Uganda in 2004 and 2005 as a consultant at the *Monitor* newspaper in Kampala.

In his departing editorial in the *New York Times* in May 2005, public editor Daniel Okrent lamented the overuse of the anecdotal lead, specifically in a story about New York City public schools: "But it isn't clear why the individual was picked; it isn't possible to determine whether she's representative; and there's no way of knowing whether she knows what she's talking about. Calling on the individual man or woman on the street to make conclusive judgments is beneath journalistic integrity."[46]

It may be easier to execute this brand of everyman journalism, or it may simply be a maturing of the circulation-challenged newspaper industry reflecting the acceptance and appeal of the intimate craft of narrative journalism. Many journalists have declared it time to move past the staccato "he said, she said, who, what, where, when, why" antiquated formula of daily journalism. It is time to raze the inverted pyramid and bury it in the burning sand. People want stories they can connect to in their newspaper. They want the news delivered in a newspaper to be personal.

The Growth of Narrative over the Years

While the increasing volume of featurized news stories running in American newspapers today is a growing phenomenon, anecdotally driven feature stories have filled magazines and newspaper feature sections for at least a generation. For years the *Wall Street Journal*'s page-one stories consistently showcased well-written narratives, quirky profiles, and everyman-driven features. Decades' worth of Pulitzer Prize–winning features have included narrative journalism of the highest quality. In 1980, one of Madeleine Blais's profiles, "Zepp's Last Stand" for the *Miami Herald,* won her the Pulitzer Prize. It is the story of an eighty-three-year-old man fighting to clear his military record.[47]

Since the '60s, hundreds of gifted writers, including Jon Hersey, Joan Didion, Susan Orlean, Gay Talese, Ted Conover, John McPhee, and Tracy Kidder, have molded magazine articles and books from meticulous reporting. These writers conjure masterful writing reflecting insight, solid information, emotion, and craft. Writers who excel in immersion journalism fill themselves up with the subject and then spin factual tales about what they have found. And their work has influenced imitators in magazines and newspapers.

"Literary journalism" and "new journalism" were the names assigned to the work of Tom Wolfe, Hunter S. Thompson, and others. For those writers at least it was a more self-conscious approach to writing, and stories mostly used a sassy, first-person "Look at me!" tone. The writing was daring, a snazzy, show-off kind of risky business where these writers knew they were breaking rules but were more concerned about expressing themselves with a dazzling story well-told than about pleasing the audience. The new narrative masters are more interested in conveying universal truths than showing off. Tracy Kidder, author and journalist, said, "I try to make the writing vivid, not flashy."[48]

Julia Keller won the Pulitzer Prize for feature writing in 2005 for her series of stories from Utica, Illinois, a small Illinois town destroyed by a tornado in the spring of 2004. More than half of the front page of the *Chicago Tribune* on Tuesday, December 7, 2004, was devoted to Keller's story, which began, "They picked at the pile, inch by inch, stone by stone, just in case. They thought they'd gotten to everyone who was alive, but you have to be sure. You had to. Buckets of debris were passed from hand to hand along chains of firefighters. It began to rain, but nobody noticed."[49] Chosen as the finest piece of feature reporting written in 2004, the story in the first paragraph did not answer any of the questions journalists have traditionally been told they should: who, what, where, when, why, or how?

Barbara Iverson, professor of journalism at Columbia College Chicago and creator of currentbuzz.org, said she remembers the morning she picked up the *Chicago Tribune* to read Keller's story. "To me that day was so notable. I thought the paper doesn't need to get news on the front page anymore. It's so different from 20 years ago. In the morning I've already been listening to the radio for 45 minutes, others are watching TV or turn on the Internet for news."[50]

What the newspaper offered that other media could not was a slower narrative about the characters involved and the world they inhabited. Newspapers, though a daily disposable, can also offer a longer shelf life for the everyman content. The featurized news stories can be reprinted in special sections, reproduced on CD-ROMs, and included in book-length anthologies and collections. In the 2005 book *The New New Journalism*, author Robert S. Boynton wrote, "We are currently experiencing the fascination with 'true stories'—news from the world—that is common during times of great unrest and turmoil."[51]

What's So New Then?

News stories today are told in real time, not always chronologically, but without the choppy, ping-pong, he said–she said, quote, exposition, nutgraph style common in traditional straight newspaper coverage of news and events. There is dialogue, drama, depth. The stories often star unofficial sources and the everyman depiction and interpretation of a trend, event, or reaction. The literary lure of writing such keenly crafted stories is what inspired many men and women of my generation to launch careers in journalism in the '70s and later. It is what kept us rewriting our stories over and over—during a pre-click, cut-and-paste era when rewriting and revising meant retyping the whole darn thing with carbon paper attached. The cadence, pacing, and drama seduced readers into caring about subjects and writers into wishing they could imitate the style. It is what Walt Harrington proclaimed "intimate journalism."[52] Alex Kotlowitz, author and journalist, said, "These are intimate stories about people who are ordinary in extraordinary circumstances."[53]

It is writing that made us swoon. And it was the exception rather than the rule. A few "chosen" writers on newspapers or magazines were deemed capable of such narrative excellence. But no longer. Most all writers are urged to tell the news in a personal way. Most writers beg for the chance. Today this genre of everyman journalism has morphed to the main sections of newspapers in the form of profiles of ordinary citizens in peril, triumph, or even mediocrity. Writers exalt anecdotes of individuals to the highest prominence in a news story. The details of the average citizen become the lead, or beginning, of the story, or an individual becomes the narrative thread pulling the story together through the writer's extensive use of quotes, dialogue, or description. This kind of journalism focuses on the tales of people affected by the news as much as it informs about the newsmakers themselves.

It is what E. L. Doctorow called "the multiplicity of witness."[54] It is what Alma Guillermoprieto, author and journalist for the *New Yorker* and *New York Review of Books,* said "is finding a way to capture humanity by very purposefully trying to blend information, observation, analysis and reaction by being very specific."[55]

Why Now?

From the 2000 presidential election and the events of September 11, 2001, to the weapons of mass destruction's mythical seduction of the press, sources in authority either were not forthcoming with answers or were not truthful. So we saw in newspapers a backlash against reporting official sources' accounts of events. The resulting rise in the use of eyewitness accounts and the stories' reliance on individuals without titles or expertise forged a path toward what author and journalist Dan Gillmor called "grassroots journalism" in his 2004 book, *We the Media.*[56]

In August 2005 Yahoo increased broadband news video with the addition of video news from CNN.com and ABC News to a provider already stocked with news from the Associated Press and Reuters.[57] At about the same time AP announced the launching of an online video news network in late 2005. According to AdAge.com, "Yahoo is the largest of the many portals that are undermining the traditional newspaper print business by enabling vast numbers of consumers to get up-to-the-minute text and video news online whenever they want it."[58]

Because print newspapers logistically were not the first outlet to deliver the daily news, the pressure for them to be different became even more intense. The answer was for newspapers to offer humanistic stories readers can't get in one click. In the 2005 "State of the News Media Report" from the Project for Excellence in Journalism, the authors wrote, "Newspapers, when compared with television and online offerings, continue to be the most thoroughly reported and transparent source of news available, covering the widest range of topics. . . . Newspapers continue to be distinguished for the depth, range and variety of their content, even on the front pages."[59]

News could be obtained more quickly from the Internet or television from anywhere in the world, so print had to offer more since it could never win the speed race. If readers were required to wait until the next day—a whole day—for the newspaper text, the writing had to deliver something more personal, more colorful, filled with word pictures and worth the wait. The stories had to have the thousand words that could match in effect and impact what the photographs conveyed in a single shot. We needed the words to be as vibrant in crafted detail as the photographs had been in chromatic detail.

Without a clear manifesto, papers already inclined toward narrative stories in their special sections appeared to adopt everyman journalism for more and more news stories on their front pages. These stories featured prominently the voices of the citizenry, creating a narratization movement in newspapers and ultimately creating community. This movement—already under way for the last ten years—says as much about our culture as it does about writers, reporters, and editors as gatekeepers who dutifully chronicle our daily unfolding history in an everyman mode. It speaks to a larger societal need to listen to the voices of everyman and to create a community within the context of journalism.

In late 2004 and 2005, the front-page news stories were about terrorism, the Iraq war, the economy, the contentious presidential election, hurricanes, and the Asian tsunamis. The stories were written with an abundance of compassion, emotion, description, and anecdotes. We could read the stories and see, hear, smell, and practically touch the individuals affected. It seemed a summary lead and straight news approach had become the exception rather than the rule.

The Need for Everyman Sources

Everyman and everywoman news is reporting through the eyes of nondeliberate, accidental newsmakers, unofficial sources—the recipients, the customers in line at the movies, not the stars on the red carpet. Why American readers hunger for stories of noncelebrity individuals raises the question of whether journalists are obliged to deliver what readers want or what they need. Can a newspaper no longer just deliver the facts? Do we require the newspaper to always tell us slower, more personal stories?

Where print journalism moves from here is critical. As keepers of the public trust, journalists need to recognize the inherent temptation to fabricate or plagiarize these kinds of stories, knowing the net worth of a treasured anecdote to a story as a pressure mounted on reporters by readers, editors, and peers. The drive to write surprising and original humanistic journalism is the monster under the bed. Narrative journalism can never be at the expense of authenticity, appropriateness, and accuracy. At a time when technology drives the economy and society, it is noteworthy that the newspaper profession, once defined by its ability to be the first and the freshest on deadline, has returned to its slower, town-crier roots.

In 1850, humanist Ralph Waldo Emerson wrote in his essay, "Goethe; or the Writer from Representative Men": "Men are born to write. . . . Nothing so broad, so subtle, or so dear, but comes therefore commended to his pen, and he will write. In his eyes, a man is the faculty of reporting, and the universe is the possibility of being reported."[60]

Journalists in the twenty-first century are forced to react much more swiftly than ever before, competing for readers' much-divided attention as they are bombarded with information messengers from cable, Internet, television, radio, and even cell phones delivering news in real time, often with an interactive component. "News was the first industry to really feel the impact of the Internet, and we've now had an entire generation grow up with the expectation of being able to have on-demand news on any subject at anytime for free," Chris Anderson wrote. "This may be good for news junkies, but it's been hell on the news business."[61]

For those who study newspapers as an ethnographer would study the artifacts of cities to understand entire societies, how we relay our immediate history and the words we choose to tell these stories provide a legacy and a tangible expression of our world views. It not only is a palpable interpretation of who we are, it demonstrates how we wish to contextualize daily history. These stories literally are how we will remember history.

Chapter 2

The Results

An Anecdotal Companion to History

He had learned further that each such story is a step in a zigzag march that takes on a discoverable direction only later, when men look back and see it as history.

—Theodore H. White, *In Search of History: A Personal Adventure*

The front page is the lobby of your newspaper, your first impression, a space that welcomes you and invites you to visit offices and apartments on different floors inside. It visually entices you like the display window of a department store. The front page announces the personality, news values, and writing styles of the paper's top editorial employees, who produce and export good journalism from all different departments inside. Because the front page is the showcase—prime editorial real estate—a makeover of its content commands our attention.

This is the holy trinity of remarkable changes in newspapers' front pages in the last few years: more features, more feature approaches to all stories, and an overwhelming rise in the voices of unofficial sources in news. It is not too far a stretch to state that the front page is a window into American print journalism and the American belief that newspapers are again the voice of the people.

Sit through an editorial meeting at any newspaper in the country, and you will see and hear editors protesting, protecting, defending, and bartering to get their departments' stories on the front page. Each editor argues a story's newsworthiness and value to readers. The editors conspire to produce a consortium of stories and visuals based on the unusual value of each story, the reader impact and consequence, the graceful eloquence of the writer, the urgency of the information, and the availability of breathtaking art—all in a package designed to serve the reader best that day.

"The notion of a Page 1 story, in fact, has evolved over the years, partly in response to the influence of other media," the *New York Times'* Bill Keller wrote in an online chat in April 2006. "When a news event has been on the Internet and TV and news radio all day long, do we want to put that news on our front page the next morning?"[1]

Journalism is changing. Still, the rate at which news happens is a constant. It may be a slow news day or a heavy news day, but it is always a news day 24/7. The deliberate and conscientious hunt for the story may be the same, but the way journalists tell the news story in print and how it is delivered have been disrupted. News is decidedly different at the curtain-raising of the twenty-first century. The evidence is overwhelming.

Methodology: How The Papers Were Chosen

For this study I chose twenty American newspapers, seeking diversity in geography, newspaper ownership, circulation, and staff size. I wanted to see if the trend of more features on the front page and more feature approaches to news was predominant only on large papers or in certain sections of the country, or if it was evident in newspapers across the country, regardless of geography, ownership, or staff size. There are four newspapers each in the Midwest, Northeast, and Southeast; three in the Southwest; three in the West; one in the Northwest; and one in Alaska. If there was a tendency in one area of the country to write one way or to cover stories with one kind of approach, then that would be reflected in the results.

No paper was unaffected by increases in the number of features. There was also a unanimous increase in the use of unofficial sources. There was no significant geographic trend toward the increases—newspapers across the country showed increases in features on the front page and also in feature leads on the front page. The six newspapers with the largest increases in the use of features on the front page were in the Southwest, West, Midwest, and Southeast. The six newspapers showing the largest increases in the use of feature leads to news stories on the front page were in the Midwest, West, Southeast, and Alaska. Over the three years, newspapers in the Northeast had a steady level of features and feature leads on the front page.

This study reflects the journalistic work of almost 6,300 newspaper staffers, including reporters, editors, copy editors, and photographers. These numbers ensure that a shift would also signify some professional tendency, rather than the work of a few influential, like-minded editors at a few newspapers who possibly attended the same conference or read the same readership studies.

Staff sizes, as measured in 2004 by *Bacon's Newspaper/Magazine Directory*, ranged from 80 at the *Anchorage Daily News* to 920 at the *New York Times*. Circulation also ranged from nearly 65,000 at the *Idaho Statesman* in 2004 to nearly 1.2 million at the *New York Times*. Altogether, this study covered front pages read by almost 7.6 million daily readers.

I also considered newspaper ownership a factor because if one newspaper chain issued an edict to cover more features or more anecdotal approaches, then all the newspapers in the chain would have similar results. Before the sale of Knight Ridder to McClatchy, at the time of this study in 2004, fourteen newspaper companies owned twenty of the newspapers studied. Gannett owned the most newspapers in the research at three. The New York Times Company, Knight Ridder, and the Tribune Company each owned two newspapers in the study. The other companies, ranging from Cox to Newhouse, had one paper each in the study.

Breakdown of Newspapers by Owners as of December 2005

Blethen Maine Newspapers: *Portland Press Herald*
Cox Newspapers, Inc.: *Atlanta Journal-Constitution*
Gannett Newspapers: *Cincinnati Enquirer, Idaho Statesman, Louisville
    Courier-Journal*
Hearst Newspapers: *San Antonio Express-News*
Knight Ridder: *Miami Herald, San Jose Mercury News*
McClatchy Newspapers: *Anchorage Daily News*
MediaNews Group: *Omaha World-Herald*
Newhouse Newspapers: *Times-Picayune*
New York Times Co.: *Boston Globe, New York Times*
Pulitzer Newspapers Inc.: *St. Louis Post-Dispatch*
Seattle Times Co.: *Seattle Times*
Tribune Co.: *Chicago Tribune, Los Angeles Times*
Washington Post Co.: *Washington Post*

Wehco Media Inc.: *Arkansas Democrat-Gazette*
Source: *Bacon's Newspaper/Magazine Directory* 2005[2]

Days of the Week Chosen and Why

With the help of two assistants trained to code the stories, I studied 20 American newspapers on eight dates—totaling 160 front pages. We measured three separate trends in close to 850 front-page stories that ran on four dates in 2001 and the same four dates in 2004 (March 1, March 15, June 1, and June 15): features vs. hard news; feature leads vs. straight news leads; and the prominence of unofficial sources. I intentionally steered away from newspapers in December or September. I avoided stories in the newspapers following the September 11, 2001, attacks and surrounding its anniversary, anticipating profiles, features, and enterprise stories related to remembrances of the attacks.

We did not measure the front pages of the weekend newspapers on Saturday and Sunday, knowing that most Sunday newspapers carry a heavy load of features. I deliberately stayed away from Wednesday, as many newspapers run features more heavily midweek or promote different sections of the paper. Tuesday, June 1, 2004, was the day after Memorial Day. One editor at the *Arkansas Democrat-Gazette* said the choice of this date shifted results, but news happens every day of the week, and even if staff writers were not available to cover the hard news events, wire stories could be used and placed on page one. Random significant dates in history demonstrate how breaking news happens every day of the week.

* Monday, May 7, 1945: Germany signed an unconditional surrender, ending World War II
* Tuesday, September 11, 2001: Thousands killed in New York, Pennsylvania, and Washington, D.C. in terrorist attacks
* Wednesday, January 4, 2006: 12 die in Sago, West Virginia, mine collapse, erroneously reported at first to be found alive
* Thursday, March 11, 2004: 191 killed in Madrid, Spain, bomb blasts
* Friday, November 22, 1963: President John F. Kennedy assassinated in Dallas
* Saturday, December 19, 1998: House of Representatives voted on 4 articles of impeachment and passed 2 of them concerning President Bill Clinton.

* Sunday, July 20, 1969: The first man walks on the moon as U.S. astronaut Neil Armstrong proclaims, "One small step for man, one giant leap for mankind."[3]

What Was Measured

After choosing the dates, we counted how many stories in total ran on the front page on each date, and tallied how many were features and how many were hard news. Then we tallied percentages of hard news and features of the total news hole. The number of front-page stories shifted from as few as four to as many as seven. For all the newspapers studied, the percentage of features out of all stories on the front page increased from 35 percent in 2001 to 50 percent in 2004.

The findings were aligned with reports from newspaper editors about their efforts to shrink the numbers of stories presented on page one.[4] My findings also were similar to the 2001 Readership Institute report on front-page content of 104 daily newspapers with circulations from 10,000 to more than 200,000. According to that study, general news accounted for 71 to 78.4 percent of the front-page content, and features plus commentary/criticism (which I considered features in my study) accounted for 21 to 27.6 percent of front-page content. The Readership Institute also had a category of "other" from .6 to 1.5 percent of front-page content.[5]

For this study, I defined a feature as a story not tied to a specific event on the previous day. Timeliness is not the main news hook. It can be a profile, trend story, enterprise piece, investigative piece, round-up, analysis, travel piece, review, commentary, anniversary story, or exclusive. It is not deadline-driven.

A feature has human interest but may not have many of the crucial elements of newsworthiness: timeliness, prominence, proximity, unusualness, diversity, consequence, or impact. It could not be branded "yesterday's news" by the following morning. It is not the most important news locally, nationally, or internationally. It can be interesting, well-written, and compelling, but it is a story that will not be easily duplicated elsewhere, and it has a looser connection to timeliness. It is part of the newspaper's branding. It is why a reader will read this newspaper perhaps, shopping for stories they cannot get online or on the television news. These are stories not exclusively related to a past event.

Tom Callinan, editor of the *Cincinnati Enquirer,* responded to the email inquiry of all the editors of the newspapers in this study with this: "'Features' seems to be a pejorative connotation. But, yes, newspapers are thinking differently about their front pages. With the information explosion of 24-hour news and pervasive Internet use, what we might term 'news' has become a commodity that readers can find many other places. Editors are thinking more about what the impact of the news is on regular readers and often this means finding a person who personifies the issue."[6]

Called an "evergreen" story in the broadcast arena, or one that has timeless appeal, a feature has a news hook that is generally human interest but can also include elements of consequence and impact, unusualness, diversity, and prominence. In this study we labeled a story a feature if that story could logically run elsewhere inside the newspaper—either further inside the A section or in a features, food, travel, metro, business, or sports section—or run on a different day.

If the story could be held one day or more without major consequence— that the paper "missed" or ignored coverage of a major story and readers were upset—or the news would not be too old or irrelevant by that time, I called it a feature. If it wasn't breaking news and readers did not need to have that information on this particular day, then it was more likely a feature. Overwhelmingly, what newspapers present on the front page now is much more often a feature story or a narrative approach to hard news.

"Soft news is considered to be less time-sensitive than hard news," wrote Michael Ray Smith in the 2005 book *Featurewriting.net: A Guide to Writing in the Electronic Age.* "Furthermore, the approach used for soft news often has richer narrative quality and allows the writer to break free of the economy of language reserved for hard news."[7]

For example, a March 1, 2001, story, "Stranded Seals Pose a Puzzle" on the front page of the *Portland Press Herald* in Maine, was considered a feature.

"Ruth Kosalka was looking out the window of her Georgetown home in mid-January when she noticed a brown, furry critter waddling toward the house." Writer Dennis Hoey continued in the next paragraph: "It was a seal. The animal slid across her yard toward a frozen pond in her backyard."[8]

In the classic text *Reporting for the Media,* authors Fred Fedler, John R. Bender, Lucinda Davenport, and Michael Drager write: "Most news stories describe recent events—meetings, crimes, fires, or accidents, for example. News stories also inform the public about topics that are important, local, or unusual. Feature stories, by contrast, read more like nonfiction short stories. Many have a beginning, middle and an end. They inform readers and viewers, but they also amuse, entertain, inspire, or stimulate. Because of these emphases, they are also called 'human interest' and 'color stories.'"[9]

In this study, a story was labeled hard news if it was timely, first of all, and contained many of the classic elements of newsworthiness. It was a story that needed to go in the newspaper that day because it was of the utmost newsworthiness and importance to the reader and could not be delayed with the same content. The paper would be "scooped" not to include it. Simply put, if the day the news happened was not critical, then it was not called hard news. But it is no longer true that most hard news stories on the front page are written in straight news style.

In the 2002 edition of the text *News Reporting and Writing,* authors Brian Brooks, George Kennedy, Daryl Moen, and Don Ranly of the Missouri Group wrote that hard news is "coverage of the actions of government or business, or the reporting of an event, such as a crime, an accident or a speech. The time element is often the most important."[10]

For example, a story of a bombing in a local school on Tuesday must go on the paper's front page Wednesday because it contains the elements of timeliness, proximity, consequence, and unusualness. In this research, this is news. A story a week later on the front page about how to prevent bombings in schools would be labeled a feature, though it is newsworthy. With a feature, the timeliness is more vague and less specific, or only loosely linked to an event. It is an enterprising, original piece of reporting, and it will likely not be printed elsewhere in other media.

In her 2005 book, *21st Century Feature Writing,* author Carla Johnson wrote: "The stories we see on the front pages are typically hard news stories, written in inverted pyramid structure. The most crucial information must be given in the first paragraph, the lead, with subsequent paragraphs arranged in descending importance of the information disclosed in them."[11] Others have similar definitions. "Journalists distinguish most frequently between the kinds of stories typical of hard and soft news, with the front pages of newspapers and top items of broadcast lineups commonly favoring the former over the latter," Barbie Zelizer of the University of Pennsylvania wrote in the 2005 anthology *The Press.*[12]

But what has been true historically in newspapers is no longer current practice. In twelve of the twenty newspapers studied, more than half and up to 68 percent of the stories on the front pages in four dates in 2004 were features, not hard news. The mean increase from 2001 to 2004 of feature stories on the front page in twenty newspapers was 55.65 percent, a startling shift.

Of the 404 front-pages stories analyzed in 2004, slightly more than half, or 203 stories, were features. That is a marked increase of close to 43 percent from the same dates in 2001 for all newspapers. In that year, the same newspapers ran 437 front-page stories, and 35 percent of those page one stories—or 154—were features, and 229 were hard news. The increases ranged from zero to nearly 225 percent. Thirteen newspapers showed percentage increases in the number of features from 25 to 100 percent.

In 2001, the percentage of front-page features of all front pages in twenty newspapers ranged from about 10 percent to more than 60 percent.

By 2004, the percentage of features running on the front pages of all twenty newspapers for the dates studied ranged from less than 30 percent to almost 70 percent.

It's All in the Lead

Not only is the front-page editorial hole shrinking—perhaps due to smaller newsprint formats on physically smaller pages, upgraded visual design, or the addition of news digests—but more of that prime front-page space is allotted for feature approaches to hard news. In 2001, of the 437 front-page stories studied, 139 had feature leads, and 298 had straightforward summary news leads. Clearly, the ratio dominance of hard summary news leads to delayed leads was more than two to one in those stories studied that year. In 2001, 31.8 percent of all stories on the front page carried narrative, descriptive, delayed, or anecdotal leads.

But only three years later, in 2004, on the same dates, the number of stories with feature leads had increased 36 percent. Of the 404 front-page stories in 2004, more than 43 percent (or 175 stories) had anecdotal, descriptive, or narrative leads, while 229 had summary leads. Now close to half the product on the front page were stories delivered with feature leads.

If the numbers seem a little off here, let me explain. Features do not necessarily have feature leads; they can have summary leads. For example, a front-page story in the *Arkansas Democrat-Gazette* on December 15, 2002, was an enterprise feature with a summary lead. The story, "Numbers of Homeless Climb during Hard Times," by Andrew DeMillo, had no tight timeliness hook, and began

"Packing shelters, abandoned buildings, makeshift tents camps and the streets, the Little Rock area's homeless population is on the rise, shelter directors and advocates for the homeless say."[13]

A front-page story in the *Omaha World-Herald* on March 1, 2001, was a news story about President Bush touring Council Bluffs, Nebraska, but with a feature lead. The story, "A Rousing Welcome in the Bluffs," by Patrick Strawbridge, had an anecdotal lead:

"Debbie Albertson voted for Al Gore.

"That fact, however, didn't dampen her enthusiasm to see President Bush during his tour of her city, Council Bluffs."[14]

Newspapers are using more of this type of feature or "second day" leads on the hard news stories than before. In 2004, the mean increase of stories on the front page with anecdotal or descriptive approaches in their leads was more than 60 percent from 2001, even with hard news or breaking stories.

The 2005 State of the News Media Report from Poynter Institute and the Pew Center showed that "looking just at news stories (excluding columns) more than a third, 36 percent, had no narrative frame. Most were simply written in the inverted-pyramid style; they described what happened yesterday, offering a grab bag of facts that did not fall into any clear narrative theme." According to the report, "After that, the most common frame was a feature style, wherein the writer told a good yarn. The approach characterized 12 percent of news stories."[15] The Poynter study looked at all stories in the newspaper, not just those on the front page. The data collected for this book reflects only the front-page stories.

The increasing popularity of descriptive, anecdotal, or delayed leads on front-page stories is noteworthy and enormous. From 2001 to 2004, newspapers demonstrated increases from 25 percent to up to 275 percent in feature leads—away from the summary, inverted-pyramid leads—in both news and feature stories. The median increase in the use of feature leads was 34 percent. Six newspapers in the study—the *Anchorage Daily News, Arizona Republic, Arkansas Democrat-Gazette, Chicago Tribune, Cincinnati Enquirer* and *San Antonio Express-News*—each increased more than 100 percent in their use of feature leads on the front page between 2001 and 2004.

The Anchorage paper had the highest percentage of feature leads, or 78 percent of all front-page stories in 2004, compared with a 33 percent total of feature leads on the front page in 2001. At the Cincinnati paper, the percentage of front-page feature leads increased from 19 percent to 45 percent in the same time period. Seventy-two percent of front-pages stories at the *Arizona Republic* had feature leads in 2004, compared to just 30 percent having feature leads on front-page stories in 2001.

At the *San Antonio Express-News*, the percentage of front-page feature leads on all stories went from 21 percent in 2001 to 61 percent in 2004. At the Arkansas paper, feature leads were used in 8 percent of the stories in 2001, and 30 percent three years later. At the *Chicago Tribune*, the percentage of front-page feature leads increased to 35 percent from 17 percent.

Four newspapers showed decreases in the number of feature leads on the front pages from 2001 to 2004—the *Boston Globe, Los Angeles Times, New York Times, Portland Press Herald* and the *Times-Picayune*—although the percentage of feature stories on the front pages of those numbers all increased in the same time period.

The Boston newspaper in the study decreased the number of front-page feature leads significantly, from 46 to 17 percent, as two of the dates in 2004 had all summary leads on all stories. The decrease was slight at the *Los Angeles Times,* where the percentage of front-page feature leads on stories went from 50 to 44 percent, still close to half of all stories. Similarly, the percentage of front-page feature leads at the *New York Times* was slight— from 38 percent of all stories in 2001 to 33 percent of all stories in 2004. A decrease at the Portland, Maine, paper was from 43 percent feature leads to 36 percent feature leads in 2004. The *Times-Picayune* continued to have a small number of feature leads on the front page with 27 percent of all stories in 2001 down to 21 percent of all stories on the front page in 2004.

Even with these decreases, this research confirms that the overall trend in sixteen of the twenty newspapers studied is that the inverted pyramid is sinking as the predominant approach to front-page news. The who, what, where, when, and why is told later. Many times the "who" stars alone in the lead. And the who is often everyman. What we traditionally have considered suitable for the front page is no longer the case in all stories.

In his 2006 book, *The Gang That Wouldn't Write Straight,* Marc Weingarten wrote: "The inverted pyramid, which was widely adapted by American newspapers, at the turn of the century, organized a story with the lead stating the salient theme in the opening paragraph, the body of the story in the middle paragraphs, and the sharp, clever, kicker at the end. The inverted pyramid, which organized the who, what, where, when and why of a story into a compact format, legitimized a story's claims to factual accuracy. It was an airtight system, and newspapers regarded it as unassailable."[16]

What was true at the turn of the last century did not hold true for this century. Just as the media environment has changed drastically to include a dizzying number of options for delivering the news, the writing styles in newspapers have changed drastically to embrace the softer, more humanistic approach to the reporting of daily events in print.

For instance, this story on the front page of the *Miami Herald* on June 1, 2001, "Schools Score High Marks but Sink in Rankings," by Charles Forelle, took an anecdotal approach to a simple numbers story:

> It looked like a report card Libia Gonzalez would be proud to take home to her mother.
>
> George Washington Carver Middle School in Coconut Grove, where Gonzalez is principal, was among Miami-Dade County's top-scoring

schools this year on the Florida Comprehensive Assessment Test. Every one of Carver's students scored at or above a key benchmark known as Level 3 on the FCAT writing test. In math, 94 percent of students met or exceeded Level 3. Statewide, 51 percent of the students were at Level 3 or above on the reading test, but 79 percent of Carvers' were.[17]

Unofficial Sources

After counting how many leads on the front page were narrative, descriptive, anecdotal, or delayed, we measured a third factor in the changing front page of American newspapers—the use and prominence of unofficial sources. I launched into this measurement because I instinctively felt I was reading one heck of a lot of anecdotal leads and comments from average citizens throughout stories. And I was right.

The voices of ordinary citizens are literally rising to the tops of stories or taking up more inches throughout the stories and newspapers in general, also validating a reverence for everyman in today's print news. Newspapers have become more democratic.

It is important for journalists and readers to examine the sourcing process. Speaking at a journalism symposium in April 2005, the *New York Times'* Phil Taubman said, "When readers begin to wonder whether sources are reliable, it is not a big step for them to start wondering if stories and newscasts are credible." Taubman was focusing mostly on the Washington press corps trend of anonymous sources, but he also touched on the sanctity of all sourcing. Taubman called sourcing "the critical transaction that lies at the heart of every story—the transmission of information from source to reporter."[18]

So if the mode of sourcing shifts in the profession and the kinds of sources sought for news and features are different now than even a few years ago, that shift must be examined, weighed, critiqued, and understood.

"A cynical school of thought would have us believe that journalists are exploiters of their sources, that they ultimately violate their confidence for the sake of an interesting story," Roy Peter Clark and Christopher Scanlan wrote in the 2006 edition of *America's Best Newspaper Writing*. But not all writers do so, and certainly not the good ones. "They honor the privilege of access by rendering the lives of their subjects with fairness, honesty, thoroughness and courtesy."[19] It is this careful consideration of a growing reliance on unofficial sources for all stories that inspired this portion of my research. Journalists' "capacity to include is perhaps their most important feature," Michael Schudson wrote in the 1995 book *The Power of News*.[20]

Measuring Frequency of Unofficial Sources

On a scale of 1 to 4 (with 1 as the least and 4 as the most), we measured the prominence of unofficial sources, with a rating of 1 used to define stories with up to one mention of an unofficial source lower in the story. Prominence means the recurring use of unofficial sources, the frequency of references in the story to unofficial sources, and the space allotted to unofficial sources in direct quotes, description, commentary, or background. It is a qualitative ranking considering the amount of space and priority in a story.

A source was considered unofficial if the person quoted was not an expert, but an observer, participant, or commentator. For instance, in a story about a parade, the unofficial sources would have been the people watching the parade—the neighbors and shopkeepers along the route. The official sources would have been the organizers of the event, the mayor, the police.

The percentage of stories using the lowest number of unofficial sources decreased 40 percent from 2001 to 2004. Put another way, 47 percent of the front-page stories in 2001 had a rating of 1, or the fewest unofficial sources. In 2004, only 28 percent of the front-page stories had the lowest number of unofficial sources used. The use of unofficial sources was increasing. The number of stories with minimal unofficial stories was decreasing. The number of stories using more unofficial sources and in higher prominence in the story increased in levels 2, 3, and 4.

A story on the front page with a prominence rating of 2 for unofficial sources had up to two unofficial sources quoted or used, with the sources assigned lower prominence in the story. For instance, if the story had a few anecdotes about an unofficial source or up to two unofficial sources quoted, but the source was mentioned rarely in the text, the rating was a 2.

In 2004, 31 percent of the stories had an unofficial source prominence rating of 2. Just three years earlier, 25 percent of the stories had a rating of 2. That was an increase of 24 percent in the use of unofficial sources.

Stories with a prominence rating of 3 I considered having at least one unofficial source in the story. But the story had an anecdotal lead featuring the unofficial source. More space and prominence were given to unofficial sources than official sources in stories with the 3 rating. These unofficial sources were mentioned higher in the stories and given more text. There was a 25 percent increase in stories with a 3 rating in 2004 from 2001. In 2004 20 percent of the front-page stories studied had a rating of 3, compared to 16 percent of the stories in 2001 with a rating of 3. The use of unofficial sources was increasing here as well.

In 2004, the percentage of stories with a rating of 4 increased an amazing 75 percent. These were the stories that most prominently featured unofficial sources. They were given the highest priority in terms of story placement, word count, and frequency of mention. Most of the text in the stories was information or quotes from unofficial sources. They were profiles or reaction stories, roundups or features based almost entirely on unofficial sources. In 2001 only 12 percent of the stories on the front page had a rating of 4. But by 2004 on the same dates, 21 percent of the front-page stories had a rating of 4 on unofficial sources.

While the largest number of stories still had a prominence rating of 1, the largest increase was in the number of stories giving the highest prominence to unofficial sources with a rating of 4. So if you think you are often reading stories about property taxes or elections with an anecdotal lead and citizen reactions sprinkled throughout the story, you are absolutely right.

I intentionally did not measure the use of official sources in this study, because it was my observation that reporters were not diminishing their use of experts and spokespersons in their stories but were only adding more unofficial voices. The use of official sources in stories will be fodder for future study. The concern in this study was not whether unofficial sources were replacing official sources but rather how many more unofficial voices were included in stories.

Unofficial sources add to the depth of the story and create different vantage points resulting in different kinds of stories. It is the realm of citizen journalism and blogging to use only unofficial sources. The profession of journalism still requires the official head count at the very least. Put simply, when covering that parade, a reporter will still get the crowd estimates from the official organizers of the parade but will more likely start the story with a reaction or comment from a person watching the marching bands from the curb.

Callinan wrote in his email: "Here's an example: When Cincinnati's Procter and Gamble bought Gillette in a $57 billion deal, it was a big news story in Cincinnati. Essentially, the deal meant Cincinnati could arguably be considered the next retail and consumer product capital of the world.

"The challenge was to connect the Real News with Real Lives with some of its 10,000 workers here and untold thousands of retirees and shareholders. The *Enquirer* focused much of its coverage on stories examining the effect on shareholders and retirees, the impact on the company and workers and reaction of regular shoppers.

"The story of how much this meant to the company's growth could have been mired in company executives and industry analysts speaking spread sheet-ese. But while readers might gloss over graphs about 'gross sales and growth strategies' they relate to familiar brand names such as 'Mach3 razors, Duracell batteries and Oral-B tooth care.' So a story and punchy graphic focused on the brands in reporting that the Gillette deal would immediately add five $1 billon brands to P&G's existing 16.

"The package included historical timelines that focused on familiar products readers grew up with (remember Foamy shaving cream?) and the report went deep into the 'what's it mean to me?' question by exploring how the acquisition could ultimately mean a real estate boost in the region as well as increased clout for Greater Cincinnati."

What the data and research in this book reveal is that editors and ultimately our culture place a premium on the personal stories of individuals, valuing them more than the predictable utterances and dalliances of prominent newsmakers or celebrities. What makes front-page news today are the stories of everyman, ordinary citizens whom journalists ideally are ordained to inform and represent. And those stories on the front page are not only about news events. The news on the front page not only validates the voices of everyman, it validates the trends, behaviors, and interests of everyman and declares them newsworthy.

"It is an effort to broaden our sourcing and bring stories home to readers' lives," Callinan wrote. "If done well, personalizing the news is good for journalism. What doesn't work is when sources who are not impacted by the story are dropped in, man-on-the-street style. They may not have to care about or even understand the issue. That's gratuitous. It's bad journalism and it doesn't serve the reader."[21]

Goodbye to Hard News?

On December 31, 2005, the City News Service of Chicago—formerly the City News Bureau—sent out its last news story. It is not insignificant that the legendary wire service, known as a bastion of hard news with famous alums such as Mike Royko, Seymour Hersh, and Kurt Vonnegut, would cease to exist after 115 years. Owned by the *Chicago Tribune,* City News shut its doors on New Year's Eve and let go its 19 employees, who would later be replaced by staff at the *Tribune*'s new Web-based 24-hour, 7-day a week continuous news desk.

In a story published in the *Tribune* on January 1, 2006, reporters Andrew L. Wang and Dave Wischnowsky wrote: "Despite the changes in ownership, the technological evolution of newsrooms and the shifting landscape of modern journalism, the core of City News' role has not strayed far from it original purpose hammered out in 1890 by six of Chicago's newspaper publishers."[22] Perhaps its 86-year-old formula of hard news, inverted-pyramid leads, and succinct summary approaches to breaking news rang its death knell. The approach no longer was valid.

The late Philip L. Graham, publisher of the *Washington Post*, called journalism the "first rough draft of history."[23] That definition can be revised today to call journalism the anecdotal companion to history. The image of journalist as credentialed professional who is the mouthpiece of the expert and the titled has given way to print journalist as a shaper of "slower" daily news.

This is news gathered carefully from unexpected corners of the world and infused with the personal stories of the real people affected directly or indirectly by the news events. Thomas Friedman claimed in his 2005 book, *The World Is Flat*, that the world has entered the stage of Globalization 3.0 and is "flattening" toward an economy uninhibited by time, space, or geography. He also wrote that the companion thrust to this era is "the newfound power for individuals to collaborate and compete globally." According to Friedman, a Pulitzer Prize–winning reporter and columnist for the *New York Times*, "Individuals from every corner of the flat world are being empowered."[24]

Newspapers have become the primary medium for delivering these intimate stories of lives explained in excerpt. For now print offers the most frequent, pluralistic, democratic engagement possible with the public. Online may be bottomless in its citizen access but only in its access to citizens who participate directly with the Web. Not everyone calls up a website, watches a television broadcast, or opens a trade magazine. In the newspaper, a reader can get a brand of story told more intimately than in a news broadcast and more reliably than in a blog. "Brand identity is a tool for capturing trust," Meyer wrote.[25] Everyman news has become the newspaper's niche.

Chapter 3

Content as Commodity

Giving Readers What They Want

Do we, as reporters, always remember that we work for our audience?

—Ken Auletta, "Whom Do Journalists Work For?"

The decline in Sunday circulation of newspapers was strongly evident when I began this study, and the slide continues inexorably even as you read this book. By now, the total will likely have dipped below the 58 million or so copies sold on Sundays in 2005, the same number as in 1985. After a slow rise until 1990, the downslide has been an undeniable pattern in the years since, a fact doomsayers and economists reiterate regularly. But it is a notion that ignores that the glass is half full and likely will not be completely empty in the near future. It also defines the water in relation to the glass, not just as water itself. It also ignores the reality that the water can be poured into another vessel. The apocalyptic view of the future of newspapers relies on the model of physical newspapers, rather than the papers' content, as the commodity.

"This combination of age, ubiquity and standardization endows the newspaper with a strong degree of familiarity," Pablo Boczkowski wrote. "Perhaps none of its features is more taken for granted than the delivery vehicle, to the point of becoming part of the term used to designate the object. This is partly related to the fact that American newspapers have always told the news in ink on paper, despite experiencing significant technological change in three centuries of existence."[1]

The view of the newspaper as defined by the limitations of ink on paper also belittles the reality that the newspaper audience—though definitely shrinking—is still huge. A Research Brief from the Center for Media Research in December 2006 reported that although regular weekly usage of newspapers declined 7.1 percent, 61 percent of consumers studied still read the newspaper weekly, compared to 6.7 percent of consumers studied who read blogs.[2]

In 2005 close to 60 percent of Americans over the age of eighteen read the Sunday newspaper. According to the Newspaper Association of America, Mediamark Research from spring 2004 showed that 60 percent of adult daily newspaper readers read general news, including the front page.[3] The number of newspapers sold each Sunday in 2005 roughly equaled the sixty million people who live in France. And also in Britain. Sixty million people in this country share music files, and more than sixty-three million people voted for *American Idol* winner Taylor Hicks in May 2006.[4] According to the 2006 Pew Internet and American Life Project Survey, sixty million Americans said they used the Internet to make a major life decision—about money, housing, health, or voting.[5] Close to sixty million Americans voted for President George W. Bush in 2004. In December 2006, sixty million people in twenty markets were part of the Sprint wireless broadband network.[6]

The newspaper death watch focuses on the loss in circulation while ignoring the sporadic gains and the niche market still engaged in reading newspapers and still craving the brand of story newspapers deliver. And not all of those readers have the same needs or tastes. The negative view also ignores the potential of newspapers to retain those same eclectic readers by carrying them to another platform with this brand of story as bait. The reader can follow the newspaper online or to whatever delivery system may be created in the next decade and beyond to a place where the number of news consumers may be increasing. It may be time to retire the adage that form dictates content and see that the same brand of content can mutate into many forms. The industry acknowledges that ignoring the dynamics of audience is suicide for newspapers. At this juncture, audiences lean toward everyman news, wherever they find it.

"Savvy publishers and editors have found that if they stop thinking of themselves as print media, and start looking at how to deliver the news and entertainment in a way that their audience wants, they are far more likely to 'engage' them and keep them engaged," Patricia Whalen of Northwestern wrote in 2006. "They know that the trend is moving toward a 24/7 news delivery mechanism that allows for mobile access and in a variety of formats—print, audio, video, photo essays, as well as a highly interactive component that allows for direct comment and inquiry."[7]

Where It Began

Research by Ruth Clark for ASNE in 1979 showed that baby boomers were drifting away from hard news and that they wanted more local news and tips they could use.[8] More than thirty years later, that study is still being quoted. According to Hazel Reinhardt, director of market research at the Media Management Center at Northwestern, "Clark argued that Baby Boomers, who were not reading at the level of their parents, wanted more soft news and feature stories. It seems the children of the Boomers, Gen Y, want even more anecdotal, feature-driven stories than their parents did."[9]

But molding the kinds of stories you run in the newspaper according to the demands of readers is not a simple process of cart, horse, and carrot. "Consumers of news expect to be surprised—by something new," Charles Layton wrote in *American Journalism Review* in 1999. "So asking people what kind of news they want is like asking them to plan their own surprise party." Layton added, "From a research and marketing point of view, a newspaper turns out to be a maddeningly complicated consumer product. When Knight Ridder asked 1,000 people their reasons for buying a newspaper, it got 188 distinct answers—far more than you'd get for running shoes or breakfast cereals or even for an automobile."[10]

In the contemporary environment of shrinking revenues and the desire to please the evolving, evaporating audiences, content has necessarily changed. "Research shows that readers find these (narrative) stories more interesting to read, but I wouldn't call that demand. Editors are trying to hold a mass audience in a segmenting environment," Reinhardt wrote.[11] Interpreting the newspaper research can be as harrowing as mapping a future from tea leaves. But the process is necessary not only for growth, but also for staving off continual decline.

"Amid the carnage of smaller newsroom budgets, buyouts, layoffs and seemingly endless prognostications of doom, opportunity lives," wrote Tim Porter in the spring 2006 issue of *Nieman Reports*. "The one-time mass media has been thin-sliced and cross-diced into me-media, an RSS feed for every person, an opinion expressed for every viewpoint offered, everyone a publisher. All that's left is journalism."[12]

That sort of journalism may equate to everyman content—local, humanistic, and democratic stories. The newspaper is not the product, the story is. At the *Atlanta Journal-Constitution* "content is just as likely to have multiple lives in a range of digital formats," David Levy wrote in February 2006 on www.apple.com.[13] The newspaper's print content is transformed into broadcast copy for other outlets as well as for satellite publishers who in turn produce newspapers for a literally moving market—cruise ships. The brand is then associated with the story, not the paper itself. With the emerging popularity of everyman journalism, the images and text readers get from a more featurized approach to stories may be enough to carry them to another form. The worth of the newspaper's brand of stories to those readers can be measured as a valuable product that exists separately from the ink on the page. And newspapers still have a large audience of readers who may not only be willing to migrate, but feel compelled to do so.

A Pew Internet and American Life study in March 2006 showed that while 71 percent of broadband users get their news online every day, 43 percent still get their news from reading the local paper. Thirty-two percent of people who get their news online go to the website of the local paper.[14] Whether in print or online, the newspaper organization is still a major contender in delivering daily content. The Newspaper Audience Database showed that in 2005, 77 percent of all adults in the top fifty markets read a newspaper at least once a week.[15]

"While the outright collapse of large news organizations is hardly imminent, as the new century progresses, it's hard to escape the fact that their franchises have eroded and their futures are far from certain," wrote Merrill Brown, founder of MSNBC.com.[16]

The Tribune Breakup and the McClatchy Purchase

A shudder went through the industry in June 2006 when plans for a Tribune Company $2 billion stock buyback and TV spinoff were made public.[17] It followed just three months after the sale of the Knight Ridder chain (with its thirty-two daily newspapers) to the McClatchy Company for $4.5 billion, and the prospect of McClatchy unloading a dozen of Knight Ridder's newspapers, from the *Philadelphia Inquirer*—which Brian Tierney later bought—to the *San Jose Mercury News*, deflated the hopes of thousands of journalists and investors assessing the future of newspapers.[18] Job cuts at major dailies such as the *Boston Globe, New York Times, Chicago Tribune, Akron Beacon Journal,* and the *Philadelphia Inquirer* in 2005 and 2006 also contributed to rampant industry near-panic.

"It's like death by drowning instead of death by fire," Stu Bykofsky, *Philadelphia Daily News* columnist, was quoted as saying in a March 14, 2006, *New York Times* article.[19] In a March 15, 2006, story on Alternet.org, Michael Stoll quoted David Satterfield, managing editor of the *San Jose Mercury News:* "I think the more concentrated you get, the more worrisome it is, just because you want to have a lot of voices out there. But with the growth of the Internet and television, you've got a lot of voices out there. The concentration of ownership in newspapers is a lot less important than it was 20 years ago."[20]

Following his May 2006 purchase of the *Philadelphia Inquirer,* the *Philadelphia Daily News,* and Philly.com for $562 million, Brian Tierney told *Advertising Age:* "I think a lot of industries like newspapers somehow see declines as an inevitable thing. I think that is crazy. I reject that and have a different perspective."[21] He may not be alone. Again newspaper watchers took notice when in April 2007 Chicago real estate mogul Sam Zell proposed to buy the Tribune Company for $8.2 billion. The move preceded more layoffs, buyouts, and industry second-guessing.

Good News with Boomers

According to the Newspaper Association of America, in 2005 adults ages eighteen to forty-nine formed the largest group of newspaper readers. The adults in that age group accounted for nearly 62 percent of the total newspaper audience, or 64.8 million readers. This age group is 55 percent of the Sunday gross newspaper audience, which totals 79.2 million readers.[22] "For all the troubling trends, newspapers still deliver the single largest audience in their markets and have by far the greatest newsgathering capacity," according to the State of the News Media 2005 report by the Project for Excellence in Journalism at the Columbia University Graduate School of Journalism.[23]

The Newspaper Association of America reported in 2005 that each Sunday newspaper had an average of 2.56 readers per copy sold, a 10 percent increase from 1994. More than 18 percent of the 789 newspapers studied by the Audit Bureau of Circulations in 2005 gained readers. That means 145 newspapers in this country increased circulation.[24]

"The newspaper industry experienced one of its most active years in modern times during 2005, as several large transactions drove deal volume above $3 billion for only the fifth time in history," according to the 2005 annual report from Dirks, Van Essen and Murray, a newspaper merger and acquisition firm.[25] In 2005, 111 daily newspapers changed hands. In the Poynter Institute's annual report, "State of the News Media 2006," the author of the newspaper section, Rick Edmonds, wrote, "Newspapers, by our reading of the evidence, are not headed for extinction by the end of the decade as some commentary has implied."[26] According to Robert Coen of Universal McCann, total newspaper advertising revenue in 2005 was $47.335 billion, compared to $46.614 billion in 2004.[27]

In May 2006, the Audit Bureau of Circulations report for the six months ending in March 2006 showed an overall slip of 2.5 percent in daily circulation of American newspapers, with a few exceptions. Gains were made by *USA Today*, the *New York Times*, the *Chicago Tribune*, the *Star-Ledger of Newark*, and the *Detroit Free Press*.[28] In the "Wall Street Transcript" of December 13, 2005, analyst Edward Atorino predicted, "Circulation will stabilize to some degree. . . . The newspaper publishing companies' online businesses are growing rapidly. So some dynamics within newspaper publishing companies are changing for the better."[29]

That change may be to shift away from newsprint as commodity to the story content as commodity, all while maintaining "journalistic excellence," a buzz phrase used as the decisive standard for bidders in the negotiations for sale of the Knight Ridder chain. According to a March 14, 2006, *New York Times* article, Private Capital Management leader Bruce Sherman wrote in a letter to investors in 2005: "Viewed from our perspective, the ability to sustain a long-term paper-based franchise while leveraging the same content into electronic distribution afford the newspaper industry the opportunity not just to survive but eventually to resume robust growth."[30] In 2006 Sherman's company, Private Capital based in Naples, Florida, held $697 million in McClatchy stock and $997 million worth of stock in Gannett Company, Inc.

A More Complex Business

In the last century, the newspaper business has been sliced and diced to suit different target audiences and please corporate owners. By comparison, a 1952 study, "The Maximisation of Profit by a Newspaper," by W. M. Corden in the *Review of Economic Studies*, appears nothing less than quaint when read today: "The newspaper's chief object is to produce the product of printed matter designed to satisfy the demands of readers. . . . If the numerous external factors influencing demand, such as competition, population and tastes, remain unchanged, then the quantity sold at a given price depends on the quality of the newspaper from the point of view of the reader."[31]

Today that definition falls short and is surely too simplistic. It could logically be changed in 2007 to "the chief objective of a newspaper is to produce the product of quality news in any format deemed fit and supply information to satisfy the demands of a splintered consumer base." The new definition would identify story consumers as active, rather than passive, appreciating their role as readers, viewers, participants, listeners, and content contributors. The profit definition for newspapers can also be modified more than fifty years later to include "If numerous external factors such as competition, population and tastes continue to shift dramatically, then the value of the news stories depends on the value to the reader."

The 1952 notion of newspaper profitability and viability is antiquated because it did not envision such intense and diversified competition from the crowded media marketplace. Newspapers and all other media must compete for "the consumer's share of mind," said Judith McHale, president and chief executive officer of Discovery Communications.[32] She conceded that competition for media consumers is shared with iPods, blogs, broadband, PDAs, MP3 players, Xbox 360, videogames, podcasts, websites, twenty-four-hour cable news, and all consumer-generated media. In 1952 the daily newspaper only competed with the network television evening news and radio news for a slice of the consumer's loyal attention.

Navigating through the mountains of this buzzing media environment requires agility. Newspapers "must be nimble and adaptive," said Dana Robbins, editor-in-chief at the *Hamilton Spectator* in Canada.[33]

Newspapers Online and on Target?

That adaptive quality includes viewing the Internet not as the traditional newspaper's greatest competitor, but as its greatest ally. A record number—fifty-five million people—visited newspaper websites in November 2005, according to the Nielsen/Net Ratings and the Newspaper Association of America's report in February 2006.[34]

For the first time, the study showed, more than one-third of all Internet users visited a newspaper website. Of the top twenty current events and news sites for December 2005, according to the same report, eight were newspaper websites. Those newspapers with popular websites include Gannett, nytimes.com, Tribune Newspapers, USA Today, Knight Ridder Digital, Hearst, Washingtonpost.com and Advance Internet.

At the *Oklahoma City Oklahoman*, registered users of the paper's website, NewsOK, exceeded the number of readers for the print version in 2006 with more than 277,000 subscribers. According to the Pew Internet and American Life Project, in February–March 2005, 72 percent of the 137 million Americans online said they get their news from the Web.[35]

"This is not the first time the newspapers have been threatened by new technology. The demise of the American newspaper has been foreseen in the years after the Marconi wireless radio, television, then 24-hour cable news," wrote Kevin Craver, a blogger on rathergate.com in his May 4, 2005, post. "Yet newspapers are still here."[36]

The emerging model of newspaper story as democratic narrative can be seen as something that could exist in any platform, a portable model applicable to any form of media, even those not yet created. This everyman journalism does already exist in many forms: broadcast documentary, streaming news video clips online, as well as in longer audio stories running on public radio stations. The journalism form also exists online as content "shoveled" from the print newspaper to the newspaper's website. But it could be more, in special sections of newspapers, take-out CD-ROMS, or sites devoted entirely to the newspaper's brand of everyman news.

It could be that the newspaper's brand of everyman news is what the reader is after, no matter how or where that story arrives in the future. Some newspaper editors appear to recognize that potential. In August 2005, Bill Keller of the *New York Times* sent a memo to his staff announcing the merging of the digital and print newsrooms in which he said, "By integrating the newsrooms we plan to diminish and eventually eliminate the difference between newspaper journalists and Web journalists—to recognize our structures and our minds to make Web journalism, in forms that are both familiar and yet-to-be-invented, as natural to us as writing and editing, and to do all of this without losing the essential qualities that make us the Times. Our readers are moving, and so are we."[37]

Two months later, *New York Times* publisher Arthur Sulzberger Jr. told *Times* reporter Katharine Q. Seelye that "At the end of the day, it is the audience we collect and the quality of that audience that is the critical factor, not the means by which we collect it." In the same story, Peter R. Kann, chairman of Dow Jones, is also quoted: "A daily print package of the most important news, insight and analysis continues to have high value."[38] The value of the journalism produced is assigned not only by the journalists, but also by the readers. Journalism is a revered transaction of information from news gatherer to audience. In turn the audience can influence the types of stories, tone of those stories, and kinds of sources used through their complaints, their accolades, and ultimately their usage behavior.

The circulation decline overall has been decades coming. The pockets of growth in the industry may well show that those newspapers that experience the increases recognize the shift in reader tastes. "You need to look to see if what you're writing is what they're looking for," *Times-Picayune* city editor David Meeks said in a speech in April 2006.[39]

In the *Nieman Reports* of spring 1999, Bill Kovach wrote, "There are limitless possibilities to redefine news in ways that will set the work of journalists apart from the babble of self-interest and self-celebration and, in the process, make the work of journalists more compelling, more connected with, and more rewarding to the public." He added, "A secure place for quality journalism in the mixed media culture of today is assured if we produce reliable information that results from a disciplined methodology and write stories filled with depth, detail and context."[40]

So What Do Readers Want?

If a reader believes a newspaper story means one brand of everyman story, then the reader will seek that brand of story. The story is the brand. "The development of brand reputations is even more important as the number of news outlets expands, because reputations based on past consumption allow a paper or program to stand out among competitors," wrote James T. Hamilton.[41] Perhaps what makes newspapers stand out among the crowded news marketplace is the ability to tell engaging, humanistic stories.

"Consumers always want great storytelling," said McHale. "That is never going away. You can always adapt content to the audience because people assimilate."[42] Thinking of the story rather than the page where it appears as the commodity that creates the relationship requires a reinvention of the newspaper culture.

"In a world in which political and commercial institutions create alternative virtual worlds that compete with the world of reality journalism presents, it is even more important that newsrooms develop a new relationship with the public," Bill Kovach, founding chairman of the Committee of Concerned Journalists, wrote in 2005.[43]

Arguments about the migration of classified ads to online, loss of overall ad revenue, circulation reporting irregularities, and the costs of paper, newsgathering, and staffing aside, circulation considerations can logically touch on newspaper content. Just as audience size in a theater can relate to the reception of a play, the content of a newspaper can logically be linked to its circulation. Unless you believe that readers buy the newspaper solely for the grocery ads or the horoscopes, the editorial content will be connected to the size and loyalty of the available audience. A newspaper considered great according to industry and audience standards in Sheboygan, Wisconsin, will never have a larger audience than a great newspaper in Seattle, Washington. Even if the Sheboygan paper is better.

It is up to editors to see the connection between content and audience. Robbins said he surveyed the top editorial and circulation managers of thirty-nine newspapers about the month's best front page for that newspaper. At only one newspaper did the top editor and the top circulation staffer agree on what had been the best front-page story. And at only two newspapers did editorial and circulation managers agree on who was each newspaper's target audience.[44]

The Readers Want Personal Stories

"Newspapers are in flux and are trying to figure out how to keep audiences," Walt Harrington said.[45] "The bigger question is if people are not interested in news they don't consider relevant," he said. Jack Hart was more straightforward. "News narrative has a way of building readership."[46] There is a correlation, but it is not proven to be cause and effect. In a story in *American Journalism Review* in April/May 2005, Rachel Smolkin wrote: "And I think there's not a clear-cut equation in which on one side of the equal sign are changes in what you write and on the other side of the equal sign are changes in the number of readers. One of the things that I'm trying to tell people and describe to people is that we're in a period of continual change and that a series of steps won't be rolled out under the heading, 'The Solution.'"[47]

According to Smolkin, a study of *Washington Post* front pages showed readership dipped 7 percent from August 2002 to February 2004, when editors said their front pages were perhaps too heavy on their Iraq war coverage. "Len Downie [the executive editor] is skeptical the correlation between news events and circulation is really that precise," Smolkin wrote. But, she added, "Downie does hope to spice up the front-page mix." The consensus, then, she wrote, was to put more local stories on page one, and to be less "dull." Less dull for readers may mean more features, feature approaches to news and stories about real people, as well as using ordinary citizens as sources more often in all stories.

The May 23, 2004, Pew Research Center for the People and the Press report predicted: "Newspapers, seeking to become more entertaining and interesting to readers, will publish more stories written in the narrative form, rather than the traditional style of presenting the facts in a straightforward manner. This trend will give newspapers more of an emotional charge and a human touch, making them appeal to readers in the way that fiction now is. As a result of this trend the use of the first person will also become more accepted and popular."[48]

Real Numbers and Real Change

Some of the 145 newspapers posting circulation gains in 2005, according to the Audit Bureau of Circulations, included the *Louisville Courier-Journal*, the *New York Times*, the *Indianapolis Star*, the *Cincinnati Enquirer*, and *USA Today*. According to *Editor and Publisher*, the *Bulletin* in Bend, Oregon, also boasted a healthy 7.5 percent Sunday circulation increase in 2005, and a 5.4 percent daily circulation rise.[49]

Sixteen of the newspapers in the study for this book are in the top fifty newspapers ranked by circulation, according to the Audit Bureau of Circulations in 2005. Three of the papers that posted increases are included in this book's data. At the *Cincinnati Enquirer*, the percentage of features on the front page increased from 29 percent in 2001 to 45 percent in 2004. The percentage of stories on the front page with narrative or anecdotal leads increased from 19 to 45 percent in the same time period at the Ohio paper.

The *Louisville Courier-Journal* showed an increase in front-page features from 10 percent for the dates studied in 2001 to 32 percent for comparable dates in 2004. The percentage of feature leads on stories on the front page increased from 15 to 26 percent for the same time period. Similarly, at the *New York Times*, the percentage of front-page feature stories went from 38 percent for the four dates studied in 2001 to 54 percent in 2004. Feature leads on the front page, though, decreased slightly at the paper from 38 to 33 percent from 2001 to 2004. But the percentage of feature leads for the entire paper remained at about one-third of all stories.

Recent readership studies—many from Northwestern's Readership Institute—bear out that content change toward more features, more narrative storytelling in all stories, and more stories about ordinary people can result in circulation boosts. What I measured on the front-page stories studied for this book correlated to those findings. I measured features, feature approaches to all stories, and the use of unofficial sources or "ordinary people" in all stories.

In the first assessment of its kind surveying 37,000 newspaper readers in this country, the Readership Institute in its 2001 report, "Newspaper Content: What Makes Readers More Satisfied" reported readers wanted more lifestyle news with feature approaches, more stories about the governing process, and more global stories with a feature approach. Readers also said they wanted more science, technology, environment, and sports stories with a feature approach.[50]

In the institute's 2001 "The Power to Grow Readership," researchers concluded that "What the research shows, though, is a strong reader appetite for news that is intensely local and personally relevant." The report continued, "Doing a better job covering ordinary people is two-fold. It means writing more stories about ordinary people engaging in ordinary, real-life activities and respecting the concerns of everyday life. In other words, writing about 'people like me.' It also means telling other stories, especially institutional and government stories in an everyday context, incorporating the voices of ordinary people, and clearly articulating 'what it means to me.'"[51]

Readers want stories with more unofficial sources. And according to the data for this book, more newspapers are giving them what they want in stories on the front page. In 2003, the Readership Institute looked at the value of feature-style writing for readers and found an appetite for narrative. They wanted news and all kinds of stories told in a non-hard news approach: "Content matters to readers and without prompting, readers recognize differences in coverage. . . . Changing content can increase satisfaction—and that satisfaction has the potential to translate into higher readership."

Readers reported that storytelling matters. "Feature-style writing is found to increase satisfaction in a variety of topic areas: politics, sports, science, health, home and food among them." These kinds of stories improve "overall brand perception, chief among them how 'easy to read' the newspaper is."[52]

The study continued, "Beyond increasing satisfaction with particular content areas, feature-style writing also improves positive brand perception. Newspapers that run more feature-style stories are seen as more honest, fun, neighborly, intelligent, 'in the know' and more in touch with the values of readers."

Editors of the 112 newspapers responding to the Readership Institute survey found the three most important changes made to the newspaper were "intensifying the local focus of the paper, increasing attention given to ordinary people and changing the culture of the newspaper," the study showed. Sixty-four percent of the 112 newspapers said they had increases in hard numbers—circulation, penetration, and readership—as a result of those specific readership building efforts.[53]

In a July 2003 Readership Institute report, one-third of the newspapers reported paying "a lot of attention" to increasing the number of stories about ordinary people. Forty-three percent of the newspapers said they increased the number of stories about ordinary people. The same percentage reported increasing the number of lifestyle stories or features in the newspaper. Forty percent reported they increased the number of stories about ordinary people in the community.[54]

Editors reported "they have done far more stories about ordinary people, more 'chicken dinner' and other hyper-local news, more feature-style stories, more story obits and more lifestyle news," according to the institute's report. "Newspapers also want to do more with features—including doing more specialty pages, anchored feature pages, more people and heart stories, more stories personalizing routine or regular events, new sections, more 'go and do' information and more entertainment news."[55]

While the findings from the Readership Institute assert that editors assume changes in content will drive circulation, we know that content is not the only factor in building circulation. If a reader can't easily obtain the paper, get it delivered, or get a response to a question, no amount of sparkling content will make that reader stay.

Journalists Weigh In

These studies show what readers prefer in newspaper content, but what do journalists think? In a May 23, 2004, study from the Pew Research Center for the People and the Press, only 15 percent of print journalists surveyed said they view declining readership as a big concern.[56]

The 2004 Pew report showed that 51 percent of the journalists at national media outlets said journalism is going in the wrong direction. A majority, or 66 percent, said bottom-line pressures are hurting news coverage. Of the nearly 550 national and local journalists surveyed, 86 percent said news avoids complex issues. More than half reported they are concerned that there is increasingly sloppy reporting. In 2004, 41 percent of national journalists and 33 percent of local journalists said problems with the quality of coverage remains a major concern.[57]

On the positive side, 42 percent of local print journalists and 31 percent of national print journalists surveyed by Pew said the quality of coverage is journalism's best performance trait. Sixty percent of national journalists reported the Internet has made journalism better—serving to augment reporting and supplement source files: "About one in five say the Internet has helped journalism by making far more information available to the public, and by helping to improve the accuracy of the information."[58]

"A related notion, mentioned about as often, is that the Internet has broadened the range of outlets and voices available to the public. This includes more points of view, deeper stories and coverage of topics and stories that otherwise would not have fit into existing time and space available," the report continued. "These changes have forced journalism to be more innovative and responsive to the public; one respondent said the Internet has 'democratized the press.'"[59]

That democratization results in a return to the historical view of journalist as public servant who provides not only what readers want, but also what they must know. What emerges is a product that is more than humanized approaches to stories and a familiarity with the lives of local citizens, it is a balance of stories judiciously weighed for newsworthiness and weighted with the necessary information. Where editors place the fulcrum in the range of stories is open to debate—balancing what readers say they want to know against what editors believe they need to know. The challenge is to keep readers level on the seesaw—staying for the desired content instead of falling off, or climbing off, and going elsewhere.

Choices and More Choices

In the December 2005 Red Smith Lecture on Journalism at the University of Notre Dame, Ken Auletta said, "Let us concede that most journalistic enterprises need to make a profit, and to make a profit they must be like supermarkets, offering a range of choices to their customers—international news, weather, sports, business, movie review, cartoons, the results of planning board meetings, etc." Auletta added, "But journalism is about sifting information, finding different voices, trying to get at the complex truth, offering context. It is not just a bird's-eye view. Live television or Webcasts—or blogs—can be like fireworks, dazzling, awesome, but soon the sky is dark again."[60]

It is up to newspapers to continue to illuminate the media landscape with good journalism, continuing to tell stories with consequence, impact, and relevance. "Perhaps most important, winning back audience through better storytelling is hard, time-consuming, and costly. As a consequence when the news industry tries to address flagging audiences, it often emphasizes concerns that are easier to manage, boosting market budgets, cutting costs, changing anchorpeople, or building a new set for the news," Rosenstiel and Kovach wrote in their 2001 book, *The Elements of Journalism.*[61]

Two years later in the Ruhl Symposium Speech in Eugene, Oregon, Rosenstiel reemphasized his points: "Journalism must remain a craft, something marinated in the street and forged by doing it rather than thinking about it. Only this will make it responsive to the public, and ensure its economic vitality."[62]

While recent statistics show the continued growth of the Internet as a news source threatens the newspaper's future, the prediction of mortality for newspapers long predates the Internet. "The daily is disappearing by way of extinction and amalgamation; its mortality rate is rising," Helen

MacGill Hughes wrote in the *American Journal of Sociology* more than sixty years ago. In her review of the 1944 book by Oswald Garrison Villard, *The Disappearing Daily: Chapters in American Newspaper Evolution*, Hughes concluded, "It is disappearing as a moral force, and the writing of editorials has become a conventional exercise that has no effect on public affairs." She added, "The readers, too, are not so robust as they used to be."[63] The newspaper naysayers are born in each generation.

The future of newspapers is not something anyone knows or can responsibly predict. The mosaic pieces of possible solutions to a shift in readership are available to the industry—circulation trends, reader studies, consideration of everyman content as the driver and considered projections about print journalism's future. No one source has provided the definitive answers, the magic pill or the crystal ball. But each newspaper can manipulate the mosaic through a kaleidoscope of practices and come up with a plan, mapping an acceptable blueprint that will please readers and ultimately the journalists and media owners who serve them.

Chapter 4

Citizen Journalism and Chicken Little

Obviously there can be benefits to getting one's news from multiple sources; others have made that case often enough that I won't bother to state the obvious anymore.

—Tom Fenton, *Bad News: The Decline of Reporting,*
the Business of News, and the Danger to Us All

✳ If citizen journalists have a patron saint, her name, unfortunately, would be Katrina. While mainstream media coverage was initially offsite and the official sources were misinformed—or misleading—during the worst natural disaster in recent history to hit American shores, citizen journalists and unofficial sources told the stories that helped refashion front-page news.

Even Sen. Patrick Leahy (D-Vermont) in his questioning of John Roberts during Supreme Court nomination hearings in September 2005 said the American public only found out about the breadth of the tragedy befalling the Gulf Coast from the media, not the federal government. Content came directly from the people involved, even if some of the reported stories later turned out to have been fueled by hysteria.[1]

That event marked the first time the big media boys, such as the *New York Times*, pleaded for input from nonjournalists. The levee of resistance was permanently breeched. On September 1, 2005, readers at www.nytimes.com were invited to "share your experiences via email or in this forum."[2] To do so, they simply clicked on the "Your Story" icon, which appeared to the left of the main story, "Higher Death Toll Seen; Police Ordered to Stop Looters," by Robert D. McFadden and Ralph Blumenthal.

After clicking, they were instructed to answer this question: "Were you affected by Hurricane Katrina and its aftermath? If so, *The New York Times* invites you to share your story. Selected stories will be published. Send an e-mail message describing what happened to *katrina@nytimes.com*. Please include information on how *The Times* can contact you with follow-up questions. Thank you."[3]

No longer was the process about reporters trying to find sources. Sources were urged to find the reporters. Either Katrina was sitting at a desk on West 43rd Street, as her email address suggested, or the email tactic was just a more efficient way to shake the bushes. But it was the first time citizen journalists were invited to the editorial meeting.

"That certainly was significant," said Dan Gillmor, author and creator of the citizen journalist project bayosphere.com. In a phone interview days after Katrina hit, Gillmor continued, "Each big event solidifies the role of citizen journalism. I think it has helped the mass media understand that listening is an important part of journalism."[4]

Chicken Little Journalism

But some of the stories told in many newspapers were not true. There is an inherent danger in publishing what I call Chicken Little Journalism, or unvetted news. That was evident with the news of Katrina. Unconfirmed reports became urban myths as stories of child rape, murders, and gang wars inside the New Orleans Convention Center and the Superdome were repeated on television reports and in print. In a September 28 interview with "Good Morning America" host Charles Gibson, *Times-Picayune* editor Jim Amoss said it was difficult to distinguish between fact and fiction because people immersed in the crisis "were predisposed" to believe that the mayhem was worse than it really was. Still, much of what was and is the meat of citizen journalist websites is accurate, informative, and non-toxic. But after Katrina, the cries that the sky was falling were louder than some of the truth.[5]

On September 29, 2005, the *New York Times* ran a story by Jim Dwyer and Christopher Drew that read like a disclaimer, if not an outright apology: "A month later, a review of the available evidence now shows that some, though not all, of the most alarming stories that coursed through the city appear to be little more than figments of frightened imaginations, the product of chaotic circumstances that included no reliable communications, and perhaps the residue of the longstanding raw relations between some police officers and members of the public."

In the penultimate paragraph of the story, a mea culpa and attempt at transparency emerged: "To assemble a picture of crime, both real and perceived, the New York Times interviewed dozens of evacuees in four cities, police officers, medical workers and city officials. Though many provided concrete firsthand accounts, others passed along secondhand information or rumor that after multiple tellings had ossified into what became accepted as fact."[6]

In his 2003 book, *Backstory: Inside the Business of News,* media critic Ken Auletta wrote that "journalism is not a walk-on profession. It requires training, just as a split end and quarterback repeatedly practice pass routes or a violinist again and again rehearses a concerto." He added, "While we are not licensed as lawyers or doctors, and not as extensively trained, we are, in effect, accredited to sort out fact from fiction, to decide what is news and what is not, what is more and also less important, what the public needs to know to make decisions in a democracy."[7]

While citizen journalists implore mainstream media to abandon the gavel of elitism and exclusion, it also bears repeating that in the childhood fable, Chicken Little was convinced the sky was falling, even though it was only an apple falling from a tree that indeed hit him on the head. Some sites and outlets are establishing new standards for contributors, as Gillmor did on bayosphere.com in September 2005.

"No longer is the audience at one end of the information pipeline. Citizen journalists and blogs have broken the monopoly of knowledge," Norman Sims said in a panel discussion at the 2006 Association for Education in Journalism and Mass Communication (AEJMC) conference.[8] Dan Gillmor called citizen journalism "the audience-producer pool."[9] The audience is not only the user, but also the producer. "User-generated content—turning the audience into the auteur—isn't exactly an online innovation," Jon Pareles wrote in the *Times* in December 2006. "It's as old as 'America's Funniest Home Videos,' or letters to the editor, or community sings, or Talmudic commentary, or graffiti. The difference is that in past eras most self-expression stayed close to home. Users generated traditional cultures and honed regional styles, concentrated by geographical isolation."[10] The boundaries of isolation have dissolved.

Understandably, the reliability and credibility of citizen journalism is a topic of debate in journalism circles, a cause for concern and a schism within journalism. What if someone intentionally publishes information that is not only wrong and inaccurate, but incendiary—or at worst, deadly? What if the result of the misinformation leads to widespread panic and violence? Or is so personally injurious it causes someone to do himself harm?

"I subscribe to the old fashioned theory of gatekeepers, those who control the locks on a canal and open then close them to best serve everyone on the way to his destination," wrote Ron Steinman, author and journalist, in the June 2004 issue of the *Digital Journalist*. "Without the gatekeeper, meaning the editor, the person with the keys to the lock, all the boats might try to come through when they want or worse, try to get through at the same time without anything to stop them. We all know the result: chaos."[11]

But when it works well, citizen journalists tell their stories with a purity of intent and a sense of social responsibility. Mainstream newspapers are attempting to mimic that intent and be more inclusive by representing more voices in the newspaper in places other than letters to the editor and calendar listings. Would American newspapers ever have opened up to have more unofficial sources without the recent loud banging at the door by citizen journalists? "Citizen journalism continues to be an evolving and frustrating concept for mainstream media," wrote Shayne Bowman and Chris Willis in *Nieman Reports* in winter 2005. "It offers the tantalizing idea of an active and engaged democracy better informing itself. It also can represent an evolving and reckless endeavor that might result in just the opposite."[12]

In April 2006, the *Times-Picayune* of New Orleans and the *Sun Herald* of Biloxi, Mississippi, each received a gold medal for public service journalism from the Pulitzer Prize board. The *Times-Picayune* staff also won a Pulitzer for breaking news "for its courageous and aggressive coverage of Hurricane Katrina, overcoming desperate conditions facing the city and the newspaper." The heroism of the *Times-Picayune* was evidenced in its embracing of unofficial voices while still refusing to be sucked into the chaos of noncorroborated urban myth that fell beneath its journalistic standards. "Readers were starved not only for food," city editor David Meeks said. "They were starved for information and the newspaper was a sign of normalcy."[13]

The people affected by the outrageous upheaval were eager if not desperate to tell their stories. Citizen journalists and credentialed journalists were eager to hear them. "In the face of Katrina's horror, I found people surprisingly eager to tell their stories," Elizabeth Mehren, New England bureau chief of the *Los Angeles Times*, wrote in the winter 2005 *Nieman Reports*. "In their terrible situation, I might have been inclined to tell a nosy journalist to buzz off. But instead they opened their hearts."[14] American newspapers ran their heartfelt stories in abundance.

The Need for Unofficial Sources

After Katrina was gone but not forgotten and Hurricane Rita headed for Texas, the September 23, 2005, *New York Times* national section ran a pair of stories on A13 under the slug, "Storm and Crisis: Facing the New Hurricane." A story by Rick Lyman on the exodus from Houston briefly told the

tales of nine people who were headed out of town. The story had no official sources, only rich description and quotes from individuals telling their
stories.[15] On the right side of the page was a story by Simon Romero
reporting from Galveston called "A Snapshot of Evacuees." The reporter
recounted the stories of nine residents who were "staying put."[16] Like the
first story, it used no official sources. While both were eloquently written
and organized, either story could have easily been a citizen journalism
blog. This kind of detailed, anecdotal writing was reminiscent of the *New
York Times'* groundbreaking obituaries after 9/11, those unforgettable
"Portraits of Grief."

But unlike the aftermath of 9/11, when the growth of grassroots journalism was still in the seedling stage, the roar and horror of all that was Hurricane Katrina unilaterally increased the journalistic reliance on ordinary
people as news sources—not by default, but by choice. They were used
more often, and their voices were nearer the lead in the story, given more
weight, more space, more time, more credibility. The event flipped the
reporting process, perhaps permanently, from top down to bottom up. It
was the crowning of the man on the street as king of the sources.

A domestic national tragedy, Katrina was the same genus of event as
9/11, but a different species. In the fall of 2001, there was no way to fill the
pages of newspapers with what seemed the biggest news of the century
with anything other than reaction and speculation from official sources.
The compelling stories of survivors and witnesses in New York, Washington, D.C., and Pennsylvania sated reader appetites in the moments, days,
weeks, and months that followed.

With Katrina, the better way to report the news was from the point of
view of the people escaping the flood, not the ones in Washington arguing
about how high the water was or whether or not the bottles of drinking
water were on their way. Everyman journalism was converging on the
Gulf Coast in every platform—from cell phone to podcast to website and
newspaper. Citizen and mainstream journalists alike were all covering the
unfolding tragedy to authenticate the true stories of evacuated and shattered residents. The exaltation of the unofficial voice across the board
secured him or her as pure newsmaker. It was that trust in the unofficial
source that led so many journalists to report their stories, believing them to
be true, not realizing the role that panic, rumor, and hysteria played in the
view of events. The immediacy, the intimacy, the informality, and the
urgency that defines citizen journalism had been spreading to newspapers
for a few years. Like it or not, Katrina made it stick.

"When there is a catastrophe, such as this hurricane, people don't
want to read a newspaper to find out how much rain fell. They want to

find out what happened to the people," said Alicia Shepard, author of *Woodward and Bernstein: Life in the Shadow of Watergate* and ombudsman at National Public Radio.[17]

That same brand of everyman news fueled by citizen journalism and the drama offered by the stories of unofficial sources was prevalent in newspapers, broadcast, and online sites following the August 2007 collapse of the 35W bridge in Minneapolis into the Mississippi River.

Responsible Citizen Input

For the three days immediately after the hurricane, the *Times-Picayune* of New Orleans was unable to create or deliver a print version of its newspaper of about 270,000 circulation in a city without electricity. Managing editor Peter Kovacs reported his staff was producing the paper online. Later, a small edition of the newspaper was printed on the presses of the *Advocate* newspaper in Baton Rouge, about seventy miles to the north.

The paper valiantly published breaking news and blogs posted on the nola.com website (an abbreviation for New Orleans, Louisiana). Editors invited readers to "share your neighborhood storm news in our local forums" and listed eight forums from seven local parishes. On the Orleans Parish forum, postings bore everything from pleas for news of missing relatives and friends to reports of stranded pets and political criticism. The traditional print newspaper existed on a blogsite and the two forms briefly worked as one.

On Monday, August 29, before the levees broke in New Orleans, the *Times-Picayune*'s online front page led with this story by Gwen Filosa:

"A 2-year-old girl clutching a bottle and ignoring her knock-off Barbie doll, running in circles around her mother. Homeless men trying to doze on the sidewalk, using backpacks as pillows. People without cars. People with cars but nowhere to go."[18] It was a descriptive, narrative lead that seemed plucked from a Tom Wolfe book.

The next day, under the head "Catastrophic," one of the three front-page stories began with a humanistic lead. This one, written by Brian Thevenot and Manuel Torres, read "As Jerry Reyes piloted his boat down St. Claude Avenue, just past the Industrial Canal, the eerie screams that could barely be heard from the roadway grew louder as one by one, faces of desperate families appeared on rooftops, on balconies, and in windows, some of them waving white flags."[19] It was one of many eloquent everyman leads on the front page that week. And it was a noticeable shift of a trend in newspaper writing that had been sliding in that direction for years.

In "Doing Well and Doing Good: How Soft News and Critical Journalism Are Shrinking the News Audience and Weakening Democracy—And What News Outlets Can Do about It" (2000), author Thomas E. Patterson of Harvard University asserted that "soft news has increased dramatically as a proportion of news coverage." He defined soft news the way I define features—not hard news and not tied to a recent breaking event. These stories, Patterson wrote, "that include a human interest element also figure more prominently in the news." In 1998, he estimated that about 26 percent of the stories were human interest, compared to 11 percent of those stories in the early 1980s.[20] What we found researching this book is that the number of features doubled from his findings in the late '90s. The stories on the front pages of many newspapers following Katrina were at least 50 percent, and sometimes up to 80 percent, human interest.

The Citizens Were the Story

Regardless of the messy finger-pointing and politicking that erupted during and after the Katrina tragedy, the immediate truth emerging in mainstream newspapers, media websites, blogs, citizen journalism sites, and mainstream television and radio was that the information Americans wanted was not coming from the White House, the Federal Emergency Management Agency (FEMA), or the embattled New Orleans mayor's office. It was coming from the flooded streets, rooftops, and shelters as well as buses and trucks headed anywhere out of town.

The coverage of Katrina "opened up moments where they were talking about those Americans whose voices are almost never heard in the media, and whose absence is always there in public discourse, said Bruce A. Williams at the University of Illinois.[21] That "opening up," however, could have a downside. "My fear is what happens when you start moving to personal stories—the triumph or tragedy of the individual—the danger is always that you get away from the structural realities. These are questions of government policy, the global economy, so it is a social scientist's endless criticism of the very way journalists go about their business," Williams said. "I think there are dangers of trivializing, so you must present the stories in an honest and accurate way to show these broader issues."

The National Radio Project out of Oakland, California, reported local stories mainstream media missed in the aftermath of Katrina in its "Making Contact" series of "Katrina Uncovers." The mission of the project, rooted in activism, journalism, and citizen participation, is "connecting people, vital ideas and important information." The project produces journalism with an advocacy component appropriately absent from newspapers but with voices from the citizenry that can no longer be avoided or ignored.[22]

The official sources surrounding Katrina were not telling the story or explaining the broader issues to journalists. So the reporters were blogging eyewitness reports. Blogsites such as craigslist.com were filling up with citizen journalism and first-person accounts.

It was the kind of authentic, first-person, passionate reporting and writing that John C. Merrill had lobbied for journalists to pursue decades ago in his 1977 book, *Existential Journalism*. "And it would seem that productive journalism, or journalism that reaches furthest toward true objectivity, would also be that which involves the interest of the reporter," Merrill wrote. "It is impossible for the journalist to detach himself from his story if he is to give an honest and full ('encompassing') account."[23]

CNN's website on September 1 and the following days of coverage hosted a blog written in the first person by correspondents including Chris Lawrence, who wrote: "It's hard to believe this is New Orleans."[24] CNN's Jim Spellman wrote: "I don't think I really have the vocabulary for this situation."[25]

It was not about official experts and their surveillance of the scene. At MSNBC.com, katrinablog captured—and continued to highlight—personal stories and daily updates. The Shreveporttimes.com hosted "Talk Back Forums" to discuss and share the latest news of Katrina. Under "More Headlines," readers could click to "Send us your memories of New Orleans."[26]

"People want to tell their stories and tell each other what they know," Gillmor said. However, he cautioned, "The tsunami had more examples of it, since [in New Orleans] the cell phone towers were out of commission and there was no power for much of it. You saw citizen journalism before and after, but the middle was missing."[27]

Still, even though the London bombings and the 2004 tsunami in Southeast Asia were milestones on the timeline of citizen journalism, the 2005 hurricane coverage in many American newspapers was undoubtedly informed by the voices and stories of the people. Americans did not want to read official spin; they wanted the truth, even though it was as raw and disturbing at times as the muck filling the streets, homes, churches, roads, and businesses throughout Louisiana and Mississippi.

On the Metroblogging New Orleans website, www.neworleans .metblogs.com, New Orleans photographer Michael Siu posted a series of images and his first-person account of what he saw Uptown on August 31. Bloggers were telling the unimaginable stories of bodies floating in the darkened water and violence, death, and mayhem at the Superdome and the convention center.[28]

"The Blogosphere and other Internet-based New Media have ended the mainstream media's monopoly on reporting the news," wrote Mark Tapscott, director of the Center for New Media and Public Policy at the Heritage Foundation, and columnist for townhall.com in a July 28, 2005, column, a month before Katrina. Writing about citizen coverage of the tsunamis and the London bombings, Tapscott said, "With sales and capabilities of video-cameras, pod and video-casting and cell phones zooming and the prospect of far more advanced tools for transmitting live-action images coming soon to the market, we now live in a world with thousands of citizen journalists."[29]

And more sprang into action with Katrina.

"With so many storytellers trying to tell stories (the Internet alone has so many separate sources of news), and with so many departing from the 'information model' of 'objective news,' journalists once again must attempt to define their craft," David T. Z. Mindich wrote in the 1998 book *Just the Facts: How Objectivity Came to Define American Journalism*.[30] Journalists for American newspapers overwhelmingly wrote the story of Katrina by telling the stories of the people in her wake.

"The best journalism is doing a better job by turning in more personal elements," said Mindich, professor at Saint Michael's College. "It does feel like democracy playing out in a better way with more immediate stories from more people." He added, "There are places where citizen journalism is important, especially if it can help bolster the directive of elite papers to do adversarial journalism and explain different parts of society to each other and have readers confront the news."[31]

Isn't that what the *New York Times* and other mainstream newspapers were doing? Perhaps it was the timing of Katrina, or the tendency in newspapers to be more anecdotal and humanistic already, but the mistrust of official sources by the public and the media seemed to only add to the trust in citizen journalism and journalism that honored the citizenry. It seemed more democratic and pluralistic and inclined toward the political in its advocacy for the citizen and shunning of officialese.

On Thursday, September 1, 2005, National Public Radio's host of *All Things Considered*, Robert Siegel, interviewed on air Michael Chertoff, secretary of Homeland Security, following an initial federal pledge of ten billion dollars to restore the city nearly destroyed three days earlier. Siegel asked Chertoff why thousands were without food and water for days at the New Orleans Convention Center after being told to relocate there.

Chertoff responded, "If you talk to someone and get a rumor or you get someone's anecdotal version of something, I think it is dangerous to extrapolate all over the place."

Siegel was insistent. "These are things coming from reporters—who have not only covered other hurricanes, but also wars and refugee camps. These aren't rumors."

Chertoff's response was terse. "I have not heard a report of 1,000 people in the Convention Center who do not have food and water."

After Siegel recounted that the reporter was at that moment on the other phone line and had his own eyewitness reports, Chertoff responded, "I can't argue with you about what your reporter tells you."[32]

Nor could the rest of the world. And some of the best reporters offering the most comprehensive anecdotal information at the time were the citizen journalists at the scene or reporters who were able to get to the scene to speak to ordinary citizens. In a story posted on September 2 on CNN.com, the lead read: "Diverging views of a crumbling New Orleans emerged Thursday. The sanitized views came from federal officials at news conferences and television appearances. But the official line was contradicted by grittier, more desperate views from the shelters and the streets."

Later in the CNN story, FEMA chief Michael Brown (who later resigned his post) was quoted as saying on a day of major unrest that included looting and brought us news images of bodies lying in the streets: "There's some really bad people out there causing some problems, and it seems to me that every time a bad person wants to scream or cause a problem, there's somebody there with a camera to stick it in their face."[33]

The power of the redefined press was working at its best to get the news out. And the power was in the hands of the people. Civic journalism "is an opening up of the process and a humanizing of who we are," said Ryan Pitts, online producer for the spokesmanreview.com, in a panel at the 2005 AEJMC conference. "We identify with these people and are part of the same community."[34] At the same conference, Jan Schaffer, then J-Lab executive director, said, "The bottom line is that citizens are both the consumers and creators of the content."[35]

Where Did Citizen Journalism Come From?

Citizen journalism had existed since before the start of the new millennium in a universe parallel to mainstream media. But there has now been significant intersection and overlapping, so much so that many fear the lines may be completely blurred in the future. Just as blogging informs newspaper writing style to make it more casual and conversational, citizen journalism by example pushes newspaper reporters and editors to include more voices and to have more unofficial sources telling their stories. And those stories are necessarily different than the traditional news stories of events, meetings, and announcements. "It is an open-source community," Gillmor said at a 2006 AEJMC panel. "We are going to have to ask more of people who are in this audience-producer pool, to be more media-literate and have a level of skepticism."[36]

The first online newspaper featuring the work of citizen journalists was OhmyNews International founded in South Korea in 2000 by Oh Yeon Ho. OhmyNews has more than thirty-eight thousand citizen reporters around the world and an estimated half a million readers every day, according to CNN in March 2005.[37] With the slogan, "Every citizen is a reporter," Ohmynews offers news and commentary from around the world, a model copied in this country by self-appointed "media foot soldiers."[38]

Wikinews—part of Wikipedia, the largest community public encyclopedia of information—promises to deliver "the free news source you can write" and enlists an army of Wikinewsies who contribute thousands of news reports.[39] Goskokie.com, BackFence.com, YourHub.com, citizen joe.org, NorthwestVoice.com, MyMissourian.com, bakersfield.com, and so many other citizen journalism sites have taken the power of the press and handed it to the people. Cyberjournalist.net, created and written by Jonathan Dube, hosts a Citizen Media Initiatives list. In September 2005, Dube listed thirty-five citizen journalism media sites in this country. By July 2006, that number had doubled to seventy-seven citizen media sites documented.[40]

"Information is coming at people in very new ways and they are bombarded with it all day," Williams said. "Right now the questions are about how media-literate the citizens are to sort out the information and understand what the rules are and how the information is passing through the gates."[41]

Showing and Telling Local Stories

Examples of the proliferation of citizen journalism are everywhere. It seems anyone who can observe a scene is invited to record the event online. Minnesota Stories is a daily videoblog that calls itself "an evolving showcase for local citizen media," bringing together "personal stories, independent films and music, hyperlocal politics."[42] It honors stories from state residents that are "the little gems that fall through the cracks of broadcast media."

In late 2005 Orato (which means "I speak" in Latin) was launched online as a site committed to "True Stories from Real People" and edited by Paul Sullivan. With a stable of more than one thousand contributing journalists—both professional and citizen—the site promised to "capture the essence and immediacy of the eyewitness to events" in a litany of only first-person stories. Under the headline "First Person Journalism 101," Sullivan posted this mandate: "It's important to remember: the story needs to be told as a kind of real-time narrative. It's more like the unfolding of a movie than the interior workings of your mind. If you've lived through Hurricane Katrina, the reader wants to live through it again with you this time. It's enormously difficult, even traumatic, but that's the difference between an Orato report and a mainstream report. These days, anyone can go to any number of news sites and get all the information: the number of people who have died, the cost, who's to blame, etc."[43]

According to the Orato website in March 2006, "The disparity between a story told by someone who had experienced the event and the version produced by traditional media was so obvious it simply could not be ignored. No matter where you live or what language you speak, we will never find a more powerful message than the one told by the human voice."[44]

Stateinformer.com recruits citizen journalists from all fifty states to contribute local news. The site reads, "Are you a news junkie? Do you want to be a citizen reporter or report on local events? This web site brings together all of the US state news into one easy to find directory. Even if you don't want to join the network as an author, we may link to your weblog if you primarily report on local events. . . . We plan to make the State Informer network one of the largest citizen journalist projects of its kind. If you already run a local news blog, or are involved in any other citizens' media project, we would love to have you become a part of our network."[45]

Front Page 2003 for Dummies is a guide to using and implementing the Microsoft Office program that allows anyone to build a website. In September 2005, the amazon.com ranking of the book was less than 4,500. For anyone with a book on Amazon, getting a ranking below 10,000 is a very good thing.[46]

On the website I Reporter, which uses the tagline "inspiring, guiding and educating citizen journalists and the news organizations that work with them," coeditor Adam Glenn wrote about how Katrina forced the "symbiosis" of citizen journalism and mainstream journalism: "I do take courage in how many of my fellow journalists have kept to their task, and instead of just packing it in are using all their energies and every means possible (especially the web and reports of citizen journalists) to get the words out on what's happening," Glenn wrote. "For me, Katrina is good evidence of the struggling corps of traditional journalists and the growing cadre of citizen journalists."[47]

Glenn's blog referred to Kaye D. Trammell, who teaches visual communication as an assistant professor in mass communication at Louisiana State University. She wrote about her experience with Katrina on "Kaye's Hurricane Katrina Blog": "We on-the-scene citizens don't mean to replace journalism. We don't have the resources. But we can provide first-person accounts in our own voices of what is happening. . . . We understand that we are trusted sources for firsthand information and want nothing more than to provide factual accounts of what is happening. Blogging will not change the world in crisis, but it will make it more human."[48]

At Medill, graduate students in the Media Management Project in the spring of 2005 created two online citizen journalism products, beep (*http://beep.dailyherald.com/*) and 2 Cents. The tag line of 2 Cents, created for the *Daily Herald* in Arlington Heights, Illinois, boasted the tagline, "You lead, we follow" and promised a mix of news, features, and profiles about, for, and by local residents. "The goal was to create a non-traditional news hierarchy in a community of 20 somethings who decide on fresh content," the student creators said in a presentation of the project to faculty, students, and industry critics.[49]

It is what many journalists fear and is what many more citizen journalists embrace: a porous entry to mainstream media where anyone can contribute to the news. And some of it could be absolutely wrong. The sky is falling.

Gillmor, in speech excerpts to the May 2005 World Editors Forum in Seoul, Korea, posted on his website, said of the motivation to do citizen journalism: "But money is not the major push behind citizen journalism. It is the entirely human desire to tell each other our stories, to help each navigate through this complex and insane world."[50]

He acknowledged the existence of the sometimes adversarial relationship between mainstream media and the citizen journalists circling the edges. In the seminal book on citizen journalism *We the Media*, Gillmor wrote: "Once mere consumers of news, the audience is learning how to get a better, timelier report. It's also learning how to join the process of journalism, helping to create a massive conversation, and in some cases, doing a better job than the professionals."[51]

Truth Floats

Boomers like me may remember a skit on a comedy television show that aired from 1968 to 1973, *Rowan and Martin's Laugh-In*. Comedienne Lily Tomlin played Ernestine, a snooty telephone operator with a nasal twang whose callous, snorting response to every inquiry was "We don't care. We're the phone company. We don't have to." As customers with no other option for phone service, we had all experienced that arrogance before the breakup of the monopoly that was Ma Bell.

Similarly, newspapers before citizen journalism and the invasion of the reader-snatchers of cable, Internet, podcasts, blogging, and even Al Gore's network of citizen journalists on current.tv, embraced a similar attitude toward the gathering and dissemination of news.[52] In the days before audience splintering, newspaper editors would decide what went in the paper by choosing who was covered, when it was covered, how it was covered, and why, without reader input of any real magnitude. Readers' personal stories were met with tolerance, if not derision.

A reader could call to suggest a story, but mostly the response was not to rush out and cover the story unless it was a very slow news day and something else fell through. There were places in the newspaper for readers' smaller stories, and it was certainly not on the front page. The reader-generated stories were mostly relegated to the inside pages. Editors and reporters figured readers were not blessed with news judgment. Journalists were information elites. Readers and citizens didn't know the handshake; no one let them in on the code. Reporters figured anyone who called with a story idea was in the self-serving business, only trying to get pictures of their kids, businesses, causes, or pets in the paper. That was the creed of most editors, who felt they did not have to heed the call. "We don't care. We're the newspaper, we don't have to."

In a speech at the Interactive Journalism Summit in August 2005, Mary Lou Fulton, the vice president of audience development at the Bakersfield Californian and creator of Northwestvoice.com, discussed this kind of dismissive attitude within mainstream media. "We've heard a lot of stories from people in the community who have interacted with other local media—*The Californian* and TV stations—and say, 'I called and I told them about my church's fundraiser and we raised $5,000. That's the most money we've ever raised for anything and we were just so excited about it and they said, 'Well that's not big enough. We don't cover that. That's not news.' Well that's the last time anybody's ever going to call that station to tell them anything, because they've just lost that trust and confidence. We wanted to take that whole thing away and say, 'You know what? If it's important enough to you that you would take the time and the effort to write something up and send it to us, and it's local, that's good enough for us.' And so we found that changing the whole conversation has been very helpful for us."[53]

Newspapers absolutely have to care today. Readers have far too many other options where their voices will be heard. They are in the position to say, "We are the readers. We don't have to read your newspaper if we don't want to." Dana Robbins, editor of the *Hamilton Spectator,* concurred. "There has been a surreal disconnect between the newsroom and the rest of the business."[54]

A New Kind of Attitude

Citizen journalists have forced an attitude change within the media, forcing outlets to embrace readers' needs for coverage and their desire to be included. Perhaps that story from a caller, that message from a blogger or podcaster, could end up as a front-page story, and perhaps it is a story that a staff short on time and resources could get no other way. The far-reaching tentacles of citizen journalism have demanded newspapers respond with stories of more people who are not officials, experts, CEOs, or politicos. Editors and reporters not only listen to what readers have to say, they solicit their stories.

Newassignment.net was slated for a fall 2006 launch. It is New York University's Jay Rosen's experiment in the collaboration of citizen journalists and paid editors. The model, simply put, was for donors to fund the reporting and writing of investigative stories that the mainstream media are missing and collaborating citizen journalists are requesting.[55] It is an experiment and may be the business model for journalism to come. Citizen journalism cannot be ignored.

Let's All Share

Good Night, and Good Luck was the first movie about journalism ever promoted with a movement of real citizen journalism. The October 2005 Participant Productions film was linked to www.report-it-now.com. The promotional site for the movie urged visitors to work as investigative reporters, acting like role models Fred Friendly and Edward R. Murrow in the CBS news show, *See It Now,* the lead characters in the feature film starring George Clooney and David Strathairn.

The site asked, "Do you know about an important story deserving of attention that the media has been missing or ignoring? Here's what we want you to do: Go out and report the truth. Film a news segment, record interviews or write about something that moves you to action—civil rights abuses, government corruption, injustices of any stripe. We will showcase your work here!"[56]

All the President's Men, the 1976 Oscar-winning movie about the efforts of *Washington Post* reporters Bob Woodward and Carl Bernstein to expose the criminality of the Richard Nixon administration, was promoted with the traditional posters of the stars, in this case, Robert Redford and Dustin Hoffman, not a call to viewers to engage in investigative reporting. Even though the movie preceded the Internet, no postcards asked viewers to send in their stories to bring down local government. Soliciting viewers to participate in journalism to promote a movie about journalism speaks to the invitation of the citizen journalist to the larger media table.

Even with the inevitable problems that may come to pass in Chicken Little Journalism, when and if citizen journalists create a community panic over a fallen apple, there is also much for newspapers to gain. Clifford Christians wrote in *Good News: Social Ethics and the Press,* "We agree that the press should be pluralistic, that it should encourage discussion and debate about pressing social needs, and that moral imperatives arising from the community should matter more than the economic and bureaucratic impulses of media institutions."[57]

The stories of the people displaced by Katrina loudly resonated with readers. It was an event that helped create the current wave of everyman journalism that David S. Broder predicted in 1987 in *Behind the Front Page: A Candid Look at How the News Is Made.* Broder included in his book excerpts from a 1979 speech he gave honoring Pulitzer Prize winners at the National Press Club. In the speech he argued that journalists need to admit to the public their editorial fallibility. They need to concede they are only doing their best under the circumstances:

"We might even encourage the readers to contribute their own information and understanding to the process. We might even find ourselves acknowledging something most of us find hard to accept: that they have something to tell us, as well as to hear from us. And if those readers felt they were part of a communications process in which they were participants and not just passive consumers, then they might more easily understand that their freedoms—and not just ours—are endangered when the search warrants and subpoenas are visited on the press."[58]

The coverage of Katrina in American newspapers was a milestone in the timeline of everyman news. America's front pages hosted multitudes of stories that resonated with the loud ring of humanity, a practice that continued long after the devastating August of 2005.

Chapter 5

What's Blogging Got to Do with It?

> Weblogs are now an established, though rapidly expanding force in news and marketing. They will continue to disrupt and challenge with a staggering pace of growth and influence.
>
> —Shayne Bowman and Chris Willis, "The Future Is Here, but Do News Media Companies See It?"

It was a peculiar intersection of the intimate and the infinite. At the 2004 Association for Education in Journalism and Mass Communication conference in Toronto, Canada, two heads of state in the Kingdom of Blog participated in a panel before a roomful of eager university journalism instructors. As they spoke, Jeff Jarvis, journalist, online consultant, and creator of buzzmachine.com, and Jay Rosen, New York University's creator of pressthink.com and newassignment.net, occasionally blogged on their websites about the real-time experience.[1] While waxing prophetic about the enormity of possibilities spawned by the Internet, the two men nearly rubbed elbows as they sent their comments into the ether.

It was an "aha" moment similar to the one Dorothy must have experienced when Toto pulled the curtain on the great and powerful Wizard of Oz. While blogging is a loud gesture without boundaries practiced by an estimated 20 million bloggers as of June 2005 on 42.3 million blogs hosting more than one million posts each day, it can also be as finite as two bloggers in a windowless hotel conference room typing on laptops within spitting distance.[2]

The "aha" happened again in March 2006 at the Women, Action and the Media conference in Cambridge, Massachusetts, where this time, the queens of bloggers were blogging about blogging. Lakshmi Chaudry, at the time, senior editor at *In These Times;* political blogger Janna Goodrich; Jessica Valenti, founder of feministing.com; and Samhita Mukhopadhyay, also of feministing.com, dispelled myths and fanned inspiration on the panel, "Web-sites of Resistance: Why Our Blogs Matter." Valenti blogged her thoughts during the session to the site that warrants 100,000 vistors a month.[3]

This concept of a hyperpersonal vision of the news in a context of infinity has forever changed the way newspaper stories are conceived, reported, and written. It has manipulated mainstream newspaper journal-ists into changing what they cover and how—from including unofficial sources to using a more conversational, anecdotal writing style. "It is the newest electronic form of street journalism," said Nikhil Moro, Kennesaw State University assistant professor in Kennesaw, Georgia.[4]

It is a separate discussion from citizen journalism. Bloggers can be citizen journalists, but not all citizen journalists are bloggers. Some journalists blog, but not all bloggers are journalists, and not all journalists blog. A does not equal B does not equal C. Blogging has influenced the tone and lan-guage of newspaper stories because of its opinion-based, casual style rooted in reaction and emotion, immediate observation, and personality-driven stories. Blogging has also influenced front-page journalism by invit-ing anyone and everyone with an opinion and an anecdote to the podium.

According to a July 19, 2006, report from the Pew Internet and American Life Project, the blogosphere is nearly gender-blind, as 54 percent of blog-gers are men and 46 percent are women. But it is young: 54 percent of blog-gers are under thirty. And only one-third of them see their blogging as journalism.[5] Blogging can offer a modern, vibrant, immediate media envi-ronment breeding refreshing, topical, sassy commentary. Bloggers offer insight and formerly inaccessible information to keep journalists at main-stream outlets on their toes. When done well, blogs "reflect better than any other medium the rich diversity of humankind," wrote Davis Merritt in his 2005 book, *Knightfall.*[6]

What I am talking about here is not what has grown to be a tiresome discussion in media circles about the viability of blogs, the ethics of jour-nalists blogging on their own, or the wisdom of mainstream pressters launching blogs for staffers. What is new to discuss is the notion that this adolescent of a media form has changed what readers expect in a tradi-tional newspaper and also how writers write and report for the print ver-sions of the product. Not expecting blogging to influence traditional media is like having the Osbournes—the whole rocker family of Ozzy, Sharon, Kelly, and Jack—move into your basement and not anticipating the daily routine to shift. The walls separating blogging from journalism are porous.

"All that material is 'user-generated content," the paramount cultural buzz phrase of 2006," Jon Pareles wrote in the *New York Times.* "It's word of mouth that can reach the entire world."[7]

"The culture is no longer a passive read-only economy. Blogs exploded the read/write capacity with text," said Lawrence Lessig, founder of Stanford University's Center for Internet and Society. Speaking at the AEJMC conference in 2006, Lessig said, "The value of the production of blogs comes from the idea that 40 million bloggers sit down and put into their own words their ideas. Creativity is democratized—anyone can express ideas. Those of us who live our lives by writing texts, our words, our text are the Latin of our generation."[8]

In March 2006, Technorati.com, a clearinghouse for websites, listed close to thirty-one million blogs in operation worldwide, with the latest surge in bloggers erupting in Cambodia.[9] According to the Pew Internet and American Life Project, thirty-two million people read blogs in 2004, a 58 percent increase over readership just a year earlier.[10] The online service, Blogger, allows anyone to build a simple weblog free of charge.[11] Blogs are an undeniable force on the culture and the media. Though blogs are not the same animals as newspapers, how can the viral nature of blogging not make newspapers change how they report and write?

"For all the talk about coming together," Lakshmi Chaudhry wrote in the *Nation* in January 2007, "Web 2.0's greatest successes have capitalized on our need to feel significant and admired, and above all, to be seen. The latest iteration of digital democracy has indeed brought with it a new democracy of fame, but in doing so has left us ever more in the thrall of celebrity, except now we have a better shot at being worshipped ourselves."[12]

With mixed success, newspapers have collided or colluded with the blogosphere. The *Austin American-Statesman* in Texas has a vibrant blog community of 875 bloggers created on the newspaper's website. Technorati.com, a blog search engine, signed an agreement with the Associated Press in May 2006 to scan and post blogs with AP links, a deal similar to the one Technorati hammered out with the *Washington Post.*[13]

BlogBurst, a blog syndication service, cemented agreements with the traditional print papers *Arizona Republic, San Jose Mercury News,* and *Des Moines Register* (all newspapers in this book's study) to publish some of the service's syndicated blogs. All of this is an effort to "give readers a news voice they never had before," Greg Sandoval wrote in a news.com column in June 2006.[14] Some blogophobes say the form is "clogging," not blogging, and see the writing form used mostly by insomniacs pontificating about their cats, their relationships, or worse—cyberbullies committing blog-bys with incendiary, violent harangues. "Blogging is opinion mixed with rumor mixed with hearsay and no vetting process," said Walt Harrington of the University of Illinois.[15]

Still others see blogging as a legitimate challenge to the way traditional journalism is practiced. "Each morning, we awake to new mountains of information. Bloggers are the new Sherpas, leading their readers through those various ranges," Hugh Hewitt wrote in April 2006. "Newspaper reporters and editors are the old Sherpas."[16] Blogging is what Mark Glaser, a columnist for the Online Journalism Review, called "journalism in an echo chamber."[17]

According to the July 2006 Pew blog study,

> Some observers have suggested that blogging is nothing more than the next step in a burgeoning culture of narcissism and exhibitionism spurred by reality TV and other elements of the modern media environment. But others contend that blogging promises a democratization of voices that can now bypass the institutional gatekeepers of mainstream media. This democratization is thought to have implications for the practice and business of journalism as well as the future of political discourse.[18]

To properly credit the blogosphere's influence on mainstream journalism, conscientious news-junkie bloggers offer perhaps what credentialed journalists have missed or should have picked up. From Trent Lott's hailing of Strom Thurmond to CBS's Rathergate regarding the Bush memo in the campaign of 2004, bloggers have force-fed key issues out into the spotlight and into the public appetite without restraint, boundaries, or traditional press credentials.

Outrage from female bloggers following an August 2006 Forbes.com article, "Don't Marry a Career Woman," by Michael Noer, caused the accompanying slide show's removal. The following day the column was downplayed from feature content to opinion and placed next to a counter-opinion written by staffer Elizabeth Corcoran. Following a piece on ABC's *World News Tonight*, editor in chief Steve Forbes issued a statement saying the piece "clearly hit a very sensitive nerve. The piece was intended to be part academic and part humorous," he said. "Instead, it profoundly offended hardworking career women everywhere. We deeply regret having done so."[19] Bloggers not only giveth to the mainstream media, but they have the power to take away.

"Pressure from the blogosphere has already forced the media to cover stories that would otherwise have been ignored," wrote Stephen Quinn and Vincent F. Filak in the 2005 book *Convergent Journalism*. "More importantly bloggers have forced news groups to admit journalistic fail-ures."[20] Blogging forces open a window—however foggy, hazy, and finger-printed—into what Americans (at least those who have a computer at home or who can make it to a public library to use one) are candidly saying and thinking. It is unrehearsed, uncensored, and, at times, unrelated to any form of newsworthiness. But blogs inspire content in the traditional press and keep new ideas circulating in an environment that can otherwise become as stale as an airplane cabin on an overseas flight. It is fresh and it is real. And it is quite possibly the germination of valid story ideas, sources, and writing styles that otherwise would not have been generated by any-one on the newspaper staff.

"Weblogs are the anti-newspaper in some ways," J. D. Lesica wrote in the 2002 book *We've Got Blog: How Weblogs Are Changing Our Culture.* The author continued, "Where the editorial process can filter out errors and polish a piece of copy to a fine sheen, too often the machinery turns even the best prose limp, lifeless, sterile and homogenized. A huge part of blogs' appeal lies in their unmediated quality. Blogs tend to be impressionistic, telegraphic, raw, honest, individualistic, highly opinionated and passion-ate, often striking an emotional chord."[21] That kind of writing is influenc-ing America's mainstream front pages by blasting open the rules of sourcing and changing the tone of writing.

"The influence of bloggers is only going to get greater and greater and I'm not convinced that's a bad thing," said Keven Willey, vice president and editorial page editor at the *Dallas Morning News,* at the 2005 AEJMC conference in San Antonio.[22]

More Grassroots Sources

With the growth of blogging and the hyperavailability of so many voices commenting on the news, newspaper journalists mimic that chorus of blogger voices by opting to highlight more Average Joe and Jane reactions in their stories with more prominence and depth. Reactions of average cit-izens used to run as a sidebar adjacent to the main news story but now often appear near the top of the story or as a larger part of the body of the main story. Everyman voices are given more space.

It makes sense that placing more people-driven, local stories on front pages is the newspapers' reaction to the ultimately democratic blogo-sphere. Blogs "are transforming the ways in which journalism is practiced today . . . by (nudging) print media to richer and more balanced sourcing outside the traditional halls of government and corporations," wrote Paul Andrews of the *Seattle Times* in the 2003 *Nieman Reports*.[23]

As editor of the *Townlight* newspaper on Townson University's campus, Brian Stelter, founder of tvnewser.com for mediabistro.com and a junior in 2005, said, "I tell my writers and editors to look for the hidden story, what you would normally find on a blog. The stories with the more personal voice are more compelling and readers want something in the newspaper they haven't read before."[24]

Bloguage

Blogs either subliminally or blatantly inspire journalists at daily newspapers to write in a mode that reflects the blogger's language, what I call bloguage. The casual tone, the frankness, and the approachable stance of blogging have turned every day in the newspaper into Casual Friday. Blogging has turned the front pages of newspapers on most days into a well of chatty feature writing, a printed conversation around the watercooler. With the deluge of blogging, writing had to change in newspapers. Expecting the informal and immediate writing style dominating the blogosphere not to influence the writing style in daily newspapers is like expecting Internet dating not to influence the culture of courtship in the twenty-first century. Many journalists have their own blogs. Journalists read blogs. Newspaper readers read blogs and have their own blogs. These are not closet bloggers. It is a difficult shift from reading bloguage to reading inverted-pyramid "sources at the White House said Thursday" writing.

In August 2004, the *Columbia Journalism Review* asked Farnaz Fassihi, the *Wall Street Journal*'s Middle East correspondent, to keep a journal of her life in Iraq. In what became a highly viral email, Fassihi wrote: "One could argue that Iraq is already lost beyond salvation. For those of us on the ground it's hard to imagine what if anything could salvage it from its violent downward spiral. The genie of terrorism, chaos and mayhem has been unleashed onto this country as a result of American mistakes and it can't be put back into a bottle."[25] It was fresh writing, candid and infectious, the stuff of blogs.

CyberJournalist.net, founded by Jonathan Dube and published in a partnership with the Online News Association, listed 180 blogs published by established news sites as of June 2006. The sites included papers from the *News and Record* in Greensboro, North Carolina, to the *Austin-American*

Statesman. CyberJournalist.net also listed 82 temporary blogs put up by news sites specifically for events, from Campaign Journal by Ryan Lizza of the *New Republic* to Diary of a Madman written by Tommy Tomlinson at the *Charlotte Observer.* Freelance personal blogs run by journalists totaled 137 in late July 2005, with a growing list of additions constantly updated.[26]

The Sticky Problem of Ethics

But it is still true that print journalism can influence but never exactly mimic—or stoop to—the by-the-seat-of-the pants, manic opinion-gushing that dominates many blogs. Nor should it. That restraint is what differentiates journalism as a profession from journalism as a hobby. "A more realistic scenario has minimedia, chiefly the blogs, influencing established major media," Cable Neuhaus wrote in the April 2005 *MediaPost Publications.*[27]

Adopting a different writing style and an open-source approach to stories is different than adopting the blogger's knee-jerk mode. The latter leaves open the possibility for violations of ethics—from accuracy to libel and fabrication. The transparency essential to newspapers is just not there in blogging. The restraint is absent as well. In a speech in November 2004 at Northwestern, Gail Collins of the *New York Times,* said, "What bothers me about it is the incredibly personal, harsh tone bloggers take. So many shriek as loud as possible to get attention."[28]

The *Dallas Morning News* under the guidance of Willey appears to be successful at inviting readers into the paper's website with the least amount of toxic backwash. The Spokane, Washington, *Spokesman-Review* invites five readers to discuss the paper's coverage on its News Is a Conversation blog as a way to increase "transparency," according to the site. "We participate, but the readers lead the conversation here," the site reads. Still, safeguards and monitors are in place.[29]

Log on late at night to a freelance blog run by an angry college student enraged about a threat to free speech and you can get mighty scared at what's out there. You may experience what Michael Kinsley, opinion editor of the *Los Angeles Times,* experienced in July 2005 when he opened and quickly slammed shut the door on wikitorials—or editorials readers write and post on the paper's website. He built a site, and they did come—about one thousand, many in the early morning hours. And like teenagers at a weekend house without supervision, the bloggers threw a party while the editors were away. Anonymous posters put up pornography. No longer

was it just an open forum for ideas or a new way for old media to participate interactively with readers. Unchecked, it was an X-rated departure
from the intended friendly swapping of ideas. It was not your mother's
newspaper.

"Unfortunately, we have had to remove this feature, at least temporarily,
because a few readers were flooding the site with inappropriate material"
was the explanation posted on latimes.com.[30] But that did not deter other
mainstream news outlets from embracing bloggers directly in their pages.
USA Today in June 2006 announced that it would start including news from
its On Deadline blog in the print edition. In March 2007, USA Today
announced more changes that included heightened blogger input. According to the site, "You're going to see USA TODAY journalists around the
site: creating profiles, joining you in conversation, asking you for your
thoughts and experiences around different stories, and looking to create
connections that help build better journalism. There's a concept here called
"network journalism"—the idea that reporting can drive readers and readers can drive reporting."[31]

"This new media environment will continue to change the notions of
community and journalism, creating fluid distinctions between the elite
and the masses," said Bruce Williams.[32] Blogging is not reporting anymore
than typing is writing. The two are different animals, as most often blogging does not offer original reporting but merely comments on the reporting of journalists. But one does influence the other. Blogging has been
met with podcasting and vlogging, or amateur video and visual coverage online. Flickr.com, youtube.com, and textamerica.com are either the
future of spontaneous photojournalism and videojournalism or just a commentary on how much spare time an individual has to sit before a camera
in his room.

Podcasts have emerged on traditional news sites as well—from
Forbes.com to Public Radio International and the Seattle Post-Intelligencer,
according to Cyberjournalist.net, which posted thirty-seven newspapers,
broadcast outlets, and magazines with accompanying podcasts. According
to Jeff South, associate professor at Virginia Commonwealth University,
"Everyone is becoming a journalist."[33] It feels reminiscent of the historical
film taken by shop owner Abraham Zapruder on the morning of November 22, 1963, as President John F. Kennedy's motorcade snaked through
Dallas's Dealey Plaza. With his Bell and Howell camera set for full close-
up from sixty-five feet away, Zapruder, who owned the shop, Jennifer
Juniors, was the only person to record the assassination.[34] His amateur
footage was instant journalism.

When the Blogline Is Blurred

At the Democratic National Convention in July 2004 and the Republican National Convention in August of that year, bloggers were given official journalism credentials. For the first time in history, they had direct access to cover stories from the conventions. They were treated as journalists. Some blogs accept advertising. Army National Guardsman Jason Christopher Hartley turned his www.justanothersoldier.com extremely candid personal posts into a book in October 2005, *Just Another Soldier: A Year on the Ground in Iraq*, after his commandeers ordered him to stop his honest and uncensored entries from Iraq. From his September 15, 2004, post came this comparatively tame entry:

> Willy's mother is dying. She has cancer and it has moved to her lungs. What especially sucks about his mother dying is that his grandmother, whom he had shared an apartment with in The Bronx for years, also passed away during this deployment. His grandmother, the tiniest cute-little-old-lady who couldn't have weighed more than 85 pounds, seemed to always be sitting in her recliner—engulfed by her recliner would better describe what I saw whenever I entered Willy's apartment—watching TV, flipping channels, looking like a delicate sculpture more than a person. Until she spoke.
>
> From that tiny throat came a voice so enormous it was like a kick in the shins for having dared think she might be feeble.[35]

It reads like a front-page newspaper feature story—without the slang. "It might be that mass media of tomorrow will evolve further toward the blogging paradigm and journalism will expand from a centralized, top-down, one-way publication process to the many-hands, perpetual feedback loop of online communications," wrote Paul Andrews, columnist for the *Seattle Times*, in *Nieman Reports*.[36]

The second annual YearlyKos convention of bloggers in August 2007 attracted not only fifteen hundred bloggers from around the world, but also seven of the eight presidential candidates for 2008. It was a vote of confidence from the candidates to the megapopularity and viral influence of blogs not only on mainstream media, but also on the politics of Americans. Hilary Clinton, Barack Obama, John Edwards, Bill Richardson, John McCain, Mitt Romney, and Rudolph Giuliani all participated in a live debate at the convention. The only front-running candidate absent was Joe Biden.[37]

Since the advent of radio, newspapers have not been the only partners ready to dance with the public. But standing so close together, each form of media influences the other and attempts to steal the reader's time and attention. It is now a crowded dance floor—that feels at times more and more like a rave—with limber and adept partners from the Internet, cable, TV, podcasts, and blogs eager to cut in and grab the reader for a twirl. Perhaps in the fight for audience, it will be as Philip Meyer wrote, "Natural selection will do the job."[38]

Chapter 6

Humanizing the News after 9/11

Perhaps we never appreciate the here and now until it is challenged, as it is beginning to be today even in America. And have we not also been awakened to a new sense of the dignity of the individual because of the threats and temptations to him, in our time, to surrender his individuality to the mass—whether it be industry or war or standardization of thought and action? We are now ready for a true appreciation of the value of the here and now and the individual.

—Anne Morrow Lindbergh, *Gift from the Sea*

✳ Writers of fiction wrestle with choices for point of view. How best to convey a story's arc, keep the reader engaged with characters, and effectively unfold the narrative? Journalists traditionally have not had these concerns; most newspaper stories are written on deadline in the third person, delivering the necessary news elements of who, what, where, when, and why featuring a rotating chorus of official sources with a backdrop of presumed detached objectivity. When events such as those that rocked the nation on September 11, 2001, consume news holes, the reverberations are felt for years. The most compelling angle on that unfolding story was either first person or through the detailed anecdotes of eyewitnesses. While the front page had been evolving for many years, the fall of 2001 seemed simultaneously to offer permission to exponentially increase the rate of change and to make it almost impossible to return to front pages offering mostly hard news.

Before the explosion of blogs and citizen journalism that we know today, the events of September 11 contributed to the news environment by allowing for news coverage to be more inclusive. The stories that day glorified the lives of ordinary citizens as front-page news. September 11 was not the sole reason for the shift, but it helped augment the spread of a style and approach that allowed the journalist to be not only a narrator, but also an emotional participant.

"Media scholars argue that the television news format for a live, breaking story causes viewers to respond on an emotional level in both positive and negative ways," Lisa Finnegan wrote in her 2007 book, *No Questions Asked: News Coverage since 9/11.* "The format provides powerful imagery—often juxtaposed with images from past tragedies—accompanied by alarmist language that triggers reactions," she wrote.[1] Print stories were just as emotional and just as vivid in their visuals.

Perhaps as much as or more than that for any other news event in recent memory, the news surrounding the events of 9/11 was emblematic of everyman news. History will put that date into perspective, but the coverage erupting from those events appears to have had an immediate impact on the tone and style of news stories to follow. "The most powerful tool we borrow is the lens through which the novelist sees the world," said Walt Harrington. "So much journalism is broken down to pieces of factual information, but humanistic storytelling is the hallmark of fiction and early journalism."[2] And it is also the hallmark of the everyman journalism that soon became more pronounced on America's front pages.

The newspaper, the Internet, television, and radio were filled with eyewitness interviews. "Most striking, perhaps were the wide number of accounts from those who had seen the World Trade Center collapse, or had in some way gained first-hand knowledge of surrounding events," according to the 2002 Pew Internet and American Life Project report.[3] It appears that because there was so much raw substance to the news from so many voices, journalists responded by matching the substance with an abundance of style. The death of so many individuals was met with an exaltation of the ordinary-man-on-the-street source to higher prominence in the news. It was similar to the narrative, highly personal tone Martha Gellhorn used in the piece called "Dachau," which ran in the *Guardian* in London in 1945. She wrote, "Behind the barbed wire and the electric fence, the skeletons sat in the sun and searched themselves for lice. They have no age and no faces; they all look alike and nothing you will ever see if you are lucky."[4]

For newspapers, September 11 was a factor for change in traditional sources for news that consistently appeared on the front page. In his 2003 book, *The Sociology of News*, Michael Schudson wrote, "Most news comes to the news media through ordinary, scheduled, government-initiated events such as press releases, public speeches, public legislative hearings or delib-erations, press conferences and background briefings for the press."[5]

But on what seemed at the time the biggest news story of the twenty-first century, the primary sources were not the official sources. For the first time, leading the way in most every newspaper were the everyman sources. The unofficial sources were compelling journalists to tell the nar-ratives of a nation horror-struck. Eyewitness accounts seemed the only proper way to convey the enormity of the story, as the whole picture was incomprehensible. And no one expert source or administration had full answers, certainly not immediately and in a manner forthcoming and reliably complete. Americans were not turning to the newspaper for the initial facts—they were glued to the television and to their computer screens. So they turned the next day to the newspaper for the emotional, personal story.

"It was a chance for journalists to report actual happenings on the ground," said Maria Hinojosa, former CNN correspondent and host for Latino USA on National Public Radio. In a speech at Northwestern in Feb-ruary 2006, she continued, "We have an 'A' on the human element. On the critical questions, I'd say a C- to B+."[6]

Immediately following the attacks, most Americans—81 percent—received their information from television, according to the September 15, 2001, Pew Internet and American Life Project directed by Rainie.[7] Eleven percent received information from the radio, 2 percent from the Internet, and only 1 percent of Americans said the information they got on the attacks came from newspapers.

Since most Americans did learn the basic facts of the story from TV, the print version needed to be different. And because of the traffic online—CNN.com tallied nine million hourly requests—websites were crashing. According to the 2002 Pew report by Alex Halavais, search engine Google printed this suggestion to visitors: "If you are looking for news, you will find the most current information on TV or radio. Many online news ser-vices are not available because of extremely high demand."[8] The next morning's newspaper needed to deliver reassurance in the form of human interest stories of survival and courage.

"With 9/11 you have this media event where the usual sources either don't have anything to say, are not sure how they will say it and it is unclear for a while just what kind of story this is," said Bruce A. Williams of the University of Illinois at Urbana-Champaign. "So that drove their desire to get at the stories of human suffering as they struggled to figure out the frame."[9]

For journalists, there was no vantage point distant or comprehensive enough to allow them to include the totality of the scenes and their implications for the nation and the world. So the next day's print stories could only be told in bits and pieces from up close, as the whole picture was a great unknown. Like the story of the elephant and the three blind men, journalists groped for understanding. They used the information given them and reported it eloquently even if no one could see or comprehend the full breadth of the mammoth from the capturing of fragments. The blanks they filled in with emotion and humanism.

The official voices and the experts were not eliminated, of course, but they shared story space and prominence with unofficial sources. It was a departure from what Schudson had claimed a decade earlier was the very definition of journalism: "Journalism, on a day-to-day basis, is the story of the interaction of reporters and government officials, both politicians and bureaucrats." He added that "there is little doubt that the center of news generation is the link between reporter and official."[10]

The most memorable stories from that day were not told in the words of President Bush or even New York Mayor Rudy Giuliani. Readers were not as deeply moved by the official responses about terrorist threats, air traffic safety, and body counts as they were the personal stories from anyone connecting to the World Trade Center attacks and Pennsylvania and D.C. crashes. They were not looking to the newspaper for speculation by sources close to the White House on how two planes could hit the towers, one could damage the Pentagon, and another could go down in rural Pennsylvania. What was memorable were the stories from the people who nearly lost their lives or who lost their loved ones. No official source reporting could have calmed or satisfied the reading and viewing public. Newspaper stories that screamed, "Officials said Tuesday," would never have sufficed.

Observers have discussed how written journalism became more descriptive and urgent as a reaction to the burning, cinematic images of September 11, and later of the Iraq war and the Israeli-Palestinian conflict. I contend the opposite; that because of the fast-forward visual and verbal urgency of news none of us could escape, the writing in newspapers slowed down, became more conversational in tone and less a ticker-tape, bulleted regurgitation. We went to the newspaper, coaxed by feature stories well told, convinced to take the time to know the people involved. News stories adopted the tone of eulogies.

Christopher John Chivers, a *New York Times* police reporter, was downtown on the morning of September 11, according to Ken Auletta. In his 2003 book, *Backstory,* Auletta wrote: "As desks and concrete and steel beams plunged to the street, he dived in to the entrance of a liquor store near Trinity Church, and soon began interviewing people huddled nearby." He later covered the story incognito from ground zero, and his eloquent diary, which reads like an Upton Sinclair novel, subsequently ran on the front page: "The inhabitants of ground zero ate together in abandoned restaurants and beside piles of putrid garbage, they fell asleep together wherever they could, they sobbed and prayed together, and as, they became familiar with Lower Manhattan's emerging landscape, they shared directions to working phones and bathrooms that were not splattered with vomit."[11]

To be sure, the detailed official accounts of how and perhaps why the events of September 11 occurred filled newspaper pages with hard news. Journalists relied on efficient reporting of the process and meticulous, accurate explanations and accounts of complicated, confusing, and often conflicting information offered by authorities with titles and expertise. It would have been irresponsible to handle the day's events only with a velvet glove of reaction and emotional human interest. But many newspapers told an adjunct story of September 11 with an everyman approach— through the eyes of a witness, survivor, or observer with detailed description in a delayed, literary style.

The front page of the *Atlanta Journal-Constitution* on September 12, 2001, was covered in large photographs and one lead story by Jay Bookman that read like the first page of a novel: "We occupy a different reality than we did a day ago. Thousands lie dead, many still buried in the smoking rubble in New York and Washington. Millions grieve. Two landmarks of the Manhattan skyline have been obliterated, and an atmosphere of war pervades Washington. A nation slow to anger has been brought to justified fury."[12]

Newsday's front page featured this story: "Bill Kelly, a day trader for Georgia, was walking by a Borders bookstore at the World Trade Center when the first explosion occurred."[13]

In the main story on page one of the September 12 *Chicago Tribune*, "U.S. under Attack," by Charles Madigan, the first extended quote in the ninth paragraph of the story (a press conference comment from President Bush ran higher up) was this: *"It sounded like an F-16 was doing a flyby," said Russ Paparo, thirty-seven, a trader at the New York Mercantile Exchange, who was just arriving to work at the trade center as the first aircraft approached. "I was standing outside and literally watched the United Airlines plane fly directly into the tower. It was a head-on collision. It was extraordinarily loud. When that happened, everybody freaked out. People were panicked. A lot of women were breaking down and crying."*[14]

Another story off the front page, in the main section of the *Chicago Tribune*, "Our Nation Saw Evil," also written by Madigan, was more descriptive: "A pall of smoke, dust and sadness settled over lower Manhattan with nightfall Tuesday as rescue workers, police and firefighters pressed their desperate search for survivors of the worst terrorist attack in United States' history, a coordinated airborne assault that destroyed the twin towers of the World Trade Center and left a portion of the Pentagon outside Washington in smoking ruins."[15]

September 11 gave birth to a hybrid of highly stylized everyman stories that used the dramatic language of fiction and could not be reduced to straightforward news summary leads. Most everyone in America—and possibly most of the world—already knew what had happened by the time the newspaper was printed. Condensing the events of the day before into a predictable five W approach—who, what, where, when, and why— would have been absurd. The best way to tell the story in a newspaper seemed to be by fanning out the scrupulously mined human details and slowly deal them to the reader like cards from a reshuffled deck. It was a move that would change newspapers for good. In the 2002 book *Journalism after September 11,* Annabelle Sreberny wrote: "The everyday, taken-for granted norms of journalism were shaken, in rushed opinion and emotion, and an effective public sphere evolved. The balance seemed to shift between the ordinary work of journalism and a kind of extraordinary writing that people seemed to need to write and others to read—writing as catharsis, writing trauma out of ourselves, trauma talk."[16] What may have resulted, also from those events, were the journalistic precedents for rushing to print with anecdote-heavy, highly personalized narrative of most all news events.

Many media observers have pinpointed the World Trade Center explosions, Pentagon attack, and Flight 93 crash as the instigations for the day journalism changed. A study from the Pew Internet and American Life Project in 2002 called much of what was emerging from 9/11 "do-it-yourself journalism." The authors of the study cautioned: "Many of these accounts do not follow the canons in fact-checking, seeking out alternative or opposing views, or attempted impartiality. They are necessarily more socially constructed, and read more like rumors, with particular aspects of the story being embellished while others are left aside."[17]

So much of what ran in American newspapers was closely related in tone and style to blogging and citizen journalism, but it was performed by professional journalists. Still, September 11 is only one influence on an evolving profession. Critics say the journalism that sprang from that day is an indictment of our nation's myopic view of the world, American patriotism, and our limited international knowledge and coverage. We only could bear to tell the news using ourselves as lead characters. But we know instinctively and intellectually that widespread institutional shifts emerge slowly and result from a confluence of events and cultural forces over time. Journalism could not have changed only because of September 11.

History teaches us as much. The 1941 December morning of the Pearl Harbor attacks cannot be identified as the single time inspiring generations of American isolationists. Nor can the appearance of TV dinners in grocery stores be diagnosed as the moment that doomed subsequent generations to become couch potatoes. And no matter how many lawsuits are filed, chubbier orders of French fries really are not the sole cause of the epidemic of childhood obesity.

The challenge of telling such a huge story in a manner that can be understood on a personal level was not new to 9/11. Bob Steele wrote about the Columbine High School shootings in "Journalism and Tragedy" on July 19, 1999: "Even though there is a tendency to switch to auto pilot on stories such as these, there is nothing simple about the role and responsibility of the journalist." He wrote later, "Our knowledge, our emotions and our reaction are a product of the information we consume. Journalism links us to this terrible incident and the issues embedded within it."[18]

But the often-brilliant personal coverage of the crisis of September 11 contributed to a metamorphosis of American newspaper coverage into the emotional, anecdotal, and descriptive newswriting common today. It granted blanket permission for all news to wear the everyman approach. What comes first? The culture where the journalists live and report stories or the stories the journalists report on while living in the culture? And did the journalists tell these kind of personal stories because the readers wanted them, or did the readers want them because newspapers offered them? The post-9/11 reader was more open to the heralding of the individual. Newspapers fed on that desire and prolonged the country's appetite for everyman journalism.

"The newspaper plays a vital function in sustaining people locally and insulating them from the larger culture of panic and fear," said Lisa Parks, author and associate professor in the department of film studies at the University of California at Santa Barbara. "In a post-9/11 moment, people are on edge and they are encountering information and stories that reinforce a sense of imminent danger," said Parks, author of the 2005 *Cultures in Orbit: Satellites and the Televisual*, dealt with different vantage points reporters take in their coverage of events. "Maybe these (humanistic) stories are a reassurance that life goes on and not all communities buy into the culture of panic and fear."[19]

The front pages of newspapers had been changing and growing more featurized for many years but had been previously stained by the influx of more sensational or celebrity-driven news. But now this was hard news with an everyman approach—about the emotional, personal narrative of the man and woman on the street encountering a real event, a national tragedy. "In most news organizations around the country, the terrorist attacks and their aftermath so thoroughly clarified the mission of journalism that many reporters and editors described the particular exhilaration of understanding exactly what the job is: the searching for vital information, the explaining of the unfamiliar, the shedding of light," Cynthia Gorney wrote in "The Business of News: A Challenge for Journalism's Next Generation," a 2002 report for the Carnegie Corporation of New York.[20]

A New Way to Portray Grief

The *New York Times*' editorial decision to run the moving snapshots of victims under the title "Portraits of Grief" is seen by many observers as a noble milestone in everyman journalism. The unconventional miniprofiles were not "standard obituaries" but an attempt, according to former *New York Times* executive editor Howell Raines, to "give some look at them [those who perished at the World Trade Center] as a living person."[21]

This portrait of Arcelia Castillo is one example of the nearly 2,000 stories the *Times* published:

> Marine Corps boot camp was an easy fit for Anthony Roman. He had already been trained by a tough, stubborn disciplinarian whom he nick-named the Colombian Drill Instructor: his mother, Arcelia Castillo.
> At home in Elizabeth, N.J., Ms. Castillo, a single mother always juggling two jobs and night school, enforced strict curfews and did not tolerate back talk or wasting money. If Anthony or his brother, Alex, broke rules, Ms. Castillo, scarcely five feet tall, would reach for her belt.[22]

In a prepared video on the *New York Times* website about the portraits with the tagline "Glimpses of Some of the Victims of the September 11 Attacks," Raines, who resigned in 2003 following the Jayson Blair plagiarism scandal, called the portraits "the purest of good journalism . . . also providing a kind of glue to a community and perhaps to a nation." He explained that the short profiles "began as an organic solution to a very real journalist problem . . . that grew out of the task of trying to report the stories of the victims." He added, because there was "so little information, we weren't able to produce a satisfactory story of that kind." So the reporters and editors at the *Times* enlisted key resources and staff to tell the stories of the unofficial sources. On the video, Raines recalls, "In my 23 years on the Times, I know of nothing that has stirred the kind of public response that these portraits have."[23]

Michael Schudson wrote, "They were a kind of journalism as tribute, journalism as homage, journalism as witness, journalism as solace, and journalism aspiring to art."[24] The portraits succeeded in the mission of bringing the victims back to life briefly in print. Ken Fuson said the appeal of the portraits was universal. "There is this yearning. Everyone is so desperately afraid they will not be remembered."[25]

It was a move that sparked a revival of lengthened obituaries of ordinary citizens in the local sections of major newspapers. These stories appealed to readers because they were personal and local and honored everyman. The innovation of running the portraits prompted many newspapers around the country to years later run stories about fallen American soldiers in Iraq—in the same tone of reverence for the individual as was evident in "Portraits of Grief." Five years after 9/11, obituaries of nonprominent citizens in major newspapers such as the *Chicago Tribune* were featured on expanded local obit pages. Teachers, volunteers, singing coaches, factory workers, all of them were eulogized in extended obituaries years after 9/11. The tone was different, more reverent, while also less formal and formulaic than that of the obituaries from a decade before. The tone was eulogistic.

"You speak differently at a party than you do at a funeral," said Bruce DeSilva, director of the Associated Press's News/Features Department. "People at a funeral and readers of a narrative have an aesthetic experience."[26]

In 2003 Carolyn Kitch of Temple University wrote that "after September 11 news media not only covered, but conducted a public funeral ceremony. . . ." Though her study focused on news weeklies, the narrative tone of eulogy was present in the stories carried in newspapers as well. She continued on to say that "this communicative process was one in which journalists shared the telling of the story with 'real people'. . . ."[27]

Roy Peter Clark, senior scholar at the Poynter Institute, wrote in 2001 about the miniprofiles that ran in the *Times:* "Each name is a story. But all the names constitute a bigger story. That bigger story, the master narrative, as some might call it, reveals what happens when so many lives and dreams are cut short. One can see the hurt and regret spread out from the center, like the spidery fissures on a broken pane of glass."[28] Each story steeped in everyman journalism tells the anecdotal accounts of a person. But all the stories together reflect a culture that is immersed in honoring the lives of individuals.

The personalized humanistic stories at the time seemed a deservedly fresh approach in 2001, but it was not the first time a story of enormous magnitude had been reported from the point of view of the ordinary people affected. John Hersey's *Hiroshima* is an example of the prosaic prototype for the kind of thoughtful storytelling that emerged from unspeakable disaster. Hersey opened chapter 1, "A Noiseless Flash," this way:

"At exactly fifteen minutes past eight in the morning on August 6, 1945, Japanese time, at the moment when the atomic bomb flashed above Hiroshima, Miss Toshiko Sasaki, a clerk in the personnel department of the East Asia Tin Works, had just sat down at her place in the plant office and was turning her head to speak to the girl at the next desk."[29]

No Going Back to Journalism as Usual

It made sense ethically and practically to respond to both history-shaking events in a more personal way. Perhaps it was a predictable way for writers to cope with the pathos. Critics said the personal writing after September 11 was saccharine, overemotional, and a corny way to break the hard news to people softly. But others saw coverage after September 11 as an opportunity to tell personal stories that had unmistakable universal appeal. It was the biggest story of the last one hundred years. Millions of Americans kept their television sets tuned into the commercial-free network and cable zones for hours and hours of that day and night. Millions more logged onto the Internet for the latest answers, updates, and visuals. Since anyone could find the shortened synopsis in bullets online or on television immediately and with constant updates, the newspaper stories were different.

The newspaper accounts were stories meant to be read aloud, stories that made readers stop and listen. The words needed to mean something grander, they needed to be profound, they had to last longer. They were historical accounts of an unimaginable assault. For the reporter, the stories had to honor the lives of everyone he could interview because he would not know if there would be a chance to interview them again. It spawned some miraculously vivid writing. It was a high point for newspaper storytelling.

"Story journalism is separate from information journalism," Zelizer said.[30] Information readers got elsewhere. Personal narratives and emotional stories they got from the newspaper. What were readers looking to a newspaper for more than a way to make sense of the suddenly changed world through story? Laurie Hertzel, enterprise editor and writing coach at the *Minneapolis Star Tribune,* said, "When you attach news stories to human beings, then it becomes more real."[31]

The content transformation of American newspapers in the last few years was a reaction not just to September 11, but also to a collection of other cultural influences. For years the pendulum had been swinging in this direction; it is September 11 that demanded the more urgent, intimate style of personal journalism as a mainstream means of reporting the news. How could the news not have changed? "Most of those who produce national news live and work in New York or Washington and so were not just reporting the story—they were living it. And everyone had a story to tell," wrote Dennis D. Cali in the 2002 *Journal of Mass Media Ethics*.[32] Christine Spolar, a veteran journalist and friend of mine who headed the *Chicago Tribune*'s Baghdad bureau during the war in Iraq, said journalists after 9/11 were "writing with the burden of history."[33]

Gregory Favre, distinguished fellow in journalism values at Poynter Institute and a veteran newspaper editor for more than forty-seven years, wrote in a September 20, 2001, column that journalists should never leave their personal feelings behind when they cover a story such as 9/11. "How else can they truly relate to the horror of what they have seen, or tell the stories behind the lives that have been lost and those that have been shattered?"[34]

In "When Evil Struck America," a CD-ROM produced by the *Chicago Tribune*, editor Anne Marie Lipinski explained in the introduction that this served as "a complete and honest picture of events," a time capsule "capturing history even as it was being made." The opening to the archives and interactive graphics is narrated by columnist Eric Zorn. He wrote: "They took flight on the ill winds of hate and vengeance on a brilliant cloudless day, they possessed a killer's cold heart and a martyr's iron will, their object no less than to destroy the American way of life."[35]

Just before the first anniversary of the attacks, the hunger for everyman stories related to the events was still strong. Alex Tizon, a reporter for the *Seattle Times*, set off to record his experiences in a series of stories, "Crossing America," about driving to New York to be at Ground Zero on 9/11. He wrote in his launching of the series on August 25, 2002: "We want to know what Americans are thinking and feeling as we approach the first anniversary of what historian David McCullough called, perhaps hastily, the worst day in American history. We want to know how Americans spent their year, and how their lives have shifted or stayed the same." He continued, "We invited you along just for the journey. More than anything, this is a road trip."[36]

Tizon's editor, Jacqui Banaszyński, former *Seattle Times* assistant managing editor/Sunday, said of the anniversary series, "This is an emotional time. And if there is anything we can tap into now, it's emotion." Speaking at the 2004 Nieman conference, Banaszynski, now on faculty at the

University of Missouri–Columbia, added, "This is the biggest news story in the history of America, so let's define it in small ways with the journalism attached."[37] Tizon's series consistently ran on the paper's front page.

September 11 helped to broaden the scope and rewrite the script of what information is deemed valid and worthy of the front page and what sources are deemed credible to deliver that information. The prejudice that hard news can only be told from the vantage point of official sources and expert commentary disintegrated along with the towers. It also set the precedent that perhaps news stories could be better told and more effective if they included the voices of more real people.

News stories written after September 11 embodied the editorial conviction that newspapers could be empathetic, informative, and humanistic in their delivery of hard news. An implied sensitivity to the dignity of the individual has prevailed since 2001 in newspapers large and small across the country. September 11 seemed to grant newspapers permission to invoke the voices of real people and include a reverence for the insights of everyman in critical stories, not just features, but news stories on the front page. The tone of the stories was more personal, emotional, and humanistic. It was a shift that was pronounced, and it is a shift that has yet to swing back.

Chapter 7

The Old, the New, the Good, the Bad, and the Long and the Short of Narrative

A narrative that has honesty and integrity is a good story based on the strength and straightforwardness of what facts you tell.

—Seymour Hersh

✳ As a United Press International reporter in Dallas in 1963, Albert Merriam Smith knew when to tell the story straightforwardly and when to break the news more gently. When the news is huge, and you are the first to tell the story to the audience, you have to be direct. Smith's first lead for the now-defunct wire service on the assassination of President John F. Kennedy on November 22, 1963, hit the news straight on—as it should have—later, in the overnight version, he let the reader down slowly. The next day's story softened the blow of the repeated news that most every American had by then seen on television or heard on the radio. Smith's first lead was eleven words dictated from a radiophone in a car six vehicles behind the president's motorcade: "Three shots were fired at President Kennedy's motorcade in downtown Dallas."[1]

About ten minutes later, Smith filed again from Parkland Hospital, where the president lay mortally wounded: "President Kennedy and Gov. John B. Connally of Texas were cut down by an assassin's bullets as they toured downtown Dallas in an open automobile today." Then he added the flair: "The president, his limp body cradled in the arms of his wife, was rushed to Parkland Hospital. The governor also was taken to Parkland." Close to midnight, Smith filed a thousand-word version that later won him the Pulitzer Prize. It began, "It was a balmy, sunny noon as we motored through downtown Dallas behind President Kennedy. The procession cleared the center of the business district and turned into a handsome highway that wound through what appeared to be a park."[2] It was personal, it was poetic, it was humanistic. It was not a hard news lead; Smith had the journalistic sense to know when to use a hard news summary lead and when to go with a narrative lead.

"Smith used 11 words to tell what happened in Dallas with authority and clarity," said Chip Scanlan of the Poynter Institute. "He did not write about what Jackie Kennedy was wearing and how he had just turned his head to look at her. If you've got news, report it. If you have stories, tell them."[3]

In *The New Front Page* (1966), John Hohenberg wrote about Smith: "What he did that day and how he did it became a classic of journalism, the basis for the Pulitzer Prize in national reporting that was awarded to him in 1964." Smith's story was a first-person account of the details of the shooting as he witnessed them, the hospital scenes and Lyndon Johnson's oath of office. It remains a model of solid news as narrative.[4]

Narrative, it had been decided, was the mode of expression for extended views into a trend, event, life, or culture told through characters in a story-line with a beginning, a middle, and an end. It is the prescription for a classic feature. It is only more recently that the salve of narrative has been applied to most all news in newspapers, delivering in print the kinds of stories that use evocative storytelling techniques to demand and hold the full attention of the reader. Narrative storytelling in newspapers is not new. What is new is the blanket use of narrative in delivering all kinds of news on American front pages. Let us have a moment of silence for the automatic inverted-pyramid approach to all news.

"There is more than enough evidence that people do want to know something more than the bare events of the day; otherwise, they would be satisfied with five minutes of sketchy radio news rattled off by a singsong announcer in a bored voice," Hohenberg wrote.[5] People's information needs have not changed so radically, but how and where they get their information has changed and will continue to evolve in the future. People still want to know more than the bulleted updates available online or in broadcast. This is where today's newspapers deliver readers a different kind of approach to news, but one with a hallowed history in print narrative.

The featurized news on today's front page pays homage to the rich roots of narrative journalism developed in the last century. From Joan Didion's 1961 *Slouching towards Bethlehem,* Truman Capote's 1966 breakthrough true novel *In Cold Blood,* and Norman Mailer's 1979 Pulitzer Prize–winning *The Executioner's Song* to Mark Bowden's 1999 *Black Hawk Down* (originally a series for the *Philadelphia Inquirer*), which tells the stories in the soldiers' own voices, remarkable narrative writing has been the continued inspiration for newspaper journalists. Even Bowden's *Guests of the Ayatollah: The First Battle in America's War with Militant Islam* (2006) is an exemplary tribute to narrative journalism. Stephanie Shapiro, a writer for the *Baltimore Sun* and author of the 2005 *Reinventing the Feature Story*, wrote, "The long view also shows that the latest tide of personal journalism also performs the same function as it did more than 100 years ago: It instructs readers on how to weather uncertain times and assimilate into society."[6]

A newspaper journalist in the '60s and '70s, author Gay Talese wrote in 2002 about his early days days at the *New York Times*:

> I wanted to write about people as people. Even when I was a daily journalist and I was stuck with hard news, I wanted to tell the hard news through people. I wanted to write about people looking outside the windows of the fire when the fire was in those neighborhood tenement buildings on both sides of the street. . . . This was not a major fire, but I wrote about the fire through the dialogue of the people talking to one another. And the firemen were down there and the dog was barking and the hoses were all over the street and traffic was blocked. It was a scene. So this one-or two-bell fire became a feature story. It was just a way of looking at the fire.[7]

Apparently thousands of American journalists also want to look differently at a fire and at every other breaking news event. "Narrative is the dominant form in American newspapers," Walt Harrington said. "We're going back to the 1960s in an effort to figure out how to take issues stories and get them palatable and more meaningful to the reader."[8]

In January 2007, *U.S. News and World Report*'s David E. Kaplan named Jon Marshall's News Gems one of the ten best blogs of 2006.[9] Marshall, a lecturer at Medill, compiles the best stories across media platforms for the Society of Professional Journalists' site. Of the top twelve stories Marshall chose for 2006, most all are examples of narrative journalism, from Jane O. Hansen's "Through Hell and High Water" in the *Atlanta Journal-Constitution*, to Paul Meyer and Stella M. Chavez's story, "Yolanda's Crossing" in the *Dallas Morning News*.[10]

Writer Beware

But there is a caveat to attach to the discussion of the widespread use of narrative in newspapers: imitation narrative journalism isn't the same as the real thing. While the motivation to write in the form is admirable, narrative is not a patina that can be applied to any surface. You can't place gold leaf on drywall and expect it to look like the Sistine Chapel. "I began my own working life in the 1970s as a writer of what was then called personal journalism," Vivian Gornick wrote in 2001. She continued, "From the beginning I saw the dangers of this kind of writing, saw what remarkable focus it would take to maintain the right balance between me and the story. Personal journalism had already thrown up many examples of people rushing into print with no clear idea of the relationship between narrator and subject; writers were repeatedly falling into the pit of confessionalism or therapy on the page or naked self-absorption."[11]

Decades ago narrative writing was an occasional dazzling distraction in American newspapers, granting its practitioners champion status in media circles. Today the explosion of news feature stories and narrative approaches to news stories in today's newspapers make them much more commonplace. The drive for narrative and even poor imitation of narrative presents a challenge to reporters at newspapers at every level on every beat. It is difficult to translate the narrative genre to daily news without making it seem forced and superficial, like stapling a beautifully crafted anecdotal lead on top of a straight news story. "The narrative that lacks vision will suffer from exactly the same weakness as an inverted pyramid story that lacks a piece of hard news. It will seem pointless," author Jon Franklin wrote. "Worse, narrative, being by nature stronger, will seem not only pointless but also vacuous and self-indulgent."[12]

To avoid that cursed label, traditional immersion narrative journalism presupposes in-depth reporting as it borrows techniques of tension, conflict, character establishment, plot, and scenes from fiction. The masters of the craft, from Mailer to Talese to Susan Orlean, take no shortcuts. Merely transplanting the narrative form by placing it over daily journalism—a school board meeting, a police story—risks putting the writer in an awkward position, like a preteen trying on a vintage heirloom wedding dress. Sometimes it won't fit and it just won't work.

"You could write news as a policy story and it would be hard to get people to care, but it becomes more relevant with narrative. And if a narrative story fails, it fails more spectacularly than any other kind of story in the newsroom," said Laurie Hertzel.[13]

If the Narrative Fits, Print It

And sometimes, when the reporting is thorough and the writing is superb, it works masterfully. This is what the buzz is about—being able to translate newswriting into this literary form and to have it be memorable and appropriate. "In this sense all journalism owes New Journalism a debt, for its adherents recognized that television's vivid and instantaneous reporting required written journalism to change. It could no longer count on being first with a fact, it had to provide something more than fact. . . . People came increasingly to written journalism for more the pleasures of reading and less for simple facts they once did," wrote Jack Fuller.[14]

Many say narrative has improved the quality of today's papers. "Newspaper journalism is vastly better today than when I was young," said Mailer, one of the founders of the *Village Voice,* in his keynote at the 2004 Nieman Narrative Conference.[15] Roland Schatz, founder of Media Tenor International, a newspaper content analysis service with offices in Switzerland and New York, agreed that the tendency for more narratives in newspapers today can be a sign of quality. "Newspapers have a bigger variety of stories now because the way it was done 30 years ago is no longer. Then people were looking at the newspaper in the morning to find out what happened yesterday. Now there are more trend and feature stories on the front page because the need is to be able to deliver background and information with a long term perspective."[16]

Good narrative writing is not often—if ever—writing you can find in TV news scripts, blogs, or Internet news sites. Some sites such as www.sixbillion.org[17] succeed in narrative storytelling through blogging, streaming video, and photographs, but they do not come close to the precision and writerliness of the long-form narrative of print journalism. This is a form of storytelling suited to print—it requires a longer time to read and an investment of the reader's attention. This is writing that requires a newspaper's investment of capital in talent and resources. And it pays off in terms of goodwill with readers.

In his 1997 credo, *Intimate Journalism: The Art and Craft of Reporting Everyday Life,* Walt Harrington wrote: "I believe that fair, accurate in-depth, sophisticated narrative reporting of everyday life is prima facie good for readers. They read it. They like it. They respond to it. I believe the reporting of everyday life is prima facie good for newspapers. It expands their mission. It touches their readers in the heart, as well as the head."[18] Nearly a decade later, it appears many newspaper editors and writers agree.

There is the possibility that daily narrative journalism can succeed often. Reporters can deliver hard news stories on the day's current events that can be told in no other media better. While few deny that narrative informs daily journalism now more than ever, the argument today is, does it always belong in daily news? As the movement builds momentum in newsrooms across the country, narrative has become the "cool" way to produce daily journalism. "More and more news organizations have become more and more tolerant of literary journalism on the news pages and even the front pages. We see a new definition of what is news and how news is to be written," said David Abrahamson, a colleague and associate professor at Northwestern's Medill School, at the AEJMC conference in 2005. He calls it the trend of the "diverted pyramid."[19]

The Society of Professional Journalists offered its members day-long narrative writing workshops along with a slew of online tips and strategies for narrative in three cities in the summer of 2006. The words of *Los Angeles Times* editor John Carroll are paraphrased on the SPJ site: "narrative writing should not be confined to massive enterprise stories."[20] In language that can sound like evangelism, June Nicholson and Deb Halpern Wenger went even further: "Become a champion of narrative writing in your newsroom. Begin talking about narrative writing across departments. . . . Discuss how stories could be different using the narrative journalism approach."[21]

Evidence of the growing push for narrative in newspapers is seen in the healthy number of editors, writers, and authors who have descended on Harvard's Nieman Narrative Conference in Cambridge each year since 2001 (more than one thousand in 2005 and more than nine hundred in 2006). Some observers argue this conference has been the moving force behind the newspaper shift toward features and the erosion of the dominance of the inverted-pyramid approach to news. It can be argued that a group of influential writers and editors set the bar for the industry. In what Malcolm Gladwell calls the influence of connectors and mavens in his book *Tipping Point*, these writers determine the style for the industry.[22] These writers are the influence leaders, and the rest of the country's writers are the followers.

In the Narrative Digest on the Nieman site, *Pittsburgh Post-Gazette* writer Bob Batz Jr. wrote about returning to work after the 2001 Nieman conference and starting what he called "a narrative cell" of "The Storytellers" at his paper, similar to groups at such papers as the *Mankato Free Press*, the *Clarion Ledger*, the *Arizona Republic*, the *Wisconsin State Journal*, and the *Akron Beacon Journal*. "I think we keep the narrative flame burning at our paper," he wrote.[23]

Judges Fan the Flames

Since 1979 when Jon Franklin won the first Pulitzer awarded for feature writing for his story in the *Baltimore Evening Sun* about a brain surgery that failed, twenty-six writers from fifteen newspapers have won the top award in the feature-writing category, all for stories in the narrative style. Eleven of those Pulitzers have gone to writers on six of the twenty newspapers included in this book's front-page analysis study: the *Chicago Tribune, Los Angeles Times, Miami Herald, New York Times, Seattle Times,* and *Washington Post.* Two of the papers—the *New York Times* and the *Los Angeles Times*—have won several Pulitzers for features. New York boasts four; Los Angeles has three (as does the *Baltimore Sun*). The other categories of reporting honored by the Pulitzer—public service, breaking news, investigative reporting, explanatory journalism, beat, national, and international reporting—have an astounding number of narrative approaches to those stories. (I excluded from my tallying the categories of editorial writing, criticism, and commentary, as those are by nature subjective.) In 2005, of the sixty-seven stories awarded the top prize in those categories, forty-nine had narrative or descriptive approaches. That means 73 percent of all the winning stories had anecdotal or narrative leads. The winning stories were in the *Boston Globe, Wall Street Journal, Star-Ledger,* and *Newsday,* in addition to the *New York Times* and *Los Angeles Times.* Nigel Jaquiss, who won for investigative reporting at *Willamette Week,* did not have anecdotal or narrative approaches to the three stories he wrote about the thirty-year cover-up of a child molestation by former Oregon governor Neil Goldschmidt.

Paul Pringle of the *Los Angeles Times* won the Pulitzer Prize in 2004 in the breaking news category for his coverage of local wildfires. His story, "What Do You Save from a House Full of Memories?" ran on October 27, 2003, and began this way:

"Their house would collapse in a smoking ruin, and tears would stain their faces for hours afterward, but at least they had their family pictures.

"'That was what we took,' Miguel Mejia, a security guard in his 30s, said as he wiped his eyes."[24]

The Pulitzer Prizes awarded in April 2006 showed a reverence for serious reporting and hard news, but they also celebrated anecdotal and featurized leads.[25] David Finkel of the *Washington Post* won a Pulitzer for explanatory journalism for his story, "U.S. Ideals Meet Reality in Yemen," which ran December 18, 2005. Finkel's story began:

"On the first day, which would turn out to be the best day, the one day of all 180 days when everything actually seemed possible, the president of Yemen hadn't yet dismissively referred to an American named Robin Madrid as an old woman."[26]

Dana Priest's beat reporting award at the *Washington Post* was for straightforward, dogged reporting on the White House and the CIA. James Riesen and Eric Lichblau of the *New York Times* earned the national reporting award for their stories uncovering the National Security Agency's program of citizen surveillance.[27]

According to David Carr of the *New York Times* in a column on April 24, 2006, "Some observers on the press side saw the awards as a recognition that the split between the government and the press, which many thought had been papered over during the Bush administration, had widened again."[28] You could also view the awards as the committee's nose-thumbing to the kowtowing to official sources and the benedictions from spokesmen and experts that defined earlier decades of journalism.

The feature writing award to Jim Sheeler of the *Rocky Mountain News*, still and again celebrated the kind of writing and approach that defines everyman journalism. Sheeler's November 9, 2005, story, "Final Salute," about a pregnant widow retrieving her Marine husband's body after he was killed in Iraq, began, "Inside a limousine parked on the airport tarmac, Katherine Cathey looked out at the clear night sky and felt a kick."[29]

Nicholas D. Kristof's Pulitzer for commentary writing in the *New York Times* also embodied the tenets of everyman journalism. Reporting from Tama, Sudan, Kristof wrote on November 20, 2005: "So who killed 2-year-old Zahra Abdullah belonging to the Fur tribe?"[30]

The editorial writing Pulitzer awarded to Rick Attig and Doug Bates of the *Oregonian* was for a series on the Oregon State Hospital. The January 9, 2005, story began this way:

"Eva York died in a bathtub in 1896 at the Oregon Asylum for the Insane. After an inquest, which absolved the hospital staff of any blame, no one claimed her corpse, so she was buried in the asylum cemetery and forgotten."[31]

True, the Pulitzer is not the only barometer of good writing in journalism. Great writing that appears in a digital format is honored by the Online News Association, as well as by several other organizations from the National Association of Black Journalists to National Headliner Awards. Each year the George Polk Awards and the Livingston Awards honor outstanding journalists across all platforms. A 2004 Polk Award went to Paisley Dodds of the Associated Press for his Haiti coverage. One of his award-winning stories from Tabbare, Haiti, began this way:

A teenage looter banged away on a grand piano dragged into the courtyard. Presidential documents, baby rattles still in their wrappers and broken plates lay scattered around. Nabokov's "Lolita" sat on a shelf in the library.

As Jean-Bertrand Aristide arrived in Africa seeking refuge Monday, it looked as if a tornado had blown though his private villa back home. Haitians upended furniture, smashed glass, picked over his books and tossed presidential correspondence from file cabinets.

"It's our own system," said one man, Junior Jean, 23. "As soon as a leader falls we loot his palace."[32]

A narrative approach to news is what gets noticed, what gets kudos, what gets rewarded nationally, what gets nods at the paper, what gets its writers promotions. It means the top writers at the most respected newspapers in the country are leaning toward narrative in daily beats and longer investigations to tell the story.

It means more stories have narrative approaches and everyman appeal, so more of this genre will end up on the front page. Many editors and reporters at the four-star newspapers where many more reporters aspire to work lean toward writing these kinds of stories. It means judges at numerous journalism organizations as well as the Pulitzer judges (arguably the top talent in the industry, including four-star editors and academics from Columbia University and the *Chicago Tribune)* applaud and appreciate narrative. Otherwise, nearly three-quarters of all the Pulitzer Prize–winning stories would not be in the narrative style.

"The stories and narratives that journalists coin from the raw material of incidents and events are the stories and narratives that produce a common sense of citizenship, and that's true on both the national and the regional level, whether you're talking about the *Wall Street Journal* and the *Washington Post* or—well, the *Piedmont Herald,*" said Henry Louis Gates Jr., chair of the Pulitzer Board and Harvard University professor, at the Pulitzer Prize luncheon in May 2005.[33]

In her 1991 book, *Winning Pulitzers,* Karen Rothmyer wrote, "As Pulitzer envisioned it, and is still the case, the prizes seek to reward outstanding examples of journalism through an annual competition. The criteria used by the judges emphasize the qualities valued by Pulitzer, specifying in all categories that preference will be given to work 'characterized by high quality of writing and reporting.'" Overall, she wrote, the stories that win the awards "have set standards of excellence that have affected the whole profession."[34]

So if Pulitzers set the standard for excellence, and the reporting Pulitzers are awarded for stories written as narrative, then it is not too bold a leap to assume that the standard of excellence for newspapers today includes stories told in the narrative form with the elements of everyman journalism. In a 2005 study of thirty-one Pulitzer Prize–winning feature stories (chosen over twenty-five years), published in the winter 2005 issue of *Newspaper Research Journal,* authors Jeanie McAdams Moore and Chris Lamb identified trends with stories carrying specific themes such as life-and-death struggles and good against evil. Most all of these stories were tales of ordinary citizens.

"The Pulitzer rules dictate that the award for feature writing should go to a distinguished example of feature writing, giving prime consideration to high 'literary quality and originality.' Although judging 'quality and originality' must be a supremely subjective matter, a few people have attempted to explain what was meant by the terms. . . . Accompanying descriptions often included adjectives like 'compelling,' 'gripping,' and moving,' words that are commonly used to describe popular works of fiction."[35]

If papers more often win Pulitzers for the narrative approaches in news, then a newspaper will push narrative stories with its writers in order to be considered top tier. It would be difficult to find a writer working on a newspaper who at some level has not fantasized about winning a Pulitzer at some point in his or her career. It would be equally difficult to find an editor working on a newspaper who does not aspire to have the paper lauded with a Pulitzer Prize. Who doesn't want to be good at what she does? Even Katharine Graham, the late publisher of the *Washington Post*, wrote, "To love what you do and feel that it matters, how could anything be more fun?"[36]

"A good paper has a culture of excellence," Leonard Downie Jr. and Robert Kaiser wrote in *The News about the News*. "The people who work for it know the difference between thorough, resourceful, tough-minded journalism and pap. A weak paper doesn't challenge itself or its readers."[37]

Does Narrative Always Equal Good?

Observers could then contend that a definition of good journalism has evolved into journalism with a narrative approach more often than a straightforward, summary presentation of facts. Modern newspaper journalism is as much about telling memorable stories as about telling the news of what happened. You could argue that good newspaper journalism equals narrative everyman journalism.

The thread of narrative is behind this front-page news story on September 28, 2004, in the *Washington Post* by Steve Fainaru that began: "The convoy stopped in a single-file line: a half-dozen U.S. Armored military vehicles and one gray Nissan pickup truck, all of them idling in the dirt lot in the insurgent-controlled slum called Sadr City."[38]

It is also a way to tell what could have been a routine local fire story without injuries, as writer Kelly Benham did for the *St. Petersburg Times* on September 20, 2002: "She built the house just the way she wanted it. She set out a couple of plants and propped up a white ceramic angel high atop the entertainment center."[39]

Perhaps it is this writerliness, this touch of the unexpected that brings readers back to the newspaper when they can get their news in so many other outlets so much quicker. They associate the newspaper now with narrative approaches—that is becoming the newspaper's niche, the newspaper specialty. "Writing that's personally engaging, that communicates an impression from one human being to another, increases the chances that the important information you're presenting will be received," wrote Perry Parks in 2006. "Public affairs news will get more interesting immediately if reporters stop separating news and features in their minds and just find the best way to tell the truth."[40]

Readers Like Narrative

"I think feature stories bring in readers," said Dawn Fallik, a reporter for more than fifteen years and most recently at the *Philadelphia Inquirer*, a paper that has won two feature writing Pulitzers. "The narrative storytelling allows for layers that straight news does not." Her stories for the *Inquirer* filed from India following the tsunami in January and February 2005 gave readers "an amazing experience," she said. Chronicling the work of two Philadelphia doctors who went back to their native India after the disaster, Fallik said, "Readers got very involved with these people's lives. I think people read the stories for the same reason they read for fun— the people become characters they are attached to. Newspapers allow people the joy of reading something like a very short story, and narrative in newspapers allows for that quick satisfaction."[41]

Boston Globe education editor Linda Wertheimer wrote a three-part narrative series in 2001 when she was working at the *Dallas Morning News*. She followed college student Netreia McNulty throughout her freshman year at the University of Texas at Dallas to write about her experiences. Wertheimer said in all of her career, it was this kind of work that prompted the most reader response. "People are looking for something that has more meaning than TV news. People are mesmerized by real life." She added, "I don't think we'll ever stop covering hard hews, but readers want to see us cover what was on TV the night before, but better. They want to see a story about persons affected by this a day or a week later."[42]

Writers Like Narrative

"I won't do a story unless I can figure out a narrative," said Alex Kotlowitz, author and journalist who has written for the *Wall Street Journal* and the *New York Times Magazine*. "They are intimate stories. What adds to the power is that they are true stories, and what can be more powerful than what is authentic and genuine?"[43]

Katherine Boo, Pulitzer Prize–winning writer for the *New Yorker,* said in a speech at Northwestern in November 2005, "Finding the narrative means floundering about and winnowing in." Whether immersed in stories about poverty or recovery from Hurricane Katrina, "You take a large social phenomenon such as job loss in America and turn it into a story people who don't want to read about job loss in America want to read," Boo said.[44]

Writers like to write these kinds of stories. Readers enjoy the engaging style. The genre is rewarded by editors and awards committees. It is satisfying to editors and publishers. So what's not to love? The problem with narrative in daily newspapers is that it can be so well or so poorly executed. And a story with a forced narrative gives the entire genre a bad name. The approach feels clichéd and overused. Rather than profound, the story is profoundly inappropriate.

"You can get too far with the soft approach. We just want to get narrative added to the mix. There is no inherent conflict between fact and story, there are many different ways to communicate the truth," said Ken Fuson of the *Des Moines Register.* "Sometimes there is no universal truth. Sometimes it is just a parade."[45]

In a 2002 series, Fuson followed an ex-convict through eight chapters of narrative. The story began, "Bob Fitzlaff knows the tricks of the con man's game. Talk fast. Stay patient. Keep moving. When opportunity knocks, pounce."[46] Fuson's use of the narrative approach was appropriate and powerful, not misused. Mark Masse of Ball State University said, "In order to go beyond informing to enlightening and have an impact on someone's world view, then the writing has to have this kind of power."[47]

In 2002 reporter Bill Reiter of the *Arkansas Democrat-Gazette* wrote a seven-part story about Edith Ware. Ware had been fourteen in 1927 when a lynch mob "descended on her neighborhood." That story began like a novel written in the present tense in which a picture begins to emerge. It is much more than simply a delayed lead to a news story, it is recreation of history.

> Edith Warre's father arrives at the Christian Science Church for his night job as a janitor.
>
> The white stucco building is at 20th and Louisiana streets just south of downtown Little Rock, near where the Governor's Mansion will stand.
>
> Henry Ware is a black man with reddish hair. He sees his boss, the white pastor.[48]

This is a powerful narrative told in a nontraditional format for a daily newspaper. This is a profile built on recollections; the writing is intentionally literary and dramatic, and it draws in the reader. But not every story can achieve that goal. "If every story on the front page of the *New York Times* was literary journalism it would be unreadable. If every story was a 2-inch brief, it would be unreadable," said Carl Sessions Stepp, of the University of Maryland, speaking at an AEJMC session in 2004. He continued, "The dueling theology of inverted pyramid vs. literary journalism needs to be reduced. We need to take risks, try more forms, use storytelling that is visual, that relates to the reader. It is vital if we are to restore vitality to newspapers."[49]

Narrative journalism is a good thing, but it should not completely overwhelm other kinds of news stories. While it is often the prevalent form on some newspaper front pages, as demonstrated in this study, perhaps it should not be the only way newspapers tell stories. "There is more than one way to tell a news story," Scanlan said. "We need to honor both forms, because writers need narrative skills as well as declarative skills. We are focusing on storytelling in newspapers because it may be impossible for the industry to survive without it."[50]

The rise in popularity of narrative journalism in daily newspapers is peculiar to print. Television, radio, and online news are not predominantly relating news in the narrative form. This means the function of newspapers has moved past the telling of news, a regurgitation of events. Newspapers are filling a more humanistic role and playing storyteller to our culture. In *The Elements of Journalism,* Kovach and Rosenstiel wrote, "As we discuss technique, it is vital to remember that form can never determine substance—technique should never alter the facts. The journalist's use of narrative forms must always be governed by the principles of accuracy and truthfulness outlined earlier here." Those principles are outgrowths of the definition of journalism. "Journalism is storytelling with a purpose. That purpose is to provide people with information they need to understand the world. . . . Part of a journalist's responsibility, in other words, is not just providing information, but providing it in such a way that people will be inclined to listen."[51]

Shorter Narrative

While the twenty newspapers studied for this book showed an overwhelming increase in the use of news features and narrative approaches to hard news on front pages, at least two newspapers are on record as taking shortened versions of features and running with them. These are featurized shorter stories or "bits" of news. Weakening circulation at the *Los Angeles Times* in the past few years, according to the October 23, 2005, *Wall Street Journal,* has influenced a shift toward shorter stories. "They want shorter stories and more regional reporting in the intensely competitive bedroom communities around Los Angeles," the *Journal* reported.[52] "In the five years since the Chicago-based Tribune Co. bought the Times, the paper has won 15 Pulitzer prizes, but it has suffered large circulation and advertising losses." As a result, editor Dean Baquet was quoted as saying he wanted to run shorter stories and more popular stories in the newspaper to pull in readers.

At the *San Jose Mercury News* in 2005, before the Knight Ridder sale, the shift was toward "chunky bits" on the front page and throughout the paper, according to Pamela Moreland, assistant managing editor. "We're getting away from the traditional story and into fast reads, with timelines and lots of Q and A's." Moreland said front-page stories also are accompanied with a "Why It Matters" graphic, which is two sentences on why the readers should read the story. According to Moreland, "This is what the reader wants. And we are learning how to report differently. You can't just report the city council meeting anymore" and write it with a summary lead.[53] So narrative, even short narrative, is preferable to the straightforward summary news approach. Long or short, it is an attempt by newspapers to deliver a product that differentiates them from their faster digital media brethren.

Stu Wilk, *Dallas Morning News* managing editor, wrote in *APME News,* spring 2003: "We've been emphasizing unique and unduplicated Page One Content. We feel it's crucial that we differentiate ourselves from other media, and one way to do that is to provide something of value on the front page that readers won't find anywhere else."[54]

"What we are asking for is a piece of your day," said Bruce DeSilva of AP. "We are competing with tv news, soap operas, videogames, computer games." Because of so much competition for your time, energy, and attention, the newspaper has to deliver a more engaging and compelling product. "Any event that happens over the course of time has the arc of narrative."[55]

What Is the Price of a Good Anecdote?

To the shame of all writers, some journalists recently have prized the vehicle of narrative over the truth it should convey. And their downfalls have been chronicled with much fanfare. The clouds cast on the profession in the last several years by Jayson Blair, *USA Today*'s Jack Kelley, the *Boston Globe*'s Patricia Smith and Mike Barnicle, and the *Chicago Tribune*'s Uli Schmetzer (whose 2004 fabricated source was uncovered by blogger Tim Blair) form a shadowy reminder that style cannot trump substance.

"Truth is a documentary, physical reality—as well as the meaning we make of that reality, the perceptions we have of it," Harrington wrote in the spring 2004 issue of *River Teeth*, a narrative nonfiction magazine. "It's not one or the other. It's both, entwined. We cannot know the 'essence of truth' if we are cavalier about 'literal truth.' That belief must be what defines us as journalists, and our credo must be: When accuracy and art conflict, accuracy wins. . . . We can't pretend away that some of our craft's famous liars were reaching for this form of journalism."[56]

In the classic 1984 book *The Literary Journalists,* editor Norman Sims wrote: "A mandate for accuracy pervades literary journalism, according to its practitioners." Sims quoted John McPhee: "The nonfiction writer is in communication with the reader about real people in real places. So if those people talk, you say what those people said. You don't say what the writer decides they said. . . . You can't interview the dead. You could make a list of the things you don't do. Where writers abridge that, they hitchhike on the credibility of writers who don't."[57]

"Although attitudes have changed, plagiarism remains widespread," Fred Fedler wrote in the spring 2006 *Newspaper Research Journal.* According to Fedler, "The problem is difficult to stop because plagiarism is difficult to detect. Only the most blatant examples may be noticed, and their exposure often seems accidental noticed by readers as often as by editors."[58]

Will Narrative Keep Growing?

The undeniable pull of narrative journalism is one magnet drawing a reader to the newspaper, but it won't hold the paper forever in a reader's hands. In 1994 Chris Harvey wrote "Tom Wolfe's Revenge" for *American Journalism Review.* In the essay he says, "Only a visionary could have predicted his impact on journalism would be lasting. Yet today, elements of the New Journalism that Wolfe so tirelessly promoted have become as commonplace as the pie chart in many newspapers, ranging from the *New York Times* to the *Oregonian* to the weekly *Washington City Paper.*"[59]

More than a decade after Harvey wrote that, Wolfe's influence has only increased. Harvey predicted: "Many journalists say the narrative form Wolfe, Talese and Capote helped popularize will be only one of the forms in newspapers of the future. . . . The short, inverted pyramid form will continue to be needed for some stories written on deadline."[60] Yes, some stories are written in the old format, but not all, not most, not even many.

Whether narrative journalism is the hope, the wish, or even the fear of the industry, the reality is that more newspapers are employing more narrative approaches. They are doing so through an expansion of the number of features on the front page and an increase in the narrative, featurized approach to hard news. There is no denying that the cheerleaders for the form are shouting into the industry megaphones. "News narrative has a way of building readership," said Jack Hart of the *Oregonian*. "There will be some point where we will not deliver stories in newsprint, but the story will never disappear."[61]

Examples of daily narrative are in almost every daily newspaper in the country every day. Their subjects range from profiles of soldiers to profiles of widows. Though the subjects are disparate in every way, the narrative style is consistently humanistic. The stories are about everyman and everywoman. Consider the November 16, 1997, story by Mark Bowden for the *Philadelphia Inquirer* that became the book *Blackhawk Down*. The headline read: "Reliving a Firefight: Hail Mary, Then Hold On" and began this way:

"Staff Sgt. Matt Eversmann's lanky frame was fully extended on the rope for what seemed too long on the way down. Hanging from a hovering Blackhawk helicopter, Eversmann was a full 70 feet above the streets of Mogadishu. His goggles had broken, so his eyes chafed in the thick cloud of dust stirred up by the bird's rotors."[62]

Eight years later, on November 20, 2005, Mary Schmich wrote in "The Journey of Judge Joan Lefkow" for the *Chicago Tribune*:

"Joan Lefkow thinks back now on a story her mother used to tell about their Kansas farm. She recounts it in the cadence of a Bible parable:

'There hadn't been rain. Then there was rain and everyone was happy. Then a hailstorm ruined the crops. My father looked out the window and said, 'The Lord giveth, and the Lord taketh away.'"[63]

Both journalists are nimble in their use of language and their adroit propulsion of the narrative. Neither is the kind of story you will get online or on the 10 P.M. television news.

"In the profession itself lies our greatest hope," wrote Will Irwin in 1911 in a series on journalism excerpted in the book *Killing the Messenger: 100 Years of Media Criticism*, edited by Tom Goldstein. Irwin continued, "In spite of all our commercial tendencies, its personnel and intelligence are improving year by year."[64]

In the 2001 anthology *Writing Creative Nonfiction*, Beverly Lowry wrote about her experience covering the aftermath of the Oklahoma City bombings:

News is plot, what happened last night or this afternoon or is in process right now. News breaks fast, somebody writes it up, the gun's barely fired before the world's clued in. Story's a wider map and involves any number of whys, relating to personal history, family background, the times, place, cultural background, the detached perversity of genes. Story makes a stab at explanation, figuring out how such or another wonderful or terrible thing could have happened. News enjoys a brief shelf life, turns stale fast, grows a quick crust. Story addresses complicated possibilities and reasons, therefore lasts longer, maybe forever."[65]

News can be delivered more quickly to the audience by other media than by a newspaper in at least a hundred, perhaps a thousand ways. The newspaper has to deliver a story form that is worth the wait, a slower read, a better written narrative. Narrative journalism is an attempt to make the newsworthy print stories more permanent or at the very least to have the stories so painstakingly reported and written last longer than a junk email before it hits the trash bin.

If newspapers are the only physical space available where daily news exists beyond the Internet and the airwaves—where its immediate evaporation is only a click away—then perhaps narrative newspaper journalism is the news we keep. Perhaps it is the story form that Ezra Pound referred to when he said, "Literature is news that stays news."[66]

Chapter 8

Diversity of Thought Shifts Content

Everyman's story is worth our attention. We are a disconnected, mobile, alienated society and we need human connections. Being able to pick up your local newspaper and feel connected to your community—that is the role and purpose we should play.

—Walt Harrington

The *Boston Globe* ran a lead story Monday, October 24, 2005, in the City and Region section about the disappearance of a local woman two weeks earlier. It had a compelling anecdotal lead.

No one can find Lynn Moran.
    Not the strangers that combed the waterfront weeds in Portland, Maine, near where the 24-year-old Shrewsbury woman disappeared two weeks ago. Not her family, which has offered a $10,000 reward to anyone with information about her whereabouts. Not her friends who spend their days tacking photos of the petite Moran in New England storefronts. Not the police in Portland, who suspect foul play and who have assigned nine detectives to the case.[1]

Inside the section was a smaller story on the murder of an African American Roxbury teen: "An 18-year-old man was shot to death Saturday night in Roxbury, in the city's 58th homicide this year, two more than at this time a year ago, Boston police said yesterday."[2]
    The approaches were different, the placement was different, the editorial importance assigned to the stories was different. And the difference is not

just that the Roxbury story had a hard news approach and the Shrewsbury story had a softer news approach. Yes, the story about Lynn Moran was more humanistic, detailed, and descriptive, which aligns it with the trend of an increase in a feature approach to hard news. The story of the Roxbury teen was terse and used an inverted-pyramid approach. But one was about a wealthy woman in a wealthy section of town, and one was not.

Perhaps more personal information for the teen story was unavailable— no one was home; no calls were returned. Perhaps staffing was short. Perhaps no official sources called the reporter back on the Roxbury story. Perhaps more details were available on the Moran story. It is idealistic to assume that every story, headline, and photo, as well as their placement will be fair. Some slights of judgment are unintentional. Some omissions are not sins but only the results of harried reporters writing on deadline.

The shift to everyman news challenges journalists to include a breadth of unofficial sources who represent a diverse society, and it challenges the industry to make everyman news truly democratic and potentially include news of every man and every woman regardless of race, age, education, background, religion, disability, sexual orientation, and point of view.

It is admirable to have more front-page news harbor a broader range of story types with more unofficial sources. The trend supports a more inclusive attitude toward news and storytelling, and it points to a corresponding trend in the diversification of newsrooms. But diversity of voice in the paper comes from a diversity of thought in the newsroom, not strictly a diversity of personnel. "Everyone is under pressure to hurry up and do it fast," said E. J. Graff of the Brandeis Women's Studies Research Center. "It's harder to stop, think, and come up with a range of good sources instead of simply calling the usual male suspects. That won't change until someone says you have to do better."[3]

It is stereotyping to perpetually assign an African American reporter to cover hip-hop, a disabled reporter to cover wheelchair basketball, or a Latina reporter to cover the local traditions for *La Quinceañera*. The goal is to have the stories that matter to different aspects of the community covered in the newspaper by all reporters.

"Diversity reporting is an extra value worth considering for every news story reported," wrote Leigh Stephens Aldrich in *Covering the Community: A Diversity Handbook for Media*. "This means making an effort to include the total community . . . but not including the total community leaves the general public in the dark about events and issues that are vital to all."[4]

A staff representative of the community is not the norm; in print, most of the reporters and editors are white males. "Because most news workers are white and male, the result is an unrecognized media tilt toward their world as norm. A powerful, unconscious belief system guides news judgment and choices about whose stories are deemed important and whose are overlooked," Sally Lehrman, diversity chair for the Society of Professional Journalists, wrote in a July 2005 report for the Knight Foundation.[5]

"Our failure to embrace diversity is principally a failure to see other people as human as ourselves, a weakness that is not easily transcended through repeat coverage of parades and festivals," Perry Parks wrote in *Making Important News Interesting.* Parks continued, "The way to engage readers in a story of diversity—or for that matter any of the routine event stories that interns and weekend reporters are so often sent out to cover—is to tell the story of a person."[6] Others agree.

"You have to tell the story of the people with the best story to tell," said Laurie Hertzel of the *Minneapolis Star Tribune.* "And that person is not always the predictable official source you always turn to for a reaction. Diversity has to do with different kinds of stories, but the voice of the paper is determined by the editors."[7]

Newsroom Realities

In a December 2004 study from the Readership Institute at Northwestern, "New Readers: Race, Ethnicity and Readership" showed that 81 percent of people who work in newsrooms are white, as are more than 80 percent of newsroom supervisors. "There is a correlation between the proportion of a particular racial/ethnic group in the workforce and how much that group is covered (i.e., mentioned in stories and shown in photos) in the content."[8]

A May 2006 Readership Institute study showed little improvement. The percentage of women news executives at 137 newspapers with circulations over 85,000 increased to 29 percent in 2006, from 27 percent in 2003. "In editorial, 39 percent of the managing editors are women, but only 26 percent of those at the top of the news department are."[9] The percentage of female managing editors decreased.

Noting the historical tilt of newspaper coverage toward a white, male norm, former Knight Ridder White House correspondent Jodi Enda wrote in 2002, "That has changed dramatically, though not dramatically enough. The overarching voice remains that of the white man." Enda, former president of Journalism and Women Symposium, wrote, "Still, the presence of women and racial and ethnic minorities in newsrooms and on editorial pages has prompted media outlets to pay more attention to such issues as racial profiling and date rape, raising public awareness to a level that could provoke change."[10]

This is not a new idea, but it bears repeating. "Getting more minorities in the newsroom is a target, but not the goal, of diversity. The goal is a more accurate news organization," wrote Bill Kovach and Tom Rosenstiel in *Elements of Journalism.* "The goal of diversity would be to assemble not only a newsroom that might resemble the community, but one that is also as open and honest so that this diversity can function. It is what we call intellectual diversity, and it encompasses and gives meaning to all the other kinds."[11]

Race and Gender Issues

Gender and race are only two floodgates that need to open to raise the awareness of diversity at a newspaper to a higher sea level of inclusion. If you think of a newspaper as a ship transporting information and opinions through a canal to a wider ocean, then the ship must go through a series of locks, or flights, of varying levels. In the process the higher sluice gates are opened, the lower sluice gates are closed, and a lock fills with water, allowing the ship to pass through onto the higher level. The transition is not complete until the ship reaches the necessary water level and is ready to sail away and be absorbed into the media consciousness of a wide audience.

There are many different levels of locks. The transition period of raising the ship to the next level may be as slow as dripping water or as swift as a tidal wave. Some newspapers never even realize the ship is on a different water level than the rest of the world. But it is a process of diversifying the newsroom physically and intellectually that is ethically necessary.

"Anecdotally, women journalists (and journalists of color, male and female) have unlimited stories of ways they have made differences in news content—topics covered, sources consulted and quoted, storytelling approach, how stories are covered and illustrated—and how newspapers are managed," wrote Christy Bulkeley in 2002. "Presence of women as sources doesn't guarantee, of course, differing points of view from those expressed by men or determine what's news anymore than absence of women negates these possibilities," Bulkeley wrote. "But arguably, presence increases possibilities."[12]

It is possible to assume that with more people in the newsroom of different backgrounds, circumstances, and DNA, there would be an eclectic and variable mix of deadline-driven stories as well as more timeless features. It is reasonable to expect that all news would just be human and fair. And it is logical to think that the more diverse newsrooms become, the more newspapers will reflect a democracy and pluralism of voice, approach, and sourcing.

"For some journalists of color, the 'desire to make an impact' appears to be tied to a personal commitment to improve the coverage of their own racial and ethnic communities," wrote Lawrence T. McGill in "Newsroom Diversity: Meeting the Challenge," a Freedom Forum project in 1999.[13]

The American Society of Newspaper Editors has a goal of parity of newsroom staffs with their communities by the year 2025. ASNE reported in its annual newsroom census in 2005 that 13.42 percent of the more than 54,000 newsroom employees were minorities; 39.9 percent of the reporters were women; and 34.8 percent of newsroom supervisors were women. These are only slight increases over the previous year.[14] It is a reasonable assumption that more women and minorities in newsrooms would increase the diversity of sources. "The source selection, then, is a key component of the final product," Cory L. Armstrong wrote in 2006. "For years, media scholars have suggested that women are underrepresented, miscast or missing completely from news coverage—a term often called 'symbolic annihilation.' These researchers suggest that news sources lack diversity, favor male sources and reinforce the chauvinistic viewpoint that should be seen as subordinate to men."[15]

But a diversity of sources can be required. Reporting on a wider array of issues, events, and trends from across the community can result in a broader range of everyman news. "The best diversity programs do more than bring varieties of human beings in the workplace," Lehrman wrote. "They embody the conviction that diversity enhances the work environment and the product itself—whether it be a car, pancakes and syrup, life insurance or a newspaper."[16]

The Gatekeeper Matters

More than half a century ago, sociologist David Manning White studied the process of wire story selection in "The Gate Keeper: A Case Study in the Selection of News." By examining the editorial choices of "Mr. Gates" in 1949, Manning White found "that basic journalistic beliefs were involved in decisions, but the process was rather subjective and depended on the gatekeeper's experiences, attitudes and expectations."[17] In 1991, Glen L. Bleske revised the study with "Ms. Gates Takes Over," and found "several comparable dimensions including gender, journalism experience, historical time period, news technology differences and organizational size."[18]

The person editing determines the types of stories that run, where they are placed, and who is assigned what story. In *Front Page Women Journalists 1920–1950*, author Kathleen A. Cairns wrote that women newspaper journalists after World War I were tapped to cover softer news. "The human interest emphasis enabled them to capitalize on the longstanding notion that women could write this type of story better than men, and the goal of objectivity allowed them (women) to argue that newspaper managers should use objective and fair criteria in hiring new reporters as well as in publishing stories."[19]

"For many years women were trained within a specific, narrow category of 'women's journalism,'" wrote Deborah Chambers, Linda Steiner, and Carole Fleming in the 2004 *Women and Journalism*. They continued, "The fact that women were taught to write specifically as women for women perpetuated the myth that to be a real journalist, dealing in hard news, you had to be male."[20] Luckily the influence of that stereotype has diminished, and both men and women journalists write features and hard news. But the mythology behind the gender divide still resonates, even though readers may be unaware of the historical professional divide. "Running through most American writing on news is the assumption that there are two kinds of news, variously called 'hard' versus 'soft,' 'important' versus 'interesting,' 'news,' versus 'human interest' and 'information' versus 'story,'" wrote Elizabeth Bird and Robert Dardenne. "There is little to suggest that audiences experience the world so neatly divided."[21]

In the twenty-first century, as more women occupy copydesk slots as well as edit, report, and assume management positions in American newspapers, the lines have been blurred, crossed, and in some cases trampled or eliminated. Kay Mills in *A Place in the News: From the Women's Pages to the Front Pages* wrote in 1988: "In the news business, this does not mean women bias their coverage; it does mean they broaden it. . . . Anecdotal evidence is compelling that the presence of more women assigning, writing and editing the news has altered the definition of news, although not firmly enough."[22]

The fair sourcing of news stories along gender lines is an issue that has been tackled frequently in recent years. Shesource.org, a project of Women's Funding Network, the White House Project, and Fenton Communications in New York, defines itself as an "online database and resource for journalists" with the intention of "closing the gender gap in news media." According to the website, "Too many journalists do not quote women as experts simply because they do not know any women who are experts in the fields that they cover."[23]

An October 2005 study by the White House Project, "Who's Talking Now: A Follow-up Analysis of Guest Appearances by Women on the Sunday Morning Talk Shows," or a parade of personalities Calvin Trillin once called the "Sabbath gasbags," showed a paucity of women sources. In the study of five shows on ABC, NBC, CBS, CNN, and FOX, women made up only 14 percent of all guests from November 2004 to mid-July 2005. "In short, our findings continue to show that women are vastly under-represented in this popular forum for debate, and therefore remain largely invisible to the greater public," wrote Marie Wilson, president of the White House project. "The sooner we have a more representative offering of female leaders speaking on behalf of their constituencies, the closer we will be to having a true democracy."[24]

The same gender imbalance is unfortunately also found in print. A 2005 study from the University of Missouri–Columbia School of Journalism, showed a ratio of 4 to 1, male to female sources in news stories and a ratio of 2 to 1 in photographs. Of the 4,851 individuals mentioned in one news-papers' stories, 79 percent of the sources were men, compared to 18 per-cent women. The researcher, Maria Len-Rios, also noticed that female news staffers were more likely to notice the lopsided coverage than male journalists.[25]

In March 2005 at the Women, Action and the Media conference, author and journalist Jill Nelson said in her keynote that there has been a distinct and intentional "silencing of diversity and the voices of women." She added, "It is important that we not censor ourselves and take a stand. We must refuse to be shunted to the soft lifestyle stories."[26]

The Project for Excellence in Journalism found in "The Gender Gap: Women Are Still Missing as Sources for Journalists" (2005) that women were a source for more than half the news stories in the lifestyle section. "Overall, 41 percent of print stories contained at least one female source, and 19 percent reached the higher threshold of citing two or more," the study reported. "Nevertheless, print stories were still half as likely to con-tain a female source as a male source (88 percent cited at least one male source). . . . It is not simply that wire stories use fewer sources. The same kind of gap did *not* occur with male sources."[27]

According to Jennifer L. Pozner, executive director of Women in Media and News, relying on a narrow source list is as much about time and staffing as it is about intent, and it is an imbalance that can be deliberately corrected.

Anyone can report using diverse sources and get balanced stories—it just takes more time, more effort, more digging . . . and more resources. That's why I usually talk about the problem of women's under-representation as sources and experts in news as attributable to a variety of issues: there's the individual biases of some reporters and editors, of course, but there's also corporate media consolidation that has led to major downsizing in newsrooms and "profit-enhancing" budget cuts leaving reporters and producers to have to file more stories in fewer hours and days than they used to, with smaller budgets for research, ESL translators, and the like. Sometimes, reporters and producers have no problem treating biased double standards about women as newsworthy—other times, good journalists are trying to do solid reporting, but they have little to no time to expand their Rolodex, so they end up relying on the same five white men in suits that they've quoted for the last ten years.[28]

Pozner founded Women in Media and News in 2002.

We created the POWER (Perspectives of Women Expand Reporting) Sources Project, which connects journalists and media producers with a national, diverse network of female experts, from women in politics to plumbing, teaching to tech work. The POWER Sources Project is a utilitarian resource for media makers, helping them to find articulate, qualified women ready to speak on record, on a huge range of topics. Anyone can do balanced, accurate, non-sexist reporting . . . they just have to have the resources available to do that.[29]

In response to the gender gap in sourcing and coverage of women's issues, Rita Henley Jensen in 1999 became editor-in-chief and creator of Women'sEnews, a nonprofit online news service that "is the definitive source of substantive news—unavailable anywhere else—covering issues of particular concern to women and their allies," she wrote.[30] (I am a regular contributor to Women'sEnews.)

"Covering stories often missed by behemoth commercial news outlets is precisely why Women's Enews exists," Jensen wrote in 2002. Jensen wrote that the opportunity to edit the paper "tapped my personal and professional frustration with the failure of commercial media to adequately report on many issues critical to women's well-being. Not only did I think welfare reform—an issue affecting millions of poor and low-income women—had not been well-covered, but I believed that reporting by the mainstream media often failed to convey essential information and perspectives about women's medical care, reproductive rights, job bias, wage discrimination, and child care."[31]

The tendency to choose as a source one gender or race over another is a pattern of behavior with which reporters have been comfortable, and it has been widely accepted and, until recently, unchallenged. An August 2005 study of male and female sources in newspaper coverage of the 2004 Senate races by Eric Freedman, Frederick Fico, and Brad Love, all of Michigan

State University, showed "male nonpartisan sources appeared more frequently and prominently than female sources. Female reporters cited male nonpartisan sources more often than did male reporters; reporters of both genders cited female sources equally rarely." The researchers added, "The findings also suggest that the comparatively small proportion of female expert sources appearing in such stories may affect the information readers receive—or do not receive—and reflect on how journalists regard their roles in covering key elections such as Senate races." According to the study, "Studies that explored gender diversity of sources have consistently found dominance by males."[32]

News and Race

Even when and where diversity of story choice and source is deliberate, stories can be stereotypical and predictable—the plucky survivor, the heroic victim, the rags-to-riches tale. An August 2005 study by Ilia Rodriguez of the University of New Mexico, "'Diversity Writing and the Imaginaries of Liberal Multiculturalism in the U.S. Mainstream Press," analyzed the award-winning news stories in the 2002 and 2003 ASNE diversity writing category. Rodriguez found that the narratives of the stories tended to support the ideology of adhering to the American dream to achieve success and offer no real insights and surprises.[33]

But the winning six-part series "Along Martin Luther King: A Passage to Black America," by Jonathan Tilove of Newhouse News Service, was different. (Tilove turned his stories into a book in 2003.) "Source selection, hence, opens space for the characterization of a community that avoids easy categorizations. Instead, the series deepens our understanding of these communities as ideologically diverse, racialized, politicized, intellectual, conflictive and vibrant, with both progressive and conservative elements," she wrote. Rodriguez added, "In sum, even when Tilove's approach reproduces the black/white paradigm that overlooks the presence of other racial and ethnic groups, his stories depart from predictable narratives in which the American dream ideology imposes closure and ready-made understanding for the white, European-American middle class reader."[34]

This is precisely what researchers were writing about as early as 2001. "A lack of full understanding of the complexity of America means that the news media may offend, however unintentionally, and so may drive away minority readers and viewers who are making up larger and larger proportions of the population," wrote Edward C. Pease, Erna Smith, and Federico Subervi in the "News and Race Model of Excellence Project" in October 2001.[35]

The important study of five newspapers over fifty-two issues in a year covered more than forty-five hundred stories and photographs in "minority-related coverage." The study showed that while the largest percentage of stories with minority elements were in the sports and entertainment category at 40 percent, the number of human interest features, 12 percent, was higher than the number of crime stories at 11 percent.[36]

"Although many feature stories centered on cultural events, such as Black History Month and Cinco de Mayo, others were 'color-blind' stories depicting racial and ethnic minorities as everyday people in everyday situations, such as a story on people seeking greater meaning in their work and careers," according to the Pease study. Most of these stories, or 68 percent, were 10 inches or longer. The newspapers studied—the *South Florida Sun-Sentinel*, the *Seattle Times*, the *San Jose Mercury News*, the *News-Journal*, and the *Dallas Morning News*—all expressed a commitment to diversity in another portion of the study.[37]

"Obviously news coverage is a product of many factors that have nothing to do with newsroom commitment to diversity. Deadlines, staffing levels, beat structure, uncooperative sources, the newspaper's reputation in communities of color and even the way news is defined in different newsroom all pose challenges to more inclusive coverage," according to the study.[38]

Coverage of Poverty Issues

At the March 2006 Women, Action and the Media conference in Cambridge, Claire Cummings, founder and publisher of Survival News, said, "Poverty and low income women are the elephants in the room. They are invisible to mainstream media." What coverage of Katrina did—at least briefly—was to raise the issue of poverty by bringing the images to the forefront. "It was poor, black people, and mostly women, who were suffering the most."[39]

Diane Lewis, a *Boston Globe* reporter speaking at the same WAM panel on poverty and women's issues, added, "When you look at print and what gets in, there is a misperception about who reads the news. They don't think people we are talking about are their readers." Reporters in the newsroom doing the stories aren't in poverty, Lewis said. But they don't need to be to bring the issues of poverty to the newspaper.[40]

The point of diversifying newsrooms is to eliminate one-shot stories, biased language, and stereotypical coverage and to promote the use of sources from all segments of the community. The reason that doesn't happen, many say, is because newsrooms are not diverse. But all that is needed is the intention to be inclusive with all sources and open-minded about nontraditional story ideas. It is diversity of perspective that guarantees diversity of content.

"Many of the reasons offered to explain such slow progress in expanding news coverage of an increasingly multicultural America and in getting journalists of color into the news business are the same today as in 1968," according to "The News and Race Models of Excellence Project" by Pease, Smith, and Subervi in 2001. "News businesses 'can't find' minorities who want to work in journalism and have trouble keeping the journalists of color they do recruit. That also was an explanation for why study after study of news content in America showed there was so little content in newspapers and TV news about people of color—typically less than 10 percent of the total newshole or newscast, several content studies have found—and why so much of that content was negative and reflected poorly on people of color: just not enough minority journalists in the newsroom."[41]

The goal is editorial reach to embrace and represent more kinds of voices in the newspaper. The result, in the best of all possible worlds, would be to regularly print stories on the front page and elsewhere in the paper that begin to represent the community and larger world as they are, telling stories from all areas that have gone unreported.

"The news business, once populated mostly by white men, has been transformed by an influx of women and people of color," wrote Leonard Downie Jr. and Robert Kaiser in *The News about the News*. "These journalists have helped expand the definition of news to include more of the realities of life in an increasingly diverse nation."[42] To declare transformation complete and full diversity of stories a reality is to picture newsroom utopia. But change in content is not accidental; it is deliberate. Some newspaper companies have taken aggressive initiatives to include more diverse points of views and stories that reflect more of the readers' lives than the editors and reporters' lives. It has resulted in more features of different types and more voices in the paper.

"In most ways, today's papers are more featurized than the older ones, and features have changed," Carl Sessions Stepp of the University of Maryland wrote in 2002. "Gone for the most part are 'women's pages,' social and personal items and full-page daily photo-spreads." He wrote that "trend stories and bright writing abound."[43]

Stepp studied ten newspapers in May 1963, September 1963, and January 1964, and then revisited them during the same months in 1998 and 1999. What he found was that "front pages are more featurized" with more 'soft leads.'" He also found that diversity in the newspapers increased. The number of female bylines was up to 29 percent from 7 percent. The photographs in the '60s period showed forty white faces and five non-white faces. In the '90s, the papers showed forty-two white and sixteen nonwhite faces in the newspapers.[44]

While any newspaper reader can cite improvement and a move toward inclusiveness of more voices in the paper, much remains to be done. "There are still so many stories that are not being told by traditional media. When I look at how America is changing, I see so much to report and many different ways of telling the stories," wrote Retha Hill in "Women in Newspapers: Still Fighting an Uphill Battle" (2002). She continued, "Reporters always tell the story the same way. They all share preconceived notions about, for example, African-Americans. The *Washington Post*'s coverage of African Americans is anthropological. The paper explains African-Americans to the larger white society. . . . When you have a big coverage tent like a daily metropolitan newspaper, you skim the surface when telling stories about people outside of the primary audience. You end up translating for white Americans what other people around them are doing and saying."[45]

Other Areas Lacking in Coverage

In 2000 the Annenberg School for Communication at the University of Southern California completed a follow-up report on "Lesbians and Gays in the Newsroom 10 Years Later." From the survey of more than 350 gay and lesbian journalists in newsrooms around the country, the researchers found: "While coverage of lesbians and gays has shown improvement over 10 years, these journalists say there is still a way to go. They rate much of current coverage as just fair to poor, especially of local issues affecting lesbian and gay communities. The response suggest mainstream media reacts to stories that reach national consideration but is falling short in its attention to home turf gay and lesbian communities. Coverage of lesbians and lesbians and gays of color is rated at the very lowest level."[46] A newspaper has to do more than cover the annual local gay pride parade and offer updates on the same-sex marriage issue to consider itself fair in its reporting of the gay community. "The media field's imminent power of consecration—the power to say who and what is important, and what we should think about important things and people—is based on its own legitimacy, which journalists have collectively accumulated in the course of history," wrote Patrick Champagne in 2005.[47]

Some newspapers such as the *Chicago Tribune, San Francisco Chronicle, New York Times,* and *Boston Globe* succeed in representing the gay community in stories where the issue or the subject matter is not a gay issue. Feature stories, wedding announcements, reaction stories, and stories on parenting and education all include gay and lesbian couples as a norm. Their voices were included in the stories because they had something relevant to say, not because they reacted to a specific issue in the gay community.

The disability community is traditionally underserved by the media in sourcing as well as by the distortion of the stereotype of the "supercrip"— a person with disabilities who is framed as able to overcome all obstacles to become superhuman. According to The Center for an Accessible Society, a 1999 study by Beth Haller showed that "a major finding of this project is that during the entire year of 1998, the four major television networks presented only 34 disability-related news stories, many of which were clustered around two or three news events." Haller added, "This research helps us interpret the meaning of news sources in stories about disability issues." She went on to say that "A major finding is that 70 percent of the stories has no identifiable source with a disability in it. . . . The print journalists were much more likely to use people with disabilities as examples in their news stories rather than as sources. About 56 percent of the news stories used a person with a disability as an example."[48]

Religion is another area in which newspapers succumb to the habit of using stereotypes for sources and consider sources only on obvious stories where religion is directly related to the issue or event. Beyond the Christian right and formulaic stories about religious holidays or traditional practices, sources with a diversity of religious viewpoints are not regularly sought out by reporters.

Unless directed otherwise, many reporters would not intentionally seek a source who is Muslim on a general economic or retail story because they wouldn't consider it necessary. "Muslims also complain that many American journalists who are writing about them have little understanding about their religion or their culture," wrote Joyce Davis, deputy foreign news editor at Knight Ridder Newspapers, in 2003. "Muslim Americans have many stories to tell. . . . They need to document a unique part of American history. Journalists must find a way to tell those stories."[49]

Going Local

Many newspapers have been bullish on diversity and expanding coverage by introducing specific initiatives aimed at coverage being more local and inclusive. In October 2003 Gannett Newspapers rolled out its "Real Life, Real News: Connecting with Readers' Lives" campaign to all its newspapers. Jennifer Carroll, director of news development; Anne Saul, news systems editor; and Ann Clark, news executive, led the Train the Trainer sessions, according to the company's website. The sessions "include descriptions of the elements of Real Life, Real News, including overviews on the readership issue and circles of life. The session will discuss approaches including breaking news, daily key-topic coverage, exclusive enterprise and First Amendment efforts. The training will explore Moments of Life and the importance of Real Life, Real News in utilizing all platforms and means of delivery."[50]

One year later, E. J. Mitchell, managing editor of the *Detroit News,* told a group of Gannett editors at the UNITY 2004 News Watch meeting: "As we rolled out Real Life, Real News, we asked everyone in the newsroom to help us compile a Moments of Life calendar. Actually, there are two different lists. One consists of seasonal Moments of Life, from applying for summer camps in February to the opening day of the deer season in November. We also have a lengthy and comprehensive list of collective experiences broken down by convenient categories—such as parenting, life passages and first-time events." In the speech printed on the Gannett website, Mitchell wrote, "At the daily news meetings, each department marks the stories that have Real Life, Real News content. As a result, the number of stories in that category has grown exponentially."[51]

At Knight Ridder newspapers before the sale in 2006, the fifth of seven tenets of journalism was listed on the website as "People Like Me." That category was defined by an editorial staff that "understands what's of special interest and importance to people of the area," wrote Jerry Ceppos, vice president of news for the chain, on the company's website in spring 2004.[52] The first tenet, of course, is storytelling.

The *Post-Crescent* in Appleton, Wisconsin, asked its readers to share their views of newspaper content by answering these questions online: "What types of stories and information from your community would you like to read more about in The Post-Crescent? Are there any types of news or information The Post-Crescent could carry that would prompt you to make sure you didn't miss the newspaper that day?"[53]

In an attempt to be more global in its everyday reporting, the *Atlanta Journal-Constitution* launched "Atlanta and the World" in February 2002, an initiative that won the paper a perspective award from Associated Press Managing Editors in 2003. "We write about issues concerning culture, heritage and identity and try and do so in a manner that transcends the insidious 'us and them' mindset that often permeates coverage of ethnic communities. We do this largely by telling stories that focus on people who make up the mosaic of metro Atlanta," V. Raman Narayanan wrote in 2003.[54]

The Goal vs. Reality

Good work continues in this area with leagues of academics and professionals pushing for initiatives in the newsroom as well as research into diversity coverage. "Is it possible to even have excellence in journalism without bringing diversity into the newsroom?" asked Alice Tait, professor at Central Michigan University, and coordinator and coauthor of the ALANA project of Ethnic Media in America. ALANA, an acronym for African, Latino, Asian, and Native American, is a three-part series of compiled research looking at the question of the media image of theses sectors of society in "mainstream news, information and entertainment content."[55]

Karla Garrett Harshaw, editor of the *Springfield News-Sun* in Ohio, and the first woman of color to be ASNE president, said in her speech to the group in 2004, "We need to reach out to all people if we are to have meaningful coverage. It's not just our mission to cover their problems, but to mainstream their voices into all aspects of coverage, whether on education, government matters or business."[56] While many editors and media insiders express the desire to have more diverse coverage, it is not always put into practice, as we have seen.

"Should news trends continue, however, the reflection of America's culture, economy and politics in newspapers, magazines and on broadcast networks will remain as white as ever," Lehrman wrote in the Knight report. "Today, in 2004, even though media executives have pledged their commitment to diversity for more than two decades, a single perspective dominates mainstream media newsrooms: at least 87 percent of newspaper editorial employees and 92 percent of network news sources are white. Two thirds are male."[57]

"We always say there has to be diversity because our readers want to know what life is like in other communities," said Ken Fuson of the *Des Moines Register*. "Diversity of thought is good."[58]

On the American Society of Newspaper Editors website, the mission is straightforward: "To cover communities fully, to carry out their role in a democracy, and to succeed in the marketplace, the nation's newsrooms must reflect the racial diversity of American society by 2025 or sooner. At a minimum, all newspapers should employ journalists of color and every newspaper should reflect the diversity of its community."[59]

But the utopia does not necessarily emerge.

From 1999 to 2003, Tracy Everbach, assistant professor at the University of North Texas, studied an all-women management team at the *Sarasota Herald-Tribune* in Florida. The team consisted of the publisher, executive editor, managing editor, and two assistant managing editors. In her report,

Everbach found that "women bring different perspectives to the work-place than men and different perspectives to news than men," as she said at a panel at AEJMC in August 2005.[60]

What she found pierces a hole in the theory that a newspaper's coverage of all communities is linked directly to a diverse management team. She found that the female management "did have somewhat of an effect on content and on series and issues. But in the day to day coverage, they picked the same national stories and the same kind of city news in the metro section." She added, "In the sports department there was one woman and there was still hardly any coverage of female sports."[61]

Without the realization of physical diversity in the newsroom, only a mandate toward diversity of thought and deliberate inclusion of all types of sources and story ideas will truly democratize American newspapers. It is a challenge to everyone in the newsroom—from management to reporter to copy editor—to maintain open minds and a shared determination to gather stories outside the comfort zones of tradition. "As more and more information is printed, broadcast, faxed, phoned and sent over the Internet, being a passive mirror is less and less relevant," David Mindich wrote in 1998. "With so much news and so many storytellers, there must be something more than passivity for responsible journalists to offer."[62]

Stories and sourcing that are diverse do not spontaneously generate in newsrooms. Journalists must actively pursue them. "Overwhelmingly we are presented with the images and lifestyles of the middle class in both news and entertainment," wrote Deepa Kumar in 2004. "If we claim to live in a democratic society where the majority should have a stake in decisions about social life, we need to challenge this state of affairs."[63]

While the move toward personal stories in newspapers demonstrates a desire by journalists to tell stories of the individual, diversity in journalism is about more than just choosing someone off the street for an anecdotal lead. It is about highlighting and fully representing the voices of everyman in news.

Chapter 9

The Therapeutic Story Flow Model

It is a truism that the story of anyone's life is not the story of one person alone.

—Myra Schneider and John Killick, *Writing for Self Discovery*

✳ "Read two newspaper articles and call me in the morning." It is not possible that a doctor you visit for a stomachache will suggest you derive an alleluia miracle cure for your ailment from reading newspaper narratives. But it is possible that the growing influence of the narrative therapy movement on cognitive science, neurophysiology, psychology, sociology, gerontology, oncology, and cardiology over the last forty years can be linked to newspaper journalism. Bear with me; it is not as crazy as it seems. "Throughout history, writing has had a profound influence on the feelings, thoughts, and behaviors of individuals and entire societies," wrote Stephen J. Lepore and Joshua M. Smyth in 2002. "The effects have not always been desirable, but there is no disputing that writing has permeated and shaped every sphere of private and public life, be it spiritual, commercial, political, educational, artistic or vocational."[1]

The abridged definition of narrative therapy—a field pioneered by psychologist Ira Pogoff with his Intensive Journal Workshops in the 1960s, expanded by James Pennebaker at the University of Texas at Austin in the 1980s, and continuing today—is the study of the physical, emotional, and psychological benefits of expressive writing. And writing—about news events using the expressions of the source and the reporter—are at the core of newspaper journalism.

Journalists organize the events, insights, and experiences of others and express them in stories. The genre of everyman news illuminates the personal stories of individuals and helps writer, sources, and reader understand these experiences. It is in this way that a connection can be drawn from everyman journalism to narrative therapy and possibly its positive effects, and hence its broadening appeal.

"Why are we drawn to other people's stories? It is satisfying a basic need; seeing another human story helps us to understand ourselves in some way," said Pennebaker, now chair of the psychology department at the University of Texas and often referred to as the father of the narrative therapy movement. From his comfortable office in Austin, he continued, "We're all ambulance chasers, journalists are the worst, psychologists are right up there. We are all driving down the highway, straining our necks and slowing down. We all want to know how people felt, but not close enough for it to be us."[2]

"Scholars in recent years have thought deeply about the power of stories and realized that journalistic storytelling, and narratives in general, are crucial building blocks for society and people's understanding of it," David Craig wrote in 2006. "Whether they are giving the history of an event, sketching a biography, explaining, or making an argument, people are telling stories to themselves and to one another to create meaning in human life. Readers of news articles, features, analyses, and columns, then, are taking in fragments of meaning—whether from anecdotes and description or statements of explanation—that together help to shape the world in which they think and act."[3]

In a column about the 2007 film *Freedom Writers,* which she describes as a movie "about the power of writing in the lives of ordinary people," *Newsweek* columnist Anna Quindlen wrote, "Words on paper confer a kind of immortality. Wouldn't all of us love to have a journal, a memoir, a letter from those we have loved and lost? Shouldn't all of us leave a bit of that behind?"[4]

Story as Catharsis

The idea of a story or narrative offering more than a written regurgitation of events is not a new idea. In the late nineteenth century Sigmund Freud and Josef Breuer presented their catharsis theory, defined as working through emotional trauma with recall and ultimately by discharging, or releasing, the trauma through behavior or words. Freud "argues that dramatic scenes move audiences because they touch upon repressed emotion."[5]

Almost three decades ago, psychologist T. J. Scheff asserted that catharsis and healing were possible through a community experiencing shared entertainment events and rituals. He argued that the distancing inherent in witnessing touchstone stories told through drama, film, and literature was cathartic in itself. That is why people cry at movies, laugh at comedy television shows, and are moved by literature. Perhaps, too, that is why readers of newspapers are drawn to stories of ordinary individuals and their reactions to events.

Appropriate distancing must happen in order for the audience—or the reader—to experience a catharsis or healing of his or her own past traumatic event or life phase, he wrote. Scheff based his theories on mass entertainment such as movies, television and dramatic plays, but this central idea can perhaps be extrapolated to include mass media of newspapers and the narrative everyman stories told on those pages.

According to Scheff, the experience of sharing these stories is made more comfortable and beneficial by being in the audience, having some distance from the story, creating what is known as community solidarity. According to Scheff, "health-promoting emotional discharge can occur in response to stimuli, such as the narrative contained in plays or books, that have not been directly experienced."[6] It is not too difficult to stretch that definition of stimuli to include newspaper stories. With this theory in mind, then, the newspaper narrative becomes a point of discussion and a way for others to connect with appropriate distancing.

In her 1992 dissertation, State University of New York doctoral candidate Melanie Arline Greenburg called upon Pennebaker's studies as well as Freud and Breuer's theories to explain the release of trauma through language, ultimately "cutting the residues" of past trauma through words.[7] Whether experiencing the narrative by writing a story is cathartic or offers some cognitive or emotional relief to the reader connecting to his or her own similar experience, many scholars and professionals consider expressive writing as curative for the writer as well as for the reader.

"One idea is that translating experiences into words forces some kind of structure to the experiences themselves. Through language individuals are able to organize, structure, and ultimately assimilate both their emotional experiences and the events that may have provoked the emotions," Pennebaker wrote. In the *Journal of Clinical Psychology* in 1999, Pennebaker wrote with coauthor Janel D. Seagal, "The guiding assumption of the present work is that the act of constructing stories is a natural human process that helps individuals to understand their experiences and themselves."[8]

"Stories are easy to remember—because in many ways, stories are how we remember," Daniel Pink wrote in the 2005 book *A Whole New Mind.* "Story is high concept because it sharpens our understanding of one thing by showing it in the context of something else."[9] In hundreds of narrative therapy studies around the world, subjects in a variety of circumstances report not just a perception of benefit from writing about their lives, but measurable physical improvements.[10] Subjects who write regularly have experienced decreases in blood pressure, fewer trips to the doctor, fewer illnesses, fewer incidents of asthma, decreased severity of arthritic symptoms, shortened recovery from surgery and cancer treatments, and on and on and on. "The referential process, embodied in storytelling, is a powerful function that has potentially significant emotional and also bodily impact," sociologist Wilma Bucci wrote.[11]

So if writing is proven to be of real value to an individual, and it is the personal story that provides the benefit, it is possible that everyman news wrapped around the core of individual personal story also provides a benefit to the source, the journalist, and the reader. This may explain the growing popularity of everyman news.

The Story Flow Model for Journalism

The newspaper story told as everyman journalism serves as the organizational tool, enabling the narrative to move from source to journalist to reader. What I call the story flow model is a triad of influences, with the journalist serving as the hub, or the filter, of the story being conveyed from source to reader. A source feeds a story to the journalist, and it is a two-way interactive process as the reporter interviews, questions, and challenges the sources. The reader receives the story from the journalist in the story flow model, but everyman journalism cannot exist without the reader's input.

Unlike journalism of decades past, it is not a one-way deposition of information. The reader is invited to offer feedback and to participate in the story. The journalist's email address is often included at the bottom of each story. Newspaper websites offer blogging posts for comments on stories. Readers can create podcasts, vlogs, blogs, and next-step alternatives. They can also send money, tips, resources, offers of jobs, homes, answers. They can become part of the story flow.

The story flow for everyman journalism is filtered through a journalist, taking into account other observations, interviews, facts, data, expert commentary, and context. It is not a dogmatic story flow, but a dynamic, organic endeavor involving the source, writer, and reader. In citizen journalism and blogging, first-person narratives skip the journalist as hub and move directly to the audience. In traditional newspaper journalism, the journalist enters into the dynamic flow of the story acting as organizer for the narrative with a reverence for sources and a respect for readers. All three links in the story flow model are tied to narrative therapy and the process of redemption through story.

The First Link: The Source

The first link narrative therapy has to journalism is that the source whose story is told well often professes a deep gratitude to the journalist for exposing a truth exposed or expressing a point of view. It is the same kind of parallel relief examined in narrative therapy when the subject details his or her story in expressive writing. Read the grateful letters to the editor; ask reporters about the thank-you emails from sources who feel their stories were sincerely portrayed. Ask sources about the impact a solid piece of quality journalism has on their lives. The sources' lives may be changed as a result of the story, and only because of the story.

In 1999 journalist and author Paul Auster began the National Story Project on National Public Radio, soliciting listeners for stories. "With their help, I said, I was hoping to put together an archive of facts, a museum of American reality." He received four thousand submissions and chose fewer than two hundred. Auster wrote a book about the project, *I Thought My Father Was God: And Other True Tales from NPR's National Story Project*, in which he said, "If I had to define what these stories were, I would call them dispatches, reports from the front lines of personal experience. They are about the private worlds of individual Americans, yet again and again one sees the inescapable marks of history on them, the intricate ways in which individual destinies are shaped by society at large." Auster acknowledged the impact of these stories on the individuals who shared them, himself as editor, and on the listeners. "Words are needed to express what is in us, and again and again contributors have thanked me for giving them the chance to tell their stories, for allowing the people to be heard."[12]

The popularity of these kinds of personal stories as well as of noncelebrity autobiographies and memoirs connects to the healing quality of this brand of journalism. "The New Autobiography is a vibrantly democratic and deeply personal type of narrative writing that, while little understood, is becoming popular in our culture," author Tristine Rainier wrote. "It is new because it is being written by new voices, not only those who represent the official and dominant view from the top."[13] These new voices are the foundation of everyman journalism, and their stories offer the source, reader, and journalist a sense of redemption, the key element in the study of narrative therapy. "Story represents a pathway to understanding that doesn't run through the left side of the brain," Pink wrote.[14]

For the sources journalists choose to include in their stories, the everyman story brings validation and vindication, perhaps even real, measurable justice, and recourse where there was none. Moving from silent anonymity to an authentic portrayal of self into the public arena gives an individual the chance to be heard and possibly understood. Why else would so many people talk to reporters at the scene of a tragedy or in the darkening aftermath of sorrow? Everyman journalism brings the megaphone to every voice, amplifying the importance of personal story. It is redemptive.

"The redemptive self is an American identity. The life stories that highly generative American adults tell are as much about American society as they are about the lives of the middle aged adults who tell them," wrote Dan McAdams, professor of psychology, human development, and social policy and director of the Foley Center for the Study of Lives at Northwestern. In his 2006 book, *The Redemptive Self: Stories Americans Live By*, McAdams continued: "As such, these stories reflect the psychological efforts of individual men and women to find coherence and meaning in their lives. But as cultural expressions, the life stories of highly generative American adults also project values and grapple with issues that have been at the center of American cultural life for over 200 years."[15]

The careful detailing of a source's life through anecdote is what attracts readers to everyman journalism. "Other journalists told us they consider character as the key to pulling people into stories," Kovach and Rosenstiel wrote in *The Elements of Journalism*. "Often this is found in the minor details that make someone human and real."[16] From Watergate to the moratorium on the death penalty, instituted by some states in response to the work of colleague David Protess and others, solid journalism can bring about societal change.[17] Newspaper stories can serve as a catalyst for justice with information provided by sources whose point of view would otherwise remain unknown. The newspaper provides the source access to broad public opinion. From Upton Sinclair's *The Jungle* to Charlie LeDuff's *Work and Other Sins*, many works of nonfiction have afforded so many citizens the platinum opportunity to be known.[18]

"We need witness to our trauma, including ourselves. Writing helps sort out what happened, when and why, and gives us a way to think of ourselves not only as victims but also as people who have talents, passion, and much to offer the world," therapist Linda Joy Meyers wrote in her 2003 book, *Becoming Whole: Writing Your Healing Story*.[19]

This increase in unofficial sources in American front pages demonstrates the porous, interactive nature of everyman journalism and the reversal of what Robert McChesney called "official source stenography" that defined journalism for decades.[20] As Ronald Bishop noted in 2001, until recently, "Readers and viewers were rarely called on as sources by journalists" in media stories.[21]

It is the reversal of the top-to-bottom sourcing that is the landmark of everyman journalism and a way for people to use these stories to understand the larger world, one outcome of narrative therapy. "In a society where you have little consensus, where there is no one authoritative view, we are left to our own devices to find our place in the world and that translates into how you think of other people's lives," McAdams said. "We look at the world around us to make sense of it and in trying to find sense of it, we are creating a narrative self which shapes how we see the world. It is the nature of a democratic society."[22]

A democratization of news has been in process for years and culminates in the trend of everyman news and the inclusion of more unofficial sources. That may be the appeal of the genre—news of the individual as a form of societal therapy. "What these efforts reveal is a hunger for what stories can provide—context enriched by emotion, a deeper understanding of how we fit in and why that matters," Pink wrote. "The Conceptual Age can remind us what has always been true but rarely acted upon—that we must listen to each other's stories and that we are each the authors of our own lives."[29]

To be more relevant to our lives, the narrators of those stories and voices resonating through those stories need to be more like us. As Stephan Lacy of Michigan State University wrote in 2000, "Research during the 1970s concluded that coverage of traditional bureaucratic beats, such as police and city hall, resulted in a narrow range of official sources gaining access to news pages. . . . During the 1980s and 1990s, some newspapers expanded their definition of beats to include non-governmental and non-geographic issues and events. The motivation was to be more inclusive of sources and to explain the definition of news. A wider news net would allow more people and organizations to participate in setting the public agenda."[24] That wider news net is the foundation of everyman news.

Writer as Second Link

The second link of everyman journalism to narrative therapy is in the positive effect that the act of reporting and crafting eloquent narrative has historically had on the writer. For centuries writers have spoken and written about loving the stories they write and the work they do. It is a passion met in other creative professions where something of substance and impact is produced and perfected from a thousand disparate pieces of information and influences. If not salvation, there is at least comfort in telling some of these stories and bringing them forth into the public realm for exposure, recognition, and understanding. There is a personal satisfaction in telling the truth and writing it well. There is also a professional reward.

Journalists "offer stories that inform, instruct and enlighten a public," Jack Lule wrote. "They offer dramas of order and disorder, of justice affirmed and justice denied. They present portrayals of heroes and villains, of models to emulate and outcasts to denigrate. News and myth speak to a public and offer stories that shape and maintain and exclude and deny important societal ideas and beliefs."[25]

Journalists find catharsis in moving the story out of the notebook and into the public domain, artfully pulling together all the data, documents, sources, background details, and observations. There is a profound sense of accomplishment in manufacturing from those wild pinball elements of fact a cohesive narrative product that is engaging, useful and truthful. "This crafting is part of the process of turning something into a work of art," Joseph Campbell wrote. "I think that many people today do not realize what it means to be an artist, instead of simply a person who is writing."[26] In 1960, Ernest van den Haag wrote, "The most common of human experiences and the most trite still depend on artists and intellectuals to become fully conscious and articulate."[27]

Removing ego from the process, producing good journalism can be about the genuine satisfaction of adroitly organizing information and news into a story. There is professional pride and personal joy in transforming facts into an accurate narrative, fully representational of the people and issues involved, to be read and absorbed. The journalist feels ownership of the intellectual, creative, professional, and emotional satisfaction derived from the process as well as the final product. "I'm always trying to find a better approach to the established truth," Norman Mailer said.[28]

In his 1997 memoir, *All Over but the Shoutin'*, Rick Bragg, Pulitzer Prize winner and former *New York Times* reporter who left the paper over concerns he did not credit other reporters for their work in his stories, wrote: "I didn't get into the business to change the world. I just wanted to tell stories. But now and then, you can make people notice that something ain't quite right, and nudge them gently, with the words, to get off their ass and fix it."[29]

Where the Reader Comes In

The third link of the narrative therapy movement to journalism is in the solace and connection to community that the reader finds in the stories of others. In the Jewish tradition, storytelling offers grace and wisdom to both the storyteller and the listener. Consider the poignant and consuming news stories over the past several years that became culturally ubiquitous: Jessica McClure trapped as an eighteen-month-old in a Midland, Texas, well; the *Challenger* explosion on January 28, 1986; the murder of journalist Daniel Pearl; Elian Gonzalez's dramatic midnight scenario; Todd Beamer's pronouncement of "Let's roll" on a doomed September 11, 2001, flight; and the April 2006 release of journalist Jill Carroll.

These humanistic stories in print captured our empathy and elicited our condolences. The reader who consumes the story is connected to the chain of the story's impact. The reader becomes involved in the story if it is told in a compelling and humanistic way. The story becomes a larger narrative, stored internally, reflective of a broader reality and bearing significance for the reader. "It seems a lot of these human interest stories are almost always a redemptive narrative and people have a really strong hunger for that," McAdams said.[30]

If the journalist has written the narrative in a way that is truthful, evocative, and involving, then the reader becomes engrossed in the life of the story and can be included in the chain of redemption. Reading stories of other individuals can promote relief, wonder, insight, anger, compassion, even action. The anecdotal information from the source filtered through the journalist in this story flow model then has a profound impact on the reader. The reader may interact with the journalist in the form of direct emails or letters to the editor, offering other story ideas or sources. If given the right information, the reader can interact with the source directly, offering comfort or solutions.

"Therapeutic journalism—it's absolutely part of it," said Barbie Zelizer of the University of Pennsylvania. "People engage through personal testimony. It works if we let go of the assumption that there could be a story delivered with no personal bias."[31]

"Journalists tell stories professionally, rather than as part of daily life, but they make use of all these possibilities, sometimes writing to soothe and sometimes to enliven, sometimes to honor and commemorate, and sometimes to embolden and impassion," Michael Schudson wrote.[32] It is crucial for the story flow model to include source, journalist, and reader interactively in a reciprocal pattern.

Narrative in Medicine

This journalism story flow model mimics the dynamic relationship of narrative in medicine as explained by Dr. Jerry Vannata, Ronald Schliefer, and Sheila Crow in the DVD "Medicine and Humanistic Understanding." The model in medicine is the patient's narrative and the physician's understanding, and the ultimate power of the narrative to aid in the doctor/patient relationship. It is narrative knowledge that will promote the most effective healing. In this context, narrative is literally healing. Though stories and medicine seem odd bedfellows, the relationship between storytelling and recovery has undeniable links. "The links between storytelling, literature and medicine can present to physicians—but also to patients—ways in which practices of healing, or alleviating suffering, and of simple caring for those who suffer can be made better and more efficient," begins the video introduction. "They can help us define and in practical ways help to achieve competence in 'narrative knowledge' that contributes, often as much as 'biomedical knowledge' to the everyday goals of medical practices."[33]

In *Incidental Findings: Lessons from My Patients in the Art of Medicine* (2005), Dr. Danielle Orfi wrote, "Over the years, the histories piled up. They grew heavy and lush, widening their reach from the patient to the parents to the children and eventually to me, as we all are gradually entwined in this ever-expanding web." She continued, "These histories both enriched and burdened me. . . . I started writing about my patients, but now I realize that I'm writing about me. In a jungle they say, you often can't tell which root system connects to which leaves."[34]

In early 2007, Rush University Medical Center in Chicago began a marketing campaign surrounding rushstories.org, where you could read and watch podcasts of the stories of real patients with their doctors. The website read: "These are the people who have benefited from the life-changing experiences at RUSH. Follow their stories. Experience their journeys."[35]

Edifying Quality to Everyman Journalism

Beyond the emotional attraction to human interest stories and the notion that such stories may be appealing because they are therapeutic, cognitive theories also suggest that the tool of narrative helps individuals acquire knowledge. Framing information with a narrative, human context may be why people connect to these kinds of newspaper stories more than to other forms of journalism. Jerome S. Bruner, a pioneer in educational psychology who has been studying cognitive learning theory since the 1940s, wrote that narrative knowledge is a universal equalizer. The author of *The Narrative Construction of Reality* contends that people absorb and retain knowledge more easily when it is presented in an anecdotal, human narrative context.

In *Making Stories: Law, Literature, Life* (2002), Bruner described the undeniable influence of storytelling on the understanding of life experience. "We should not write off this power of story to shape everyday experience as simply another error in our human effort to make sense of the world, though cognitive scientists are sometimes wont to do this." He added, "All I want to say for the moment is that narrative, including fictional narrative, gives shape to things in the real world and often bestows on them a title to reality."[36]

Just as storytelling plays a large role in any understanding of society, journalism contributes to the community with stories of individuals, recently much more prominent now in American newspapers. Michael Schudson wrote, "We can speculate, without much in the way of proof, that news builds expectations of a common, shared world; promotes an emphasis on and a positive valuation of the new; endorses a historical mentality (note how much less 'dated' is a myth, novel, academic paper, or sermon than a news report), and encourages a progressive rather than cyclical or recursive sense of time."[37] Journalism offers society a chance at "shared knowledge," according to Schudson.

Journalism has traditionally been a combination of narrative knowledge and paradigmatic knowledge as Bruner outlined decades ago. According to McAdams, "Narrative knowledge explains why people do something. Paradigmatic knowledge is straight news, cause and effect. Newspaper stories pull from narrative and paradigmatic knowledge both." But what is new about the everyman news trend in newspaper journalism is that the balance has shifted to give more space, energy, and better placement to narrative knowledge. Today the paradigmatic knowledge has equal or more weight than the narrative view in American newspapers. "To the extent that journalism goes in that direction is a post-modern view that there is no authoritative truth," McAdams said.[38] News stories are then a way not only to represent the events of the world, but to make sense of the world as a writer, express one's position in the world as a source, and perceive the world as a reader.

There are significant reservations to declaring everyman news a form of cultural narrative therapy. Suggesting that all journalists are emotionally and physically healthy because of the work they do is as foolish as suggesting that all doctors are physically healthy because of the work they do.

Not all sources are grateful to be included in stories, professing gratitude for a life makeover as a result of the printed story. Many reluctant sources claim they are misquoted, that the printed newspaper stories are inaccurate, slanted, or imbalanced, and that the writers grossly misrepresented them. Not all readers are edified, enriched, or even impressed by the stories they read in the newspaper. Some never read the news story beyond the lead. Others forget the story before it is recycled. But for many readers and many audiences of news, the story of an individual or the news as portrayed through the reactions of individuals is assigned greater importance.

"As more people lead lives of abundance, we'll have a greater opportunity to pursue lives of meaning. And stories—the ones we tell about ourselves, the ones we tell to ourselves—are often the vehicles we use in that pursuit," Pink wrote.[39] This may be all mere coincidence, a confluence of trends from disconnected corners of the culture. But it is an interesting notion to connect narrative therapy and the positive aspects of a story's role in human experience to the trend toward everyman news in newspapers. A growing number of professionals in disparate fields see the role of narrative as redemptive in our culture—and many of them are emphatic about the individual's connection to story.

"We are our stories. We compress years of experience, thought and emotion into a few compact narratives that we convey to others and tell to ourselves," according to Pink. "But personal narrative has become more prevalent, and perhaps more urgent, in a time of abundance, when many of us are freer to seek a deeper understanding of ourselves and our purpose."[40]

Newspaper stories are not the printed Prozac of our nation. Sources do not give information only to feel better—some are vengeful, some are whistleblowers, some are purely narcissists. Writers do not always write stories to find some brand of social remedy—some just write for a living. Readers do not read the newspaper solely for therapy—they read to find out the score of the football game. Sometimes what appears in the paper are merely accounts of what happened the day before and the people who were there. Everyman news cannot cure the world's ills one column inch at a time, but its growing prominence in American newspapers is decidedly worth our examination.

Chapter 10

Fifteen Seconds of Fame

A Cultural Reverence for Story

When the audience becomes the producer, the audience is part of the brand.

—Peter Hirschberg, executive vice-president, Technorati

A Cultural Reverence for Personal Story
Mirrored in Advertising and TV

✳ What does voluntarily injecting botulism into your forehead have to do with everyman news? Magazine and Internet ads for Botox Cosmetic touting "Real Women Real Stories" are an investment in the belief that the individual, unofficial story can coerce anyone suffering a hate relationship with a frown line to get stiff on wrinkles. A client can log on to botox cosmetic.com and read stories such as "Laura's" or click on testimonials to be convinced that temporary and partial facial paralysis is the perfect antidote to aging publicly.[1]

The comparison to news stories is not such a stretch. Newspapers invest staff and resources in the belief that anecdotal and humanistic approaches to news may convince someone to buy and read the newspaper day after day and develop lasting loyalty to the newspaper brand, the perfect antidote to newspaper extinction. A growing number of anecdotal ads in newspapers and magazines sanctify the stories of real customers, clients, and users in story-based marketing of a variety of products and services. The ads are similar to anecdotal features that run in newspapers. Though non-news, the ads mirror the style, approach, and sourcing of everyman news. The storytelling is similar even if the spin is not.

It points to a growing appetite in the culture for the authority of individual testimony over the scripted voice of the official spokesperson. It points to the majesty of personal story as the message. On websites selling everything from Botox to weight-loss regimens (on weightwatchers.com), everyone is invited to "share your story." Why? Because people want to read what other real people have to say, whether in ads or editorial content. The ads mimic the wording and tone of anecdotal feature leads of news and feature stories running in newspapers today. They employ the same user-friendly interactive tools as blogs on newspaper websites. Marketing with stories and providing news with stories are opposite sides of a coin. They exist in parallel universes.

Newspapers observe much of popular culture through a rearview mirror—chronicling events, trends, announcements, and one thousand other daily blips after they happen or as they happen. Advertising scrutinizes popular culture through a telescope focused on a particular niche in the culture. Both are trying to react to, and perhaps predict, the audience's behavior. They are both viewing the same cultural circus. Both are trying to be as current, proactive, reactive, and immediate as possible. The shapes and trends of what they observe in popular culture are the same. The consequences of missing the events by not being tuned in enough to report what is current—or predict what is next—are disastrous for both advertisers and newspapers. It can result in a loss of relevance, credibility, reliability, and cachet.

In *The Wisdom of Crowds: Why the Many Are Smarter than the Few and How Collective Wisdom Shapes Business, Economics, Societies and Nations* (2003), author James Surowiecki wrote that instead of searching for experts, "We should stop hunting and ask the crowd (which, of course includes the geniuses as well as everyone else) instead."[2] The crowd—whether reading the front page of a newspaper or clicking on a product's website—wants to hear and read a story from a real person in the crowd. The crowd wants to read what other people in the crowd are saying, thinking, and doing. And they will listen to what the noncelebrity faces in the crowd are saying, whether it is in ads or news copy. The presence of the individual in a story is welcomed by the consumer in both venues. Even though editorial and advertising are separated ideologically and physically by both porous and impenetrable walls at different newspapers, magazines, and broadcast stations, the tone and content of the messages have become eerily similar.

The overwhelming evidence in advertising and other media points to a remarkable reinforcement of the power of the individual story as a reflection of what Americans now hold sacred. Our culture bombards all of us with minutiae about the lives of individuals—no detail too small, no stage too large. MySpace.com, a repository for the picayune, has 66 million users and adds 250,000 new users every day, according to the *Financial Times*.[3] Even Kleenex users are urged to go to the maker's website and tell their stories—worthy of tissue consumption—in the Let It Out campaign in 2007.[4]

"We look at the text of the news story or the TV show, analyzing what it says, and what it might mean for the audience. Instead we need to think of these stories as emerging out of the culture, and as then sparking a broader set of interrogative narratives and discussions among the people," S. Elizabeth Bird wrote in 2003, "And people want personal stories because they are memorable."[5]

The Ads Have Stories: From Broadband to Diamond Band

Testimonials are not a new way to sell soap. But the overwhelming bombardment of "real stories" ads and branding is significant when considering the cultural context for everyman news. This kind of marketing is ubiquitous and not unrelated to the developing appetite readers express for news told in the framework of personal stories. You can't escape the avalanche of Average Joe and Jane minutiae to sell just about anything.

In April 2006, American Express launched a My Life My Card campaign encouraging card users to submit a macro-movie to the "15 Seconds Clips Competition" as part of the Tribeca Film Festival. With a prize of $15,000 for the best clip, to be judged by directors Martin Scorsese and M. Night Shyamalan, the contest called for entries that centered on a dream, a childhood ambition, or even a perfect day. "Stories make up our lives," read the website. "Show us yours in 15 seconds."[6]

Verizon Wireless Broadband promised to be "Richer. Deeper. Broader." on www.broadbandstories.com. According to the website in August 2005, "The stories you'll see on this site are all real. Not created as advertisements. This project is meant to be a reflection of how broadband has truly come to be such a central part of our lives." The copy continued, "It is a tool for helping people express themselves and pursue their interests. In short, it's a great medium for telling stories."[7] Take out the line about broadband, and you could be quoting part of a newspaper's mission statement noted on its website or a local metro columnist's invitation for reader participation in print.

A radio and web campaign in April 2006 for Chicago Area Volvo Retailers began with a provocative first-person story about a woman about to meet a man for the first time following an email introduction by an Internet dating service. Abruptly the story ends. The listener is instructed to go the website to hear the rest. Why? The tagline instructs, "The thing about a good story—especially a life story—you want to keep it going." The ad continues, "Drive the safest care you can. Volvo. For life. Keep your story going."[8] Apparently, Woolrich Company, makers of outdoor clothing and accessories, agree with Volvo that such reminders of mortality sell since their 2006 print ad in *National Geographic Adventurer* stated, "The best stories never end."[9]

But with a Nissan Pathfinder, the owner can not only survive but "tell better stories," the heart of that vehicle's campaign since 2004. Logging on to the Nissan site, anyone can enter the chance to win three "dream adventures" in a Pathfinder by submitting five hundred words on a dream adventure. "So go on. Take control. Take advantage. And tell us your stories."[10] Even backyard grillers have caught on to the story train. In April 2006 the makers of Weber Grill created a Weber nation with a website and television ads touting, "Real people, real stories, real grills." Backed up by a national television campaign, the website encouraged grillers to submit their own stories: "If you have a Weber story like Jim's, John's, Dave's, Mike's or Jay and Catherine's, we would encourage you to share it with the world. Go to www.webernation.com and tell your story and give us your advice. Maybe we'll feature you in the next edition of this publication."[11] Is that so different from a newspaper soliciting stories and news from readers to print in a future edition? Didn't the *New York Times* ask for stories in the wake of Katrina?

White Castle, the fast-food steamers of small square burgers on mini-buns, offered a place at www.truecastlestories.com, where slider lovers could tell their stories of consumption and triumph on The TrueCraver's True Castle Stories homepage.[12] Are these stories anyone really wants to hear, let alone tell? At apple.com/switch/stories, customers who switched to Apple computers from different brands of PC deliver testimonials as "those who paved the way."

According to the website, "People write to us everyday telling us how—and why—they successfully switched from PCs to MACS. Executives. Parents, Students. Creatives. Researchers. Educators. Retirees. Thousands of you. Here are some of your true stories." What follows are folksy posts from a dad, a doc, a mom, and a music lover, all hailing from different parts of the country and all on a first-name basis with the good people at Apple.[13]

Not to be outdone in meeting the craving for customer stories, a magazine ad running in September 2005 for Microsoft Corporation's Windows XP read: "Start something memorable. Start capturing every milestone. Replaying the scenes. Adding the soundtrack. Burning your own DVDs.

Sharing the story. Start freezing time."[14] A newspaper's purpose is to capture the milestones and replay the scenes. Adding the soundtrack and burning the DVDs may be arriving in the future.

"People relate to personal stories because they're usually a funnier, sadder, more relevant, more outrageous experience than looking at a picture of someone famous," said Michele Lowe, a friend, playwright, and former senior vice president associate creative director at BBDO New York. "The real kick is that if you can use stories that are true or real people selling a particular product, then you have something that becomes dinner conversation."[15]

In the summer of 2005, advertising featuring six voluptuous real women in their white underwear (who weren't even selling underwear) became the marketing story of the year. With their "Real women have real bodies with real curves" advertising in the "Campaign for real beauty," Dove, the soap and beauty product company that probably should start selling underwear, made headlines because of its everywoman approach.[16] Newspaper columnists and bloggers waxed cruel and complimentary about the size of thighs and the importance of body image for women and girls. More than a quarter century after fifteen-year-old Brooke Shields reclined in a provocative pose in her Calvin Klein jeans, real women were selling Levi's with their personal stories. "A Style for Every Story" was the magazine and online advertising campaign in 2004 and 2005 for the legendary Levi Strauss. The print ads featured photos of ordinary people posed casually and haphazardly in the Levi's, quite unlike the deliberate stances of supermodels.[17]

Myra Stark, a member of the strategic planning office in advertising giant Saatchi and Saatchi's New York office, wrote in the 2003 brief "Ideas from Trends" that this kind of advertising as well as reality TV is part of the "democratization of celebrity." Stark wrote: "The blurring of the distinction between celebrities and ordinary people is occurring in many parts of the culture." She continued, "Just as important is recognizing the hunger for the authentic—the real—behind the real people as celebrities trend. This value of authenticity provides a clear direction for brands."[18]

Ecco, Danish shoe manufacturers, had a four-page advertising insert in fall 2005 women's magazines that read: "The soles of your feet are as unique as you are. They tell a story about who you are, whether you're a rock climber or rock star, dancer or long-distance runner, power executive or power mom." Photographs of three nonmodel Ecco wearers accompanied their narratives. On the last page, readers were encouraged to enter a contest answering the burning question: "What does your 'sole' say about you?" in one hundred words or less.[19]

And for anyone away from home trapped without the cash to pay for jeans or shoes, Western Union's 2005 TV ads for the 212,000 agents world-wide touted: "For every story, there's Western Union." Western Union president Christina Gold was quoted as saying the company intended "to create a global brand framework that relates to people on a more personal level."[20] Selling newspapers and products using personal stories as the portal may be part of the branding newspapers are looking for, as voices of the people, by the people, and for the people. It is part of what Dan Gill-mor called the "explosion of conversations."[21]

The Authenticity of Everyman Stories

The telling of others' stories has an integrity that we naturally respect whether those stories arrive in a news article, an ad on the opposite page, or in a reality show. The individual story has risen in importance in our lives and has reached the point where as a culture we no longer have an occasional yearning for a story but require a diet of storytelling. Such a craving is growing within the culture.

The abundance of reality shows on the air in the summer of 2006 points to a national appetite for the stories of the ordinary people at home, work, rest, and play and many other activities you may not want to watch. The website www.realityshows.com listed ninety-five current reality shows from the bewildering *Beauty and the Geek* on the WB to the testosterone-soaked *Pimp My Ride* on MTV.[22] Whether it is a tear-filled *Wife Swap*, or a session of home demolition and rebuilding on *Extreme Makeover–Home Edition*, it seems every network has been swooping in on the drama of ordinary life. Miracle cures and inventors were the subjects of 2006 reality shows. Donald Trump and Martha Stewart in *The Apprentice* and Paris Hilton in FOX-TV's *Simple Life* were the exemptions to the no-celebrity rule, as more abundant were the nonfamous people who filled the television screens and dominated small talk around office watercoolers each morning after. "Reality TV is an effort to turn real events into narrative," said Jon Franklin, author, journalist, and journalism professor. "It is an effort to take a collection of facts and maneuver them into a conflict. People put themselves into a petri dish and the production people maneuver the dish."[23]

Just as human and dramatic can be the reality shows that follow either the child-rearing rescues of *Super Nanny* or the singing aspirations of the next *American Idol*. A feminist version of the pop star search was the 2005 *RU the Girl with T-Boz and Chilli*. The UPN show documented the singers' nationwide hunt for a young woman to join the hip-hop group TLC after bandmember Lisa Lopez was killed in a car accident.[24] Each week young women who dream of being famous auditioned for the slot on shows in the same genre as *Making the Band, Nashville Star,* and *Popstars.* The magnetic pull of those shows—as well as shows such as *The Amazing Race* and *How to Get the Guy*—is that no one who is reaching for the stars or having their ambition or heartaches mercilessly exposed is inherently newsworthy on his or her own. It is the possibility that a story will be chiseled into a myth before our eyes that draws us in over and over again. "Reality TV is so popular because it recognizes the importance of story," said Alex Kotlowitz, author and journalist. He added, "It's a cheapened form of literary nonfiction."[25]

And if a producer of a reality show doesn't ever happen to roll into your hometown, you can make a reality video of your own, the ultimate in customized newsmaking. Personal videobiographies, what we might call vanity documentaries, are produced by companies that create DVDs and videotape of a client's life for fees ranging from three hundred to twelve thousand dollars. According to the *Wall Street Journal,* the videobiographies are becoming increasingly popular around the country. One company, MyVideoStory.com, has a clip on its website that says the company "is all about preserving the life stories of individuals. . . . Don't let the stories of your life go untold."[26]

You could join the millions on youtube.com and make a video from your computer and post it on the Internet. The range of videos is astounding. Most are jaw-droppingly inane. Participants might flex their muscles, play table tennis, talk about a recent break-up, or mimic the Simpsons. Some amateur spots end up airing in commercial breaks during the Super Bowl. All tell stories.

The seductive story of us has become such a rich part of the fabric of our culture that it would be impossible for newspapers to ignore. The message that is resonating with the audience begins with a story of an individual. When discussing an editorial product or a marketing push, the context may shift and the intention may move from one of pure information delivered to a manipulation of behavior into purchasing a product or service. But the theme of individual story at the center of the brand or newspaper remains the same. Everyman journalism is as much a symptom of a culture that craves story as it is the mode to chronicle it. It is both the message and the messenger. Journalism at this time is operating at the intersection of culture and history presenting events of our time in a package of everyman story. It is a method that meets both the professional requirements of newsworthiness and the audience's desire for the details about the lives of individuals.

It is a brand of story that literally sells.

Chapter 11

Emergence Journalism

Where We Go from Here

Let's publish the best, most interesting, most audacious stories we can on
our own terms. . . . Let's put our art—the stories we love to write, edit and
publish—on the market and see who buys it.

—Bob Baker, "It Just Doesn't Matter"

⁂ One of my colleagues at Medill, Susan Mango Curtis, has an office
two doors to the north of mine where she is always thinking ten to
twenty years ahead. In a March 2006 presentation in the senior-level elective
class, Print Media Design, her students presented final projects that included
fast-forward formats for paperless and inkless delivery of news.

"I designed a news and media viewer for the year 2020 for use in
medium- and long-range commuter rail," twenty-one-year-old Anthony
Walters explained in the text of his presentation. "The touch screen is 7" x
7", and is designed to either remain in a seat back, or snap out and be held
by the user," said the senior journalism major from Middle Village, New
York. "CommuterView is a subscription-based service. Users can add their
newspaper subscriptions to their transit fare cards using special kiosks in
transit stations. At these kiosks, users can also add media, such as episodes
of popular television shows. Using the kiosks, users will be able to cus-
tomize the news content they view to a high degree, based on their interests, age, vocation, etc."[1]

Walters continued, "CommuterView is designed to increase the readership of newspapers among commuters. . . . With CommuterView, a transit

rider could read the content from as many as 20 newspapers. In addition to the newspaper content, CommuterView allows the integration of multimedia content from a newspaper's website, such as videos, audio clips and photo slideshows. For each story in a newspaper, a feature called "Sidebar" appears in the same frame. Sidebar contains all the multimedia content associated with a given story." As Walters saw it, instead of folding the newspaper before her, a commuter would retrieve news from a screen and settle in to click and flip to the desired news. "A section called MyPage will have content based on user preferences and customization," Walters wrote.[2]

Frank Ahrens in the *Washington Post* agreed in a 2005 column that in the future there will be "paperless ways to deliver the news." He added, "Storytelling will change, as well. . . . For years, newspapers have thought of ways to deliver their news—and brand—in as many formats as possible."[3]

But the impetus to change from the daily model of ink on paper has not been forthcoming for many reasons. "Among the factors that have slowed editors and publishers' move toward the new media world is cost," Overholser wrote in the 2006 manifesto, "On Behalf of Journalism." "Even as newsroom leaders begin to understand the necessity to guide their staffs more quickly toward new models of journalism (or to allow innovators within their staffs to push toward those new models) the counting houses are often stuck in the old model. Retraining a newsroom to deliver the news online and on cell phones and iPods takes some thought and some expenditures—even as newsrooms are being forced to cut back to continue to support the old business model in ever more challenging times."[4]

Dave Pettit, of the *Wall Street Journal* online edition, said in a May 10, 2006, column that consumer demand for innovative news outlets is driving the need for change in spite of newspaper owners' reluctance. "Readers want more context and background included in news reporting. They want new ways to receive their news, on next-generation handheld devices, for instance, rather than simply on a Web page." He added, "The perfect Web site will be a mix of print news, video and audio news."[5] It will be several journalistic elements at once, and it will be what has been for several years called convergence.

The concept of convergence—several delivery modes, including print, digital, broadcast, visual, and text emanating from the same reporting across platforms—has been bandied about in journalism circles since the 1980s and has been in operation in some newsrooms since the 1990s. For the past five years or more, the buzz in journalism education has been about convergence. Educators have shifted curriculum, bolstered equipment and software, added faculty, and crossed our fingers that we are training young journalists for the profession's present and future. We demand students be adept in print, digital, broadcast, and whatever delivery mode may present itself before they graduate. While the changes have been beneficial, we have not progressed quickly enough.

"By this time 'convergence' was being used so frequently, in so many different contexts that it had largely lost its value in focusing discussions about journalism and the news media," Rich Gordon, a colleague at Medill, wrote in "The Meanings and Implications of Convergence," a chapter in 2003's *Digital Journalism*. "But at the same time, the popularity of the word was evidence of its power, especially among advocates for change in newsrooms, media companies, and journalism schools."[6]

But it is time for another phase beyond convergence journalism: emergence journalism—a journalism that is transparent, efficient, cross-platform, and inclusive. We need to accept that we do not know now where the industry will be or how news will be delivered. Reporters will need readiness for the technology with a solid aptitude in reporting and writing that is not shackled to a specific platform and does not ignore the possibilities of instant transformation from print to audio and video. But they will also need to accept the undeniable reverence for story persistent in American pop culture at this time and apply that reverence to emerging journalism.

Twenty-first–century journalists are primed to acknowledge the audience appetite for story and to perform in a variety or combination of platforms, with a sophisticated skill set grounded in storytelling for the needs of a diverse audience. Audience members also contribute and compete for conversation time with their own self-generated forms of media in blogs, vblogs, and chatrooms. To survive, we need to acknowledge that journalism is an evolving profession cracking open as forms of media delivery emerge and as a constant chorus of voices looks to correct, amplify, negate, or reconstruct everything journalists produce.

In the 2006 Aspen Institute Report titled "When Push Comes to Pull: The New Economy and Culture of Networking Technology," David Bollier quoted Esther Dyson's comments: "Commercial creators of content 'aren't simply competing with each other, nor with the people who steal their content, but with all the people producing videos of grandchildren that are of interest to exactly four grandparents (except for modern families of eight grandparents). You have a huge set of forces sucking attention away from paid-for-content—or at least, would-be paid-for content.'"[7]

These forces are bearing down on the traditional business models of newspapers. "First, print newspapers' pursuit of nonprint delivery options has not been simply a technical change to the people involved, but a fundamental cultural transformation," Boczkowski wrote. "But in doing this they have begun constructing a kind of newspaper that although it bears connections to its print predecessor, also differs qualitatively from it in its material infrastructure, editorial practices and production routines."[8] At the foundation of emergence journalism, the core content before all the bells and whistles, is the common editorial practice of everyman journalism—stories with a humanistic touch, a more complex and featurized approach to news with a broader base of sources instead of a regurgitation of events. The story solidifies the brand.

Where newspapers are in the first decade of the new millennium is not where they will be in the second. It has been a trying phase, one that demands transformation. On December 11, 2006, a project of The Newspaper Guild of America and the Communications Workers of America launched Day of Action, also called Save Journalism Day, to "alert the public that the quality and diversity of news coverage that our readers now depend on is at risk, as corporations focus on building profits, not comprehensive news coverage." On SaveJournalism.org., rallies and events from Pittsburgh, Dayton, Knoxville, and York, Pennsylvania, were listed for their focus on job cuts and "standing up for quality journalism" at a time when more than 34,000 journalism jobs had been lost from 2001 to June 2006. A flyer for the event read, "When we're gone . . . who will report the news, investigate leads, or ask the tough questions?" The flyer continued, "Fewer people in the newsroom mean less news coverage. With fewer journalists, we all suffer. With smaller staffs, editors are being forced to decide which stories not to report, cover or investigate. . . . These cutbacks aren't momentary, or due to poor economy. . . . They represent an accelerating and alarming trend by corporations to demand higher profit margins from their news operations. . . . This means that you will not only receive less news, but also you'll be less informed."[9] IWantMedia.com, run by Veronis Suhler Stevenson, the company that produces the Communications Industry Forecast each year, in December 2007 listed more than 72,000 media job cuts since 2000. Change is not imminent, but constant.[10]

The data in this book show how quickly newspaper front-page content has changed since 2001. Many of the papers included in this study changed content style and tone from 2001, with features accounting for well over half of the front-page stories on the dates studied in 2004. The *Arizona Republic* in 2004, for instance, showed 72 percent feature stories on page 1, with the *Miami Herald* running 68 percent features on the front page on the dates studied in 2004. The *Omaha World-Herald* had 64 percent features on the front page, while the *Chicago Tribune* posted 57 percent of its front-page stories as features, and the *New York Times* was not far behind at 54 percent of the front pages stories defined as features on the dates analyzed in 2004. A look at current front pages demonstrates that features are still prominent on American front pages.

An analysis of all twenty newspapers shows that the comments of unofficial sources were more prominent in many front-page stories across the country in both large and small newspapers in 2004 than in 2001. These are stories that received the highest rating of 4, or the most frequent and with most space given to unofficial sources. At both the *Anchorage Daily News* and the *San Jose Mercury News,* 50 percent of the front-page stories studied in 2004 had ratings of 4 for the prominence of unofficial sources. At the *St. Louis Post-Dispatch* and the *Washington Post,* 39 percent of the front-page stories studied in 2004 had the highest prominence given to unofficial sources. The *Chicago Tribune* front-page stories prominently quoted unofficial sources to receive the highest rating in 26 percent of the stories, while the *Seattle Times* scored highest for using the most unofficial sources in 25 percent of the front-page stories in 2004. The *Los Angeles Times'* use of unofficial sources gained it the highest rating in 22 percent of the front-page stories studied in 2004 and in the *San Antonio Express-News,* 20 percent.

What does this mean? I believe the cultural reverence for everyman narrative will continue as the demands of the audience grow louder. Newspapers are providing readers with this more personal, accessible, conversational approach to breaking news and features. Reacting to it effectively is part of what Andrew Swinand of Starcom called "The Participation Age" of media in a May 2006 presentation to the Medill faculty. It is journalism that prompts engagement and involvement.[11]

"The goal is to make content that is worth pointing to," John Battelle wrote in the 2005 book *The Search: How Google and Its Rivals Rewrote the Rules of Business and Transformed Our Culture.* "If you're feeding the conversation, the rest will then follow, including advertisers who want to be in the conversation that news stories are fostering."[12]

Readers will point to well-written, well-executed, well-sourced stories that define everyman journalism. The popularity of newspaper features stories on the front page, of humanistic approaches to news, and of a deliberately more democratic source base is a trend that can be applied to wherever and however newspapers shift delivery in the future. This brand of story and approach can be adapted to other media, and can become "liquid," as Swinand described. It is a medium that "flows" and can no longer be defined by print, audio, video, or Web, but for and by all of them.[13]

"The written word is a sacred thing and it is out there forever," author Debra Dickerson said at the Nieman Narrative Conference in Cambridge in 2004.[14] By recognizing the cultural forces at work on the media, acknowledging audience tastes and the relentless craving for story, journalists are in a better position to prepare for what lies ahead. It is a position preferable to responding to the present or playing catch-up to the past. No longer can journalists wall themselves off from readers and write only what they deem newsworthy. They must solicit readers' views about what needs to be covered, report stories using a wider range of sources, and write stories in a more humanistic and conversational way, positioning them alongside more traditional news. "The only way newspapers can bring new information is by concentrating on 'exclusives' or by taking advantage of the extra time to make more calls, gather more information and weigh more arguments to add new dimensions to their reporting," according to Rick Edmonds in the Poynter Institute's State of the Media 2006 report.[15] In other words, diverse sourcing and everyman storytelling are crucial to good newspaper journalism now and forever.

In his 2005 book, *Blog: Understanding the Information Reformation That's Changing Your World*, Hugh Hewitt wrote: "millions of people are changing their habits when it comes to information acquisition. This has happened many times before: with the appearance of the printing press, then the telegraph, the telephone, radio, television, and Internet." Newspapers, he said, "are selling the news equivalent of day-old bread—or with *Time* and *Newsweek*, week-old rolls."[16]

But here is the challenge: freshen the product with everyman stories and allow the readership base to rise and move with you to another delivery base. The consistent delivery of this type of story will allow the story, rather than the paper, to define and become the brand. Since newspapers cannot be faster than online or broadcast alternatives, they can be better— more sources, better narrative, and different approaches than a digital digest of events as they happen in real time. What was feared would happen with Internet habits—that readers would go deep on a single story because of the infinity of the Web and become entranced for hours on links and never again read a book, magazine, or a newspaper—didn't happen. Consumers clicked on what they were interested in and quickly moved on, finding answers immediately and news in real time. The depth, context, writerliness, and patience it takes to include more sources is delivered in other media beyond the Web—newspapers, magazines, documentary.

"The Web has become an alert service, the place for time-starved but news-hungry consumers," Nora Paul wrote in *Online Journalism Review*. Paul added, "As noted before, most online news content continues to be the same news text from offline displayed online. The same reporting forms."[17] Close to 73 percent of households online report they are following the news on the Internet, according to the 2006 Advertising Age Fact Pack, citing the conference board as a source for the first quarter of 2006. That percentage is fewer than the 74 percent who report they are doing work online and the 76 percent who say they are making financial transactions—including shopping—online.[18] Consumers are getting updates online and following the news there. Readers are following stories in newspapers.

"What the public needs from journalism in the early twenty-first century is improved information gathering and analyzing skills from the established press, and new means for hungry, critical, dogged information seekers, assemblers, and distributors who lie outside the circle of information elites to join the circuit of public information and debate," Carolyn Marvin and Philip Meyer wrote in *The Press*.[19] That appears to be on the minds of many in the industry. In April 2006, the John S. and James L. Knight Foundation launched the Knight New Media Center with funding of $650,000. "Our mission is to help traditional print and broadcast journalists cross the bridge into the New Media world as well as help current multimedia journalists sharpen their beat and topic expertise with a New Media frame for storytelling," reads the email from director Vikki Porter.[20]

Journalist as Ally

In the 1992 movie *Hero*, a sparkling parody of sappy broadcast journalism, Chevy Chase plays a 1940s caricature of a television news editor. In one scene, he is perched behind a large oak desk, and you can see his crisply starched shirt. When the starlet anchorwoman played by Geena Davis exits his office with a flirtatious wiggle, he grumbles, "Oh, she's just pretending to be a human being. She's really just a journalist."[21]

In this millennium, journalists are human again—fallible, not always trustworthy, but approachable and seen as receptive to the stories from the streets. Readers want to talk to reporters, email them, befriend them.[22] Newspapers want to be good citizens, not just the bearers of news. This helps shape a kinder, gentler brand of journalism. It has affected sourcing in stories and approaches to news.

In a letter to readers online in 2005, *Chicago Tribune* publisher David Hiller wrote: "We are part of the community, and we hope what you read in the paper every day is important and interesting to you (and some of it just plain fun). Whether it's an in-depth investigation of problems in the criminal justice system or a John Kass column that helps get a little boy's dog back, the news and commentary in the paper can have a real impact on people's lives."[23]

The April 2006 redesign of the NYTimes.com was also aimed at creating community and a customized news source for readers. Online readers could not only get the headlines but also see the most popular stories in lists of Most Emailed, Most Blogged, Most Searched, and Most Popular Movies. Videos were embedded in the site as well. The site also introduced the upcoming MyTimes, a personalized front page of *New York Times* news according to areas of interest.[24] The newspaper was repackaging content with story as commodity, not as words on newsprint.

Tomorrow's Sources

Newspapers have changed drastically in the last few years and will continue to evolve. The featurized format of the front page seems to fit well into this culture and its cravings for story. Though the shift has many critics, it is important that reporters, writers, and editors stay vigilant and do not allow everyman journalism to evolve into superficial, vapid happy talk. "At the heart of the change is a de-aggregation and democratization of the newspaper," wrote Scott D. Anthony and Clark G. Gilbert in the January 2006 issue of *Presstime,* the Newspaper Association of America magazine.[25] That democratization is at the nucleus of anecdotal storytelling and a broader net of sources. It is what newspapers do well and can continue to do better, with an eye toward balanced presentation and a delivery of accurate information, concise exposition, thorough explanation, and valid human interest in a mélange of diverse stories.

By taking one day in the life of a variety of print, digital, and broadcast media, Poynter researchers recently compared content and sourcing in its 2006 report. "In addition to more and deeper sourcing on major stories, newspaper stories also scored higher on our index that measured how many contextual elements stories explored to make them more relevant and useful to readers," according to the report. More than 90 percent of national newspapers, compared to 53 percent of metro papers, used three or more sources on a story. According to the report, "Yet large numbers of the public still find newspapers to be a fact-based and comprehensive news source."[26] It is a formula that appears to be used by many newspapers, and readers are responding favorably. More than 72 percent of readers surveyed in June 2005 assigned a favorable or mostly favorable rating to their regular daily newspaper, according to the Pew Research Center for the People and the Press.[27]

"Today's larger public is not a blank slate, a child, or a neurotic," Marvin and Meyer wrote in *The Press.* "The people are not retarded, or emotionally or intellectually stunted. The multiple publics of the United States need journalists who take them seriously as citizens. They deserve a journalism that shares the stage with different levels of information and different perspectives, that tells the truth about where information comes from, that corrects itself publicly, that offers what well-trained and experienced fact-finders and observers believe these publics ought to know, that expects from these same publics the resources needed to get the job done."[28]

That is not to say newspaper journalists are beyond reproach. A study by Scott Meier in the *Journalism and Mass Communications Quarterly* in autumn 2005, "Accuracy Matters: A Cross-Market Assessment of Newspaper Error and Credibility," looked at 14 daily newspapers in 12 markets and 3,287 stories. What he found was an average rate of 1.36 errors per story with an overall mean error rate of 61 percent.[29]

That number reflected a steady increase since the first study of accuracy in 1936 by Mitchell Charnley. Seventy years ago Charnley found an error rate of 46 percent. In 2005 error rates reported by sources ranged from 54.9 to 70.3 percent.[30] The kinds of mistakes most often cited were misquotations, distortion of quotes, and sensationalizing of the material. As for causes, sources most often said errors were due to a reporter's lack of understanding of the information. "More than 60 percent of local news and news feature stories in a cross-section of American daily newspapers were found in error by news sources, an inaccuracy rate among the highest reported in nearly seventy years of research," Meier wrote.[31]

In a May 2006 report by Medill colleagues David Nelson and Ellen Shearer, a study of more than 500 newspaper editors and reporters showed that 70 percent had experienced problems with sources in their careers. Thirty five percent of the journalists said they had learned that one of their stories in the past year had contained false information—either from a source or from the edited story creating a false impression. More than 72 percent of the journalists surveyed said readers had accused them of bias.[32]

"When you start uniting a series of facts you arrange them also in a story line, intellectual or temporal or both, and the story that forms reveals your interpretation of the facts you have used," journalist and author Larry Woiwode said in "The Ethics of Writing," his June 2003 World Journalism Institute Speech. He continued, "The best writers give the appropriate weight and authority within each context, to each 'fact,' never ignoring the ones that may clash with a theory they happen to hold. . . . Writers understand that facts can be sifted, sorted, set aside, deleted, altered, or shaved down to achieve a slant to match the writer's preconceptions or ambitions, or worse, his original theory."[33]

Balanced presentation of news demands journalists also diversify sourcing—and the most obvious way to do so is along gender lines. That has not been a successful mission. In its annual "Who Makes the News?" report

The Global Media Monitoring Project in 2005 showed gender balance in news is still grossly absent. Hundreds of volunteer monitors in 76 countries coded almost 13,000 stories on television, on radio, and in print on one day in February 2005.[34]

"Women's views and voices are marginalized in the world's news media," according to the report that showed 21 percent of the people featured in the news were women. "Men's voices dominate in hard news. . . . Female reporters are more likely to cover soft news." There has not been much progress in the last ten years.

In 1995, 17 percent of news subjects were women, and 83 percent were men. A full decade later, 28 percent of the news subjects were women, and 72 percent were men. Only 10 percent of news stories in 2005 worldwide had women as a central focus, according to the report.[35] Clearly the expansion of sourcing has not gone far enough on the most basic level. And levels of diversity in newsrooms have dropped below peak, according to a 2005 Knight Foundation report by Bill Dedman and Stephen K. Doig: "Among the 200 largest newspapers, 73 percent employ fewer non-whites." According to the report, "Only 13 percent of newspapers responding to the survey have reached ASNE's goal of parity between newsroom and community." And it goes on, "The share of journalism jobs held by non-whites has receded from its high-water mark."[36]

Rev. Irene Monroe wrote in *Newsweekly* about stereotypes and dismissal of coverage of the gay, lesbian, bisexual, transgender community in both the mainstream media and the gay press: "Covering the news is an arduous task when it comes to communities of color and other marginal groups within the larger lesbian, gay, bisexual, transgender and queer community around the country. One of the problems is due to the paucity of reporters of color in our newsrooms." In her May 3, 2006, column, she wrote, "Gay newspapers function as important community-based media. They will report what the larger media will not about our lives; and they are our mirrors, reflecting our lives and our stories back to us."[37]

If sourcing in newspapers is to represent society, then more effort must be made to educate journalists and journalism students on how to broaden source bases to be more fair and more inclusive of all sectors of society. "A well-functioning democracy depends on good journalism. Markets cannot function well without reliable, timely information provided by good journalism," reads the mission statement of "A Vision for Journalism Education: The Professional School for Twenty-first Century News Leaders: A Manifesto." The goal was crafted by the deans of five journalism schools— Medill, Columbia, Annenberg, Berkeley, and Harvard—and funded by the John S. and James L. Knight Foundation and the Carnegie Corporation.[38]

Newspaper journalists want to produce good journalism. Readers want to experience good journalism. Sources want to be included in good journalism. It's a win, win, win situation. "The vast majority of reporters will tell you that they entered journalism because they wanted to make a difference in the lives of ordinary people," Linda Foley, president of the Newspaper Guild and Communications Workers of America, wrote in an essay in *The Future of Media: Resistance and Reform in the Twenty-first Century* (2005). She continued, "Yet our poll indicates that 65 percent of media workers believe news organizations do not give enough coverage to stories that are meaningful to the average Americans."[39]

An underperforming media risks more than its credibility and wastes more than ink, paper, and a reader's time. "The truth, slowly emerging, is that human society cannot improve, cannot function properly, may not even be able to survive, if the media do not do their job well," Claude Jean-Bertrand wrote in the foreword to *Good News: Social Ethics and the Press* (1993) by Clifford Christians, John Ferre, and P. Mark Fackler.[40] In the introduction to the book, the authors wrote, "If the world's confusion has stiffened news reports to bloodless information bytes, communitarian journalism salutes it as a sign of cultural richness, a trove that journalists mine for insights on the ways and means of people bonded by symbol and culture."[41]

The recent growth of features and feature approaches to news and the broadening of sources are outward indications of the evolution of everyman journalism. While the future cannot be mapped with certainty, an examination of how and why newspapers arrived here helps to bring the media landscape into sharper focus. "In the mid-century move to professionalism, journalists embraced the inverted pyramid and objectivity," Anders Gyllenhaal wrote in the spring 2006 *Nieman Reports* on newspapers. "Now newspapers compete with a host of other media that feel less cold and conventional. And those Web sites, magazines and cable news outlets are winning people over in a climate of great skepticism toward the media establishment," Gyllenhaal, editor of the *Star Tribune* in Minneapolis, wrote. "One of our new goals is to make every journalistic decision with our readers foremost in mind."[42]

The proliferation of features in newspapers is a response to what readers want and has been coming for a long time. Many journalists fear features will expand to overtake newspapers so there is not a shred of hard news in their pages. But I think readers demand a balanced diet, just as they would not gorge on only mashed potatoes at a Thanksgiving buffet. They would at least like to be offered the turkey, turnips, dressing, cranberries, and broccoli soufflé. Sameness does not inspire excellence. "Over recent decades, the emphasis on short-term profitability has meant not only lack of training and frequent buyouts of veteran talent, but decreased amounts of space in newspapers and airtime in radio and television and failure to invest in new models of delivery or improvements in news—in other words 'harvesting,'" Overholser wrote in her journalism manifesto.[43]

Features Have Been Steadily Increasing

In 1926, Orland Kay Armstrong published the results of his study measuring newspaper content in 1875, 1900, and 1925 of two St. Louis newspapers—the *St. Louis Post-Dispatch* and the *Republican*. In 1875, Armstrong reported that 55.3 percent of the papers were devoted to news, 6.3 percent to features, and 9.6 percent to opinion. That would mean the newspapers contained close to 16 percent non-news. Advertising made up 28.9 percent of the newspapers' pages. By 1900 news content had the same concentration, but opinion had increased to 7.1 percent of the paper, and features had decreased to 5.5 percent of content. That would mean non-news was about 12 percent of the newspaper editorial content.[44]

By 1925, the editorial hole for news stories had shrunk to 26.7 percent of the paper. The percentage of features had nearly doubled from 1875 to 10.4 percent with 2.2 percent opinion, leaving the paper with the same amount of total non-news as in 1900. The papers in 1925 contained a whopping 60.5 percent advertising.

"Feature matter has grown tremendously in volume during the five decades under consideration," Armstrong wrote of the period from 1875 to 1925. In a text that was published more than eighty years ago, Armstrong wrote an explanation that could have been written today: "But feature matter has changed more in tone and subject matter than in volume during this time. . . . Feature matter today bears a closer relation to timely news; in fact, much feature matter today is as timely as news; and it bears the stamp of authenticity, as opposed to the 'it is rumored' type grotesque feature story of fifty years ago." In this century and particularly in the last decade, changes in newspaper content and the ratio of news to features have been shifting at an exponential rate. The trend toward more features on the front pages of newspapers begun more than a century ago has continued. Armstrong wrote, "The front page uniformly carries the news considered of the greatest general interest."[45]

What happens in the next hundred years depends on factors not yet even imagined. What we do know as journalists and consumers of news is that there will always be news. There will always be a need to know what is happening across the street or around the world. Every moment history is created, and an audience needs to know about it and is waiting to be informed, sometimes searching for the information through a variety of delivery vehicles. There will be even more vehicles in the future, many of which we can't even fathom today. And every day an observer will spread the word about the event or the idea, whether that observer and gatherer of news is a journalist, participant, or citizen journalist. Because of the kind of everyman story that readers have grown to associate with the newspaper, that news content will now be more democratic, inclusive, and anecdotal than ever—wherever it appears. "The next generation of writing stars will take the tools of narrative and showcase them in daily newspapers," said Ken Fuson.[46]

Whether the news you consume is ink on paper you hold in your hands, an image on a screen in the seat back in front of you, or audio text a narrator reads to you through an earpiece, it will be the story that matters. And it will be the story that informs you, the story you remember, and the story that brings you back tomorrow.

About 5:45 on a recent dark, blustery February morning in Chicago, I was driving my sons Weldon and Brendan to weightlifting training at the high school, where they are both on the wrestling team. A lone station wagon was double-parked in the street, its hazard lights flashing, and a newspaper delivery man was running across front yards to throw newspapers on selected doorsteps.

"That job would stink," Brendan said. "Why doesn't he just mail them?"

At first it seemed absurd. But why not just mail them? From his point of view, newspapers don't deliver the news, and he could wait a few days for whatever offerings were inside. Brendan and his generation retrieve the information they want when they want it online—and from a menagerie of sites. You might as well mail the newspaper.

His question exaggerates what we all know. On daily news, newspapers deliver the breaking news last; they are beaten every minute by Internet, television, and radio. Unless it is enterprise work, investigative stories and masterfully written narrative and opinion that the blogs, websites, and TV stations don't have time to produce, newspapers can't win. Still, newspapers can deliver the best-written story with a depth of sources and in the way the reader wants to receive it.

Everyman news has grown from a desire for newspapers to bring to the media buffet a different brand of story. It is a reaction to a cultural climate that sanctifies the story and reveres the viewpoints, input, and reactions to events cultivated from a broader range of sources. And it fills the demand for the democracy of voice. It is the deliberate reporting, writing, and place-ment of these stories in newspapers that have changed American front pages. Whether or not that has been a good thing for the media landscape is debatable. But everyman news is an undeniable reality and a measurable shift we can't ignore. The next step involves the way those stories continue to arrive. And I'll bet good money it won't be through the mail.

Data from 20 Newspapers Measuring Features, Feature Leads and Unofficial Sources

Findings for All Newspapers Studied
(*Breakdown by newspaper follows comprehensive data.*)

Newspaper name		Staff Size	Morning Circulation	Saturday Circulation	Sunday Circulation
Anchorage Daily News	Alaska	80	69,990	69,660	84,417
Arkansas Democrat Gazette	SW	180	189,213	177,879	278,370
Atlanta Constitution	SE	332	405,367	530,115	662,835
Arizona Republic	SW	380	496,373	496,373	601,885
Boston Globe	NE	390	478,735	i456,760	705,017
Chicago Tribune	MW	454	689,026	568,022	1,016,103
Cincinnati Enquirer	MW	131	189,883	215,135	318,915
Idaho Statesman	W	89	64,526	64,526	87,188
Los Angeles Times	W	588	959,863	1,011,732	1,392,544
Louisville Courier Journal	SE	161	228,809	231,835	301,426
Miami Herald	SE	214	328,124	356,238	443,752
New York Times	NE	920	1,194,491	1,088,117	1,735,059
Omaha World Herald	MW	260	214,651	216,675	268,953
Portland Press Herald	NE	106	74,130	74,130	120,583
San Antonio Express News	SW	238	228,733	263,693	362,352
San Jose Mercury News	W	362	275,567	282,413	301,346
Seattle Times	NW	264	219,941	215,604	478,612
St. Louis Post Dispatch	MW	267	255,869	255,869	459,220
Times Picayune	SE	175	259,705	276,762	309,274
Washington Post	NE	696	772,535	681,673	1,029,966
Totals		6,287	7,595,531	7,533,211	10,957,817

Source: Bacon's Newspaper Directory, 2005

Percentage of front page features vs. hard news, 2001

Percent of front
page features -
35%

Percent of front
page hard news -
65%

Percentage of front page features vs. hard news, 2004

Percent of front
page features -
50%

Percent of front
page hard news -
50%

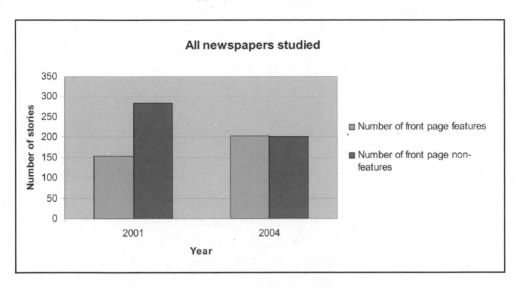

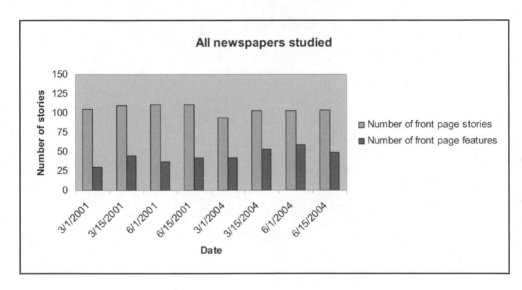

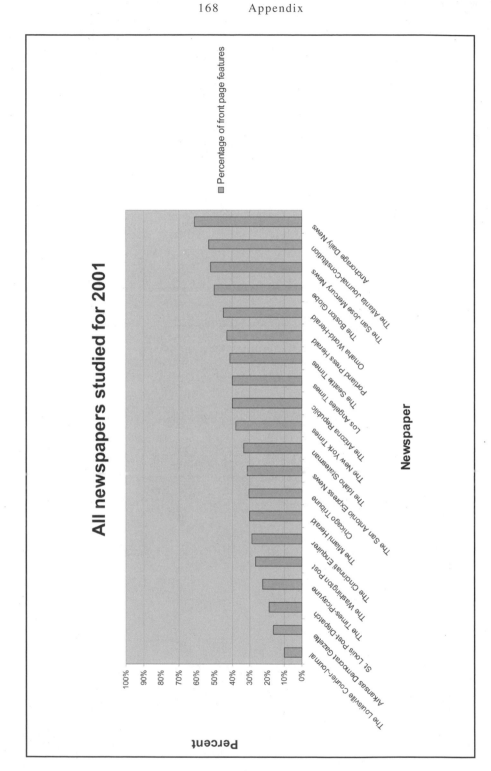

All newspapers studied for 2001

Percentage of front page features

Newspaper

Percent

The Anchorage Daily News
The Atlanta Journal-Constitution
The San Jose Mercury News
The Boston Globe
Omaha World-Herald
Portland Press Herald
The Seattle Times
Los Angeles Times
The Arizona Republic
The New York Times
The Idaho Statesman
The San Antonio Express News
Chicago Tribune
The Miami Herald
The Cincinnati Enquirer
The Washington Post
The Times-Picayune
St. Louis Post-Dispatch
Arkansas Democrat Gazette
The Louisville Courier-Journal

100%
90%
80%
70%
60%
50%
40%
30%
20%
10%
0%

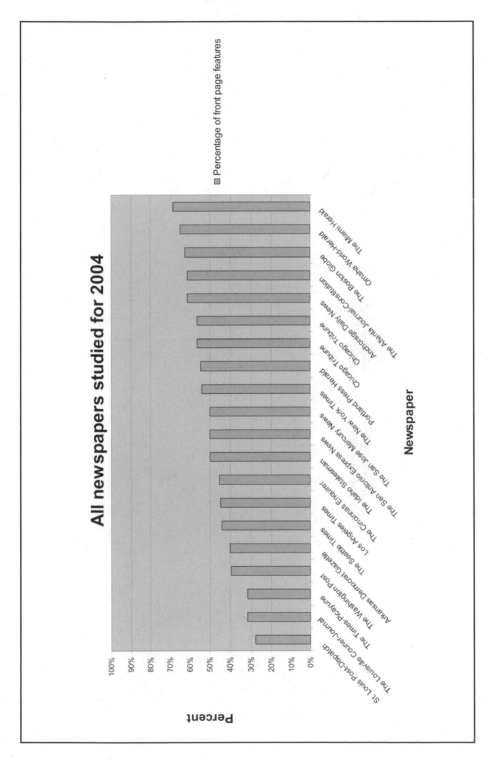

All newspapers studied for 2004

Percentage of front page features

Newspaper

Percent

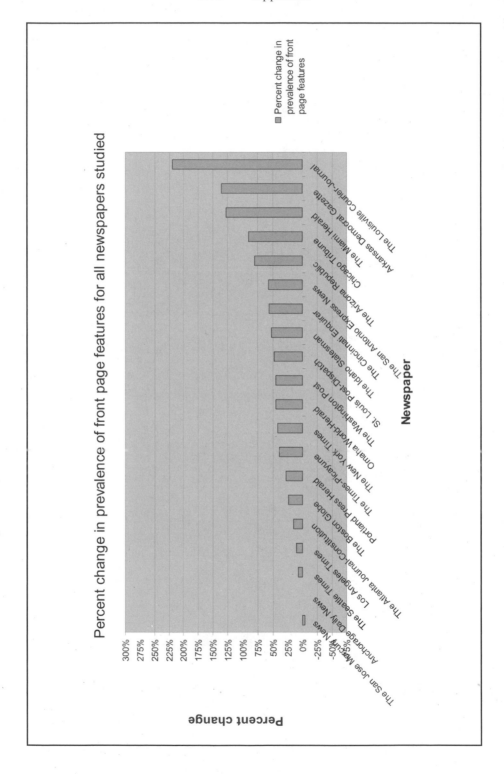

Percent change in prevalence of front page features for all newspapers studied

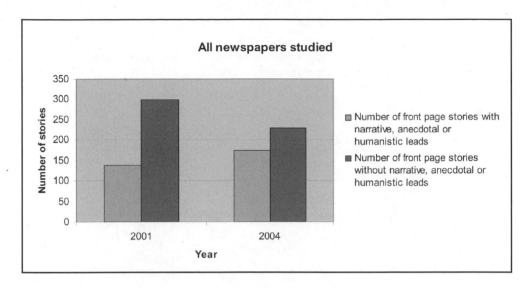

All newspapers studied

- Number of front page stories with narrative, anecdotal or humanistic leads
- Number of front page stories without narrative, anecdotal or humanistic leads

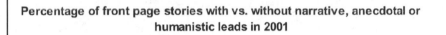

Percentage of front page stories with vs. without narrative, anecdotal or humanistic leads in 2001

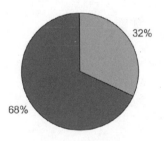

- Number of front page stories with narrative, anecdotal or humanistic leads
- Number of front page stories without narrative, anecdotal or humanistic leads

Percentage of front page stories with vs. without narrative, anecdotal or humanistic leads in 2004

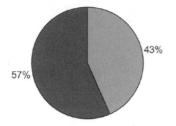

43%

57%

☐ Number of front page stories with narrative, anecdotal or humanistic leads

■ Number of front page stories without narrative, anecdotal or humanistic leads

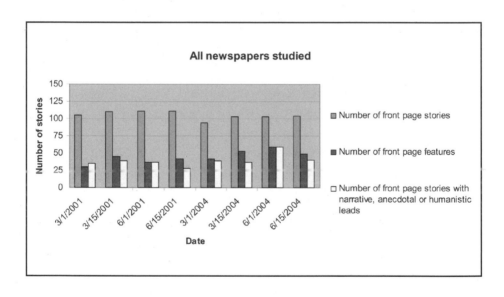

All newspapers studied

Number of stories

Date

☐ Number of front page stories

■ Number of front page features

☐ Number of front page stories with narrative, anecdotal or humanistic leads

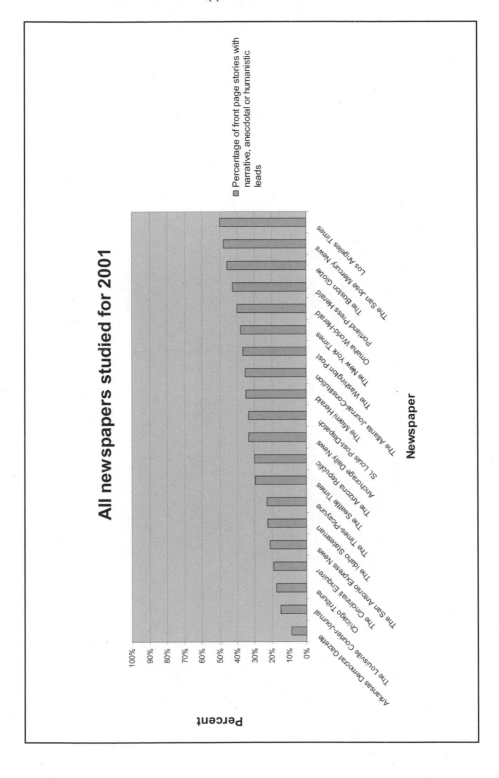

All newspapers studied for 2001

Percentage of front page stories with narrative, anecdotal or humanistic leads

Newspaper

Percent

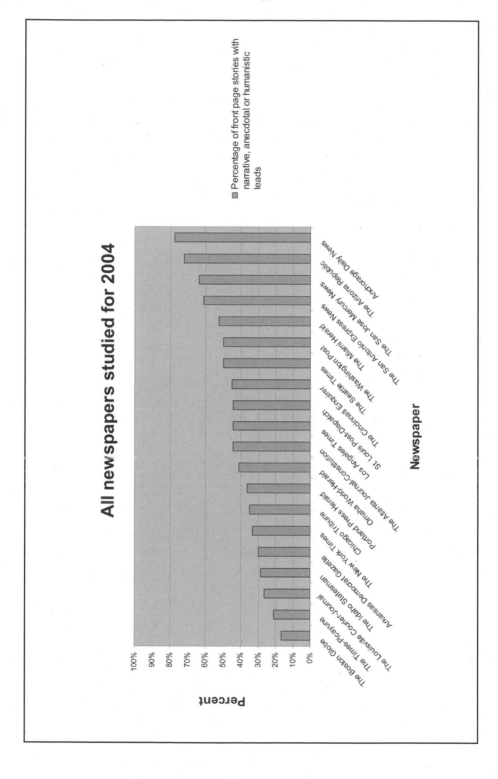

All newspapers studied for 2004

Percent

Newspaper

■ Percentage of front page stories with narrative, anecdotal or humanistic leads

The Boston Globe
The Times-Picayune
The Louisville Courier-Journal
The Idaho Statesman
Arkansas Democrat Gazette
The New York Times
Chicago Tribune
Portland Press Herald
Omaha World-Herald
The Atlanta Journal-Constitution
Los Angeles Times
St. Louis Post-Dispatch
The Cincinnati Enquirer
The Seattle Times
The Washington Post
The Miami Herald
The San Antonio Express News
The San Jose Mercury News
The Arizona Republic
Anchorage Daily News

Percent of Change 2001-2004 for Each Newspaper:
Features and Feature Leads to News

Newspaper	% Change Features	% Change Feature Leads
1. Anchorage Daily News	0 %	+136.4 %
2. Arizona Republic	+80 %	+140%
3. Arkansas Democrat Gazette	+ 135.3 %	+275 %
4. Atlanta Journal Constitution	+15.1 %	+25.7 %
5. Boston Globe	+24%	-63.6 %
6. Chicago Tribune	+90 %	+105.8 %
7. Cincinnati Enquirer	+55.2 %	+136.8 %
8. Idaho Statesman	+51.5 %	+31.8 %
9. Los Angeles Times	+10 %	-12 %
10. Louisville Courier Journal	+220 %	+66.7 %
11. Miami Herald	+126.7 %	+42.9 %
12. The New York Times	+42.1 %	-13.2%
13. Omaha World-Herald	+44.4 %	+2.5 %
14. Portland Press Herald	+27.9 %	-16.3 %
15. San Antonio Express News	+56.3 %	+190.5%
16. San Jose Mercury News	-3.8 %	+33.3%
17. Seattle Times	+7.3 %	+72.4%
18. St. Louis Post-Dispatch	+47.4 %	+33.3 %
19. Times-Picayune	+39.1%	-22.2 %
20. Washington Post	+44.4 %	+35.1 %

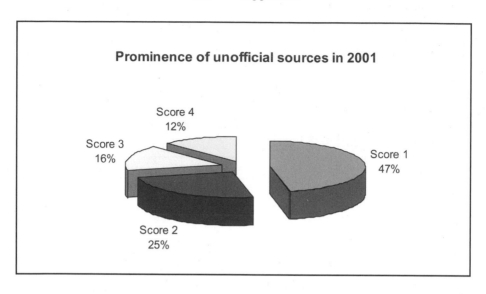

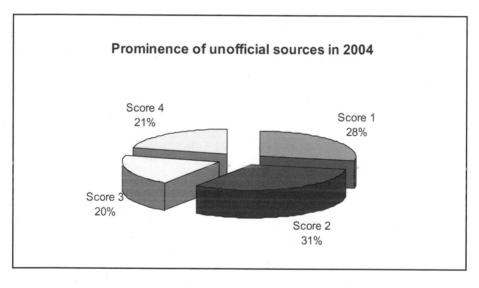

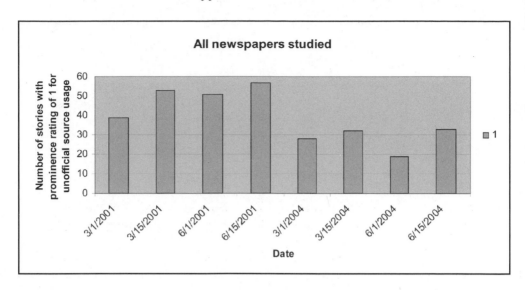

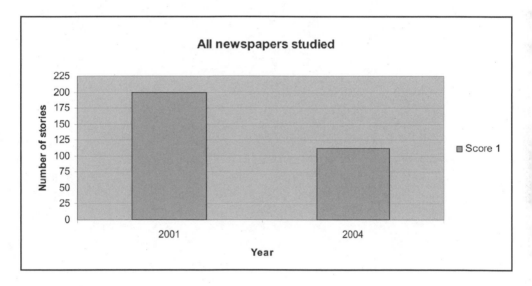

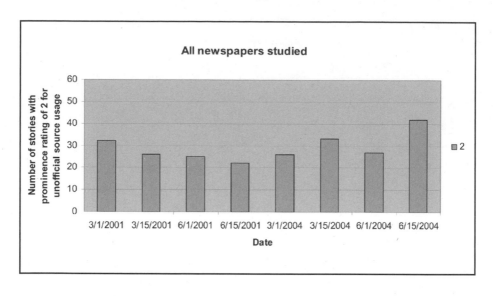

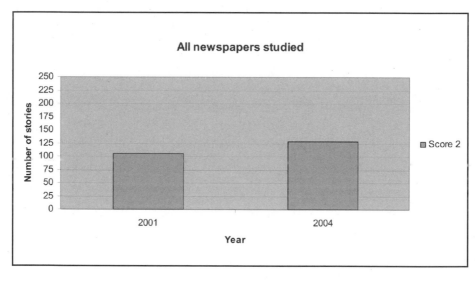

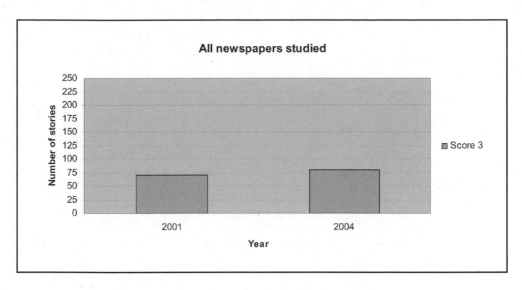

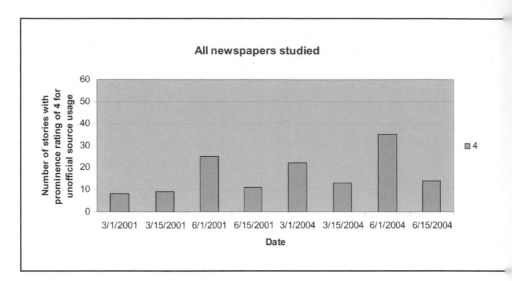

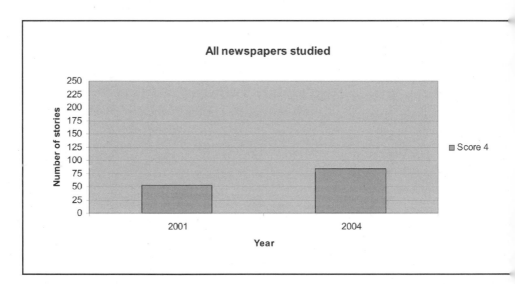

Anchorage Daily News

1. Features vs. News

These pie charts show the total percentage of front page features and hard news in 2001 and 2004. There was no change in the number of feature stories from 2001 to 2004.

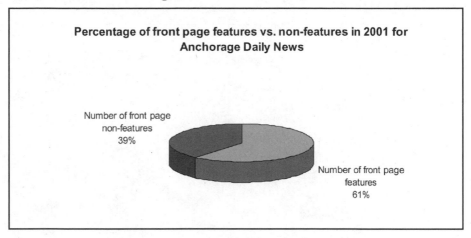

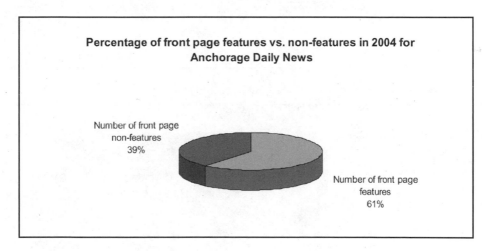

2. Feature Leads vs. Summary News Leads

This section measures all front page stories for summary news leads vs. anecdotal, descriptive, or humanistic leads on the studied dates in 2001 and 2004. There was a 136.4 percent increase in feature leads on the front page.

Anchorage Daily News in 2001 front page stories vs. feature leads

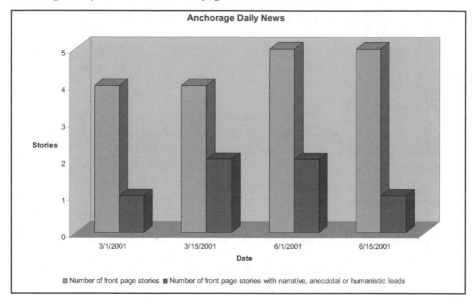

Anchorage Daily News in 2004 front page stories vs. feature leads

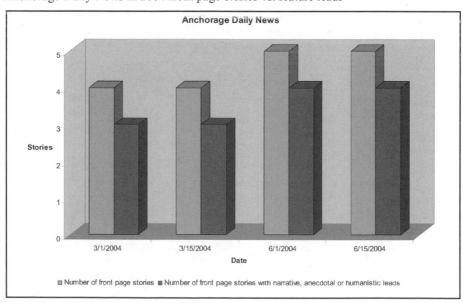

3. Use of Unofficial Sources

This section measures the prominence of unofficial sources in these same front page stories.

KEY:

    1 rating—up to 1 mention of unofficial source, lower in story

    2 rating—up to 2 mentions of unofficial sources, lower in story

    3 rating—up to 1 mention of unofficial source, higher in the story, with more graphs

    4 rating—several mentions of unofficial sources; most of story includes unofficial sources

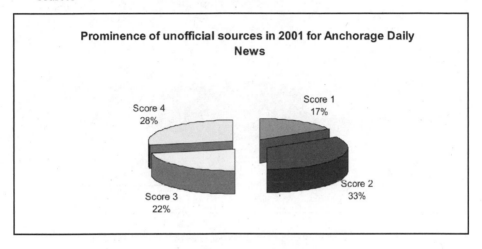

Prominence of unofficial sources in 2001 for Anchorage Daily News

Score 4 28%
Score 1 17%
Score 2 33%
Score 3 22%

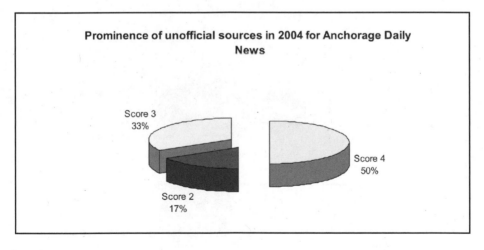

Prominence of unofficial sources in 2004 for Anchorage Daily News

Score 3 33%
Score 4 50%
Score 2 17%

Arizona Republic

1. Features vs. News

These pie charts show the total percentage of front page features and hard news in 2001 and 2004. There was an 80 percent increase in the number of features on the front page from 2001 to 2004.

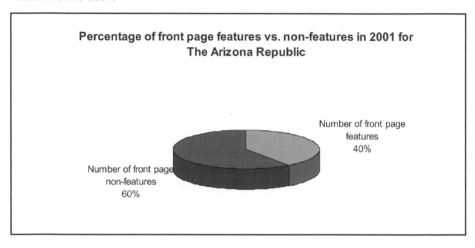

Percentage of front page features vs. non-features in 2001 for The Arizona Republic

Number of front page features
40%

Number of front page non-features
60%

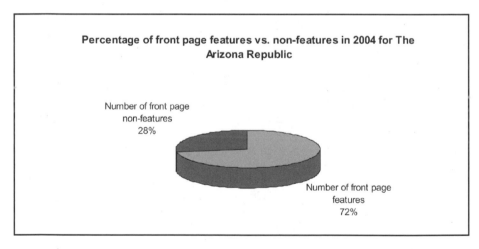

Percentage of front page features vs. non-features in 2004 for The Arizona Republic

Number of front page non-features
28%

Number of front page features
72%

2. Feature Leads vs. Summary News Leads

This section measures all front page stories for summary news leads vs. anecdotal, descriptive, or humanistic leads on the studied dates in 2001 and 2004. There was a 140 percent increase in feature leads on the front page.

The Arizona Republic in 2001 front page stories vs. feature leads

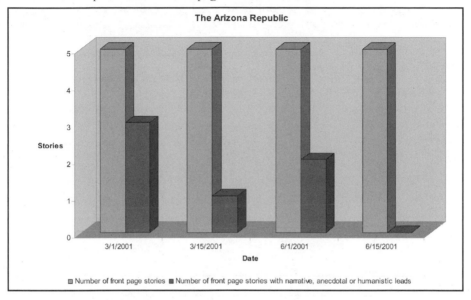

The Arizona Republic in 2004 front page stories vs. feature leads

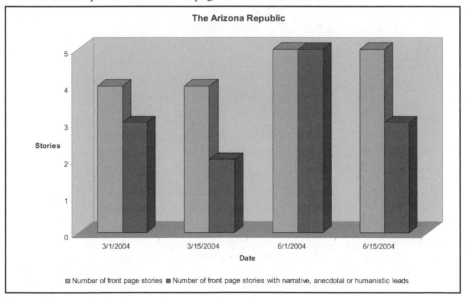

3. Use of Unofficial Sources

This section measures the prominence of unofficial sources in these same front page stories.
KEY:
    1 rating—up to 1 mention of unofficial source, lower in story
    2 rating—up to 2 mentions of unofficial sources, lower in story
    3 rating—up to 1 mention of unofficial source, higher in the story, with more graphs
    4 rating—several mentions of unofficial sources; most of story includes unofficial sources

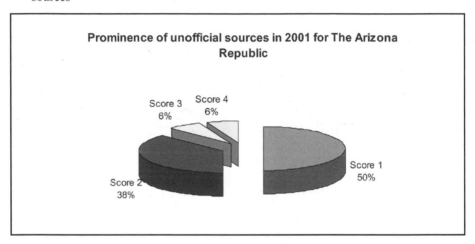

Prominence of unofficial sources in 2001 for The Arizona Republic

Score 3 6%
Score 4 6%
Score 1 50%
Score 2 38%

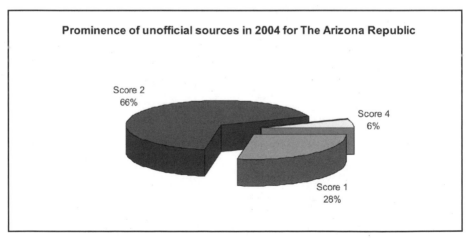

Prominence of unofficial sources in 2004 for The Arizona Republic

Score 2 66%
Score 4 6%
Score 1 28%

Arkansas Democrat-Gazette

1. Features vs. News

These pie charts show the total percentage of front page features and hard news in 2001 and 2004. There was a 135 percent increase in the number of features on the front page from 2001 to 2004.

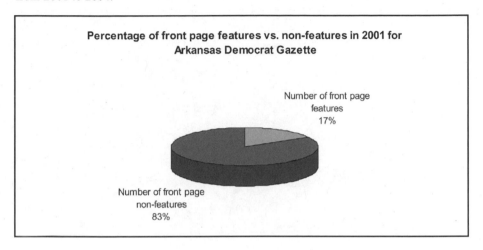

Percentage of front page features vs. non-features in 2001 for Arkansas Democrat Gazette

Number of front page features
17%

Number of front page non-features
83%

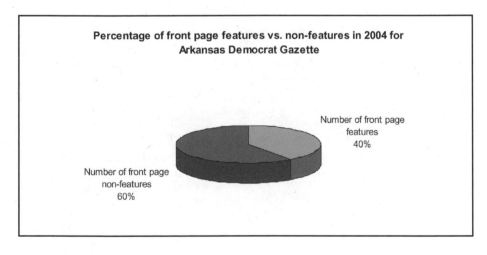

Percentage of front page features vs. non-features in 2004 for Arkansas Democrat Gazette

Number of front page features
40%

Number of front page non-features
60%

2. Feature Leads vs. Summary News Leads

This section measures all front page stories for summary news leads vs. anecdotal, descriptive, or humanistic leads on the studied dates in 2001 and 2004. There was a 275 percent increase in feature leads on the front page.

Arkansas Democrat Gazette in 2001 front page stories vs. feature leads

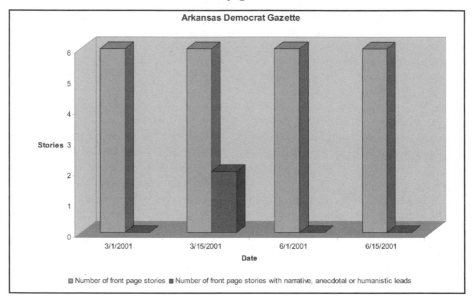

Arkansas Democrat Gazette in 2004 front page stories vs. feature leads

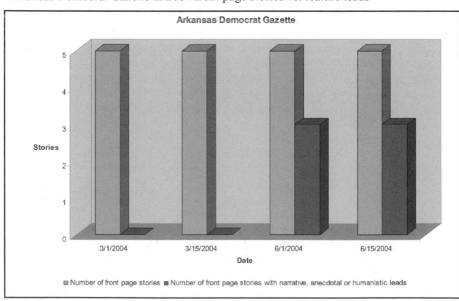

3. Use of Unofficial Sources

This section measures the prominence of unofficial sources in these same front page stories.

KEY:

1 rating—up to 1 mention of unofficial source, lower in story

2 rating—up to 2 mentions of unofficial sources, lower in story

3 rating—up to 1 mention of unofficial source, higher in the story, with more graphs

4 rating—several mentions of unofficial sources; most of story includes unofficial sources

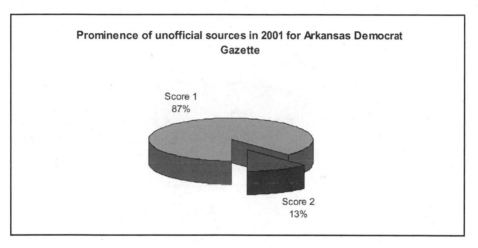

Prominence of unofficial sources in 2001 for Arkansas Democrat Gazette

Score 1
87%

Score 2
13%

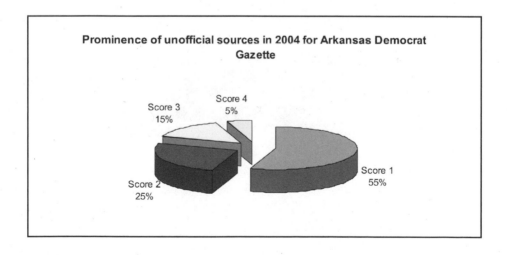

Prominence of unofficial sources in 2004 for Arkansas Democrat Gazette

Score 3
15%

Score 4
5%

Score 2
25%

Score 1
55%

Atlanta Journal-Constitution

1. Features vs. News

These pie charts show the total percentage of front page features and hard news in 2001 and 2004. There was a 15 percent increase in the number of features on the front page from 2001 to 2004.

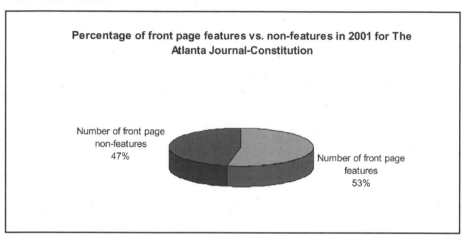

Percentage of front page features vs. non-features in 2001 for The Atlanta Journal-Constitution

Number of front page non-features 47%

Number of front page features 53%

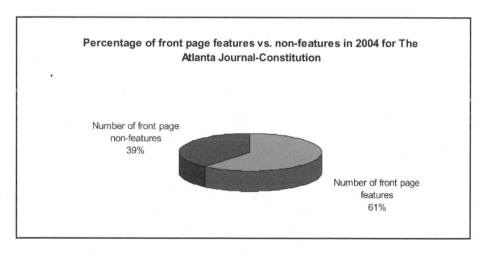

Percentage of front page features vs. non-features in 2004 for The Atlanta Journal-Constitution

Number of front page non-features 39%

Number of front page features 61%

2. Feature Leads vs. Summary News Leads

This section measures all front page stories for summary news leads vs. anecdotal, descriptive, or humanistic leads on the studied dates in 2001 and 2004. There was a 25.7 percent increase in feature leads on the front page.

The Atlanta Journal-Constitution in 2001 front page stories vs. feature leads

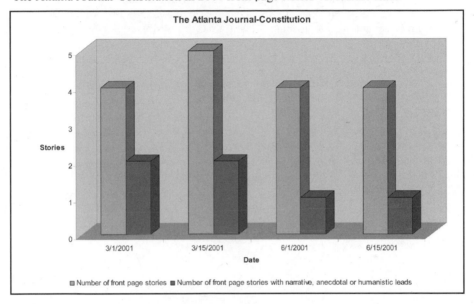

The Atlanta Journal-Constitution in 2004 front page stories vs. feature leads

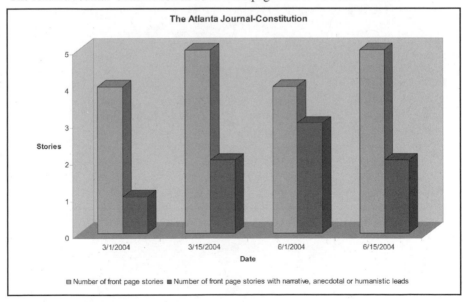

3. Use of Unofficial Sources

This section measures the prominence of unofficial sources in these same front page stories.

KEY:

    1 rating—up to 1 mention of unofficial source, lower in story

    2 rating—up to 2 mentions of unofficial sources, lower in story

    3 rating—up to 1 mention of unofficial source, higher in the story, with more graphs

    4 rating—several mentions of unofficial sources; most of story includes unofficial sources

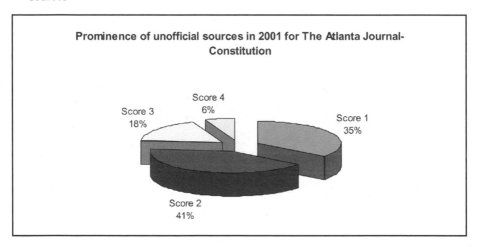

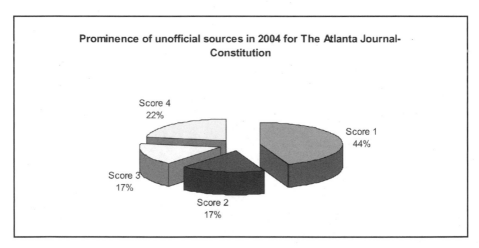

Boston Globe

1. Features vs. News

These pie charts show the total percentage of front page features and hard news in 2001 and 2004. There was a 24 percent increase in the number of features on the front page from 2001 to 2004.

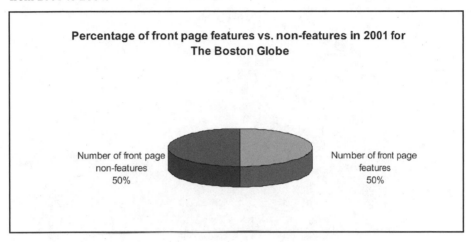

Percentage of front page features vs. non-features in 2001 for The Boston Globe

Number of front page non-features 50%

Number of front page features 50%

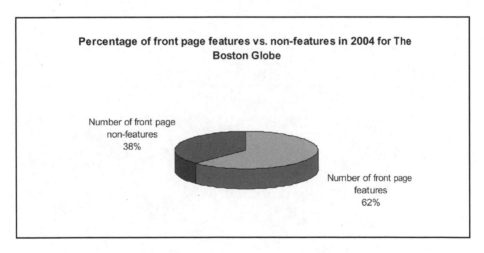

Percentage of front page features vs. non-features in 2004 for The Boston Globe

Number of front page non-features 38%

Number of front page features 62%

2. Feature Leads vs. Summary News Leads

This section measures all front page stories for summary news leads vs. anecdotal, descriptive, or humanistic leads on the studied dates in 2001 and 2004. There was a 63 percent decrease in feature leads on the front page.

The Boston Globe in 2001 front page stories vs. feature leads

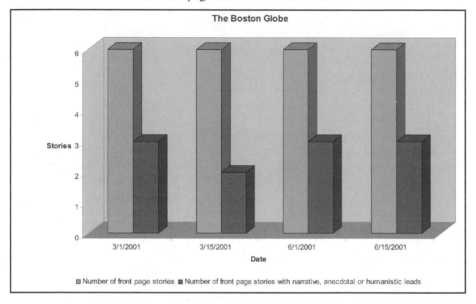

The Boston Globe in 2004 front page stories vs. feature leads

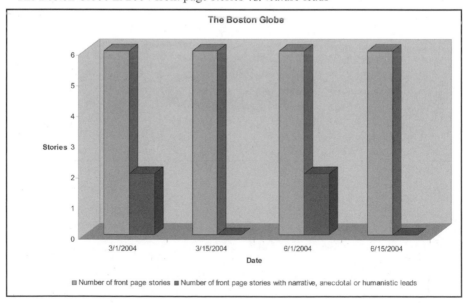

3. Use of Unofficial Sources

This section measures the prominence of unofficial sources in these same front page stories.

KEY:

    1 rating—up to 1 mention of unofficial source, lower in story

    2 rating—up to 2 mentions of unofficial sources, lower in story

    3 rating—up to 1 mention of unofficial source, higher in the story, with more graphs

    4 rating—several mentions of unofficial sources; most of story includes unofficial sources

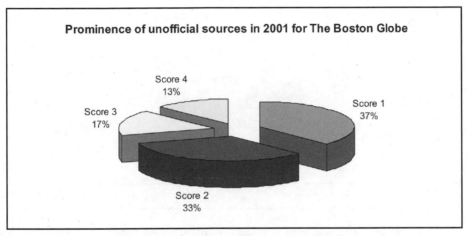

Prominence of unofficial sources in 2001 for The Boston Globe

Score 4 — 13%
Score 3 — 17%
Score 1 — 37%
Score 2 — 33%

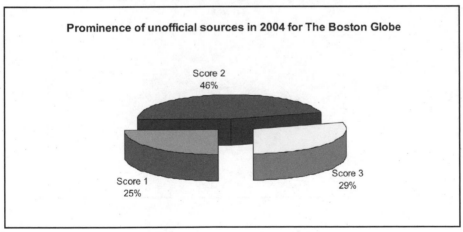

Prominence of unofficial sources in 2004 for The Boston Globe

Score 2 — 46%
Score 1 — 25%
Score 3 — 29%

Chicago Tribune

1. Features vs. News

These pie charts show the total percentage of front page features and hard news in 2001 and 2004. There was a 90 percent increase in the number of features on the front page from 2001 to 2004.

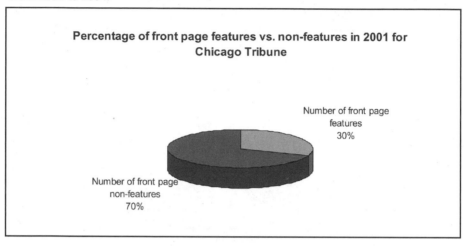

Percentage of front page features vs. non-features in 2001 for Chicago Tribune

Number of front page features
30%

Number of front page non-features
70%

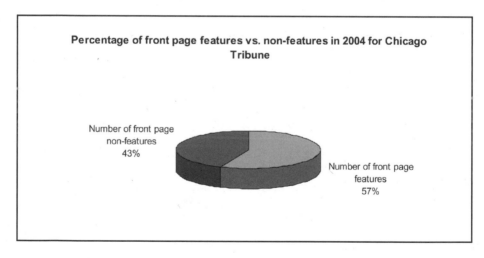

Percentage of front page features vs. non-features in 2004 for Chicago Tribune

Number of front page non-features
43%

Number of front page features
57%

2. Feature Leads vs. Summary News Leads

This section measures all front page stories for summary news leads vs. anecdotal, descriptive, or humanistic leads on the studied dates in 2001 and 2004. There was a 105.8 percent increase in feature leads on the front page.

The Chicago Tribune in 2001 front page stories vs. feature leads

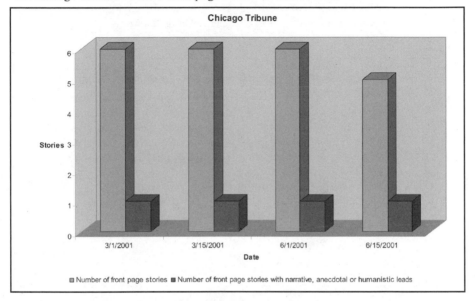

The Chicago Tribune in 2004 front page stories vs. feature leads

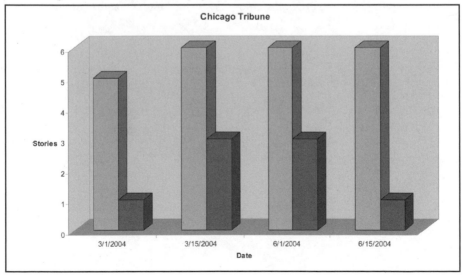

3. Use of Unofficial Sources

This section measures the prominence of unofficial sources in these same front page stories.
KEY:
    1 rating—up to 1 mention of unofficial source, lower in story
    2 rating—up to 2 mentions of unofficial sources, lower in story
    3 rating—up to 1 mention of unofficial source, higher in the story, with more graph
    4 rating—several mentions of unofficial sources; most of story includes unofficial sources

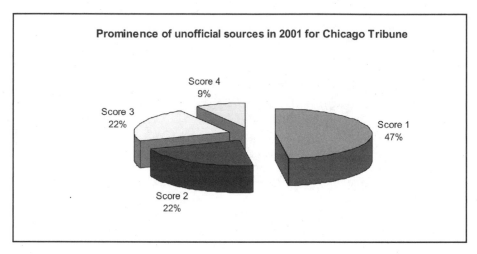

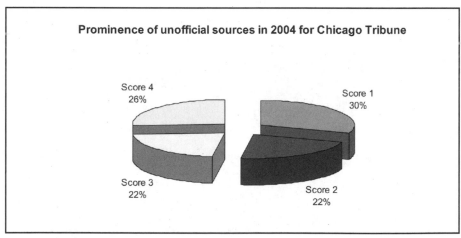

Cincinnati Enquirer

1. Features vs. News

These pie charts show the total percentage of front page features and hard news in 2001 and 2004. There was a 55 percent increase in the number of features on the front page from 2001 to 2004.

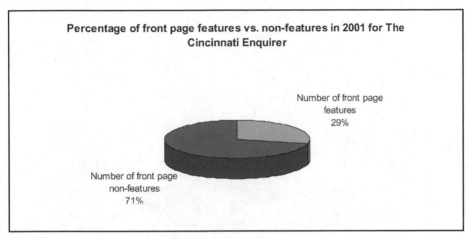

Percentage of front page features vs. non-features in 2001 for The Cincinnati Enquirer

Number of front page features 29%

Number of front page non-features 71%

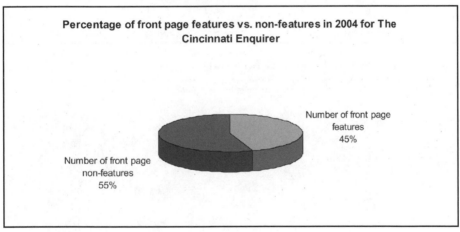

Percentage of front page features vs. non-features in 2004 for The Cincinnati Enquirer

Number of front page features 45%

Number of front page non-features 55%

2. Feature Leads vs. Summary News Leads

This section measures all front page stories for summary news leads vs. anecdotal, descriptive, or humanistic leads on the studied dates in 2001 and 2004. There was a 136 percent increase in feature leads on the front page.

The Cincinnati Enquirer in 2001 front page stories vs. feature leads

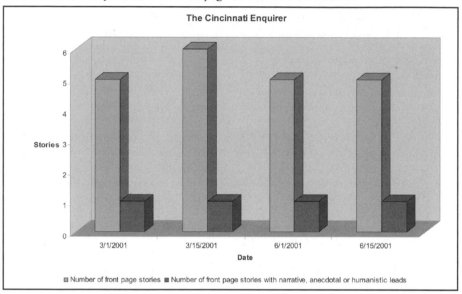

The Cincinnati Enquirer in 2004 front page stories vs. feature leads

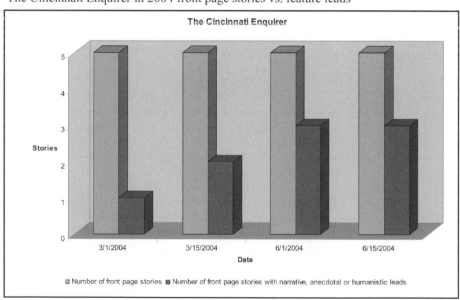

3. Use of Unofficial Sources

This section measures the prominence of unofficial sources in these same front page stories.

KEY:

  1 rating—up to 1 mention of unofficial source, lower in story

  2 rating—up to 2 mentions of unofficial sources, lower in story

  3 rating—up to 1 mention of unofficial source, higher in the story, with more graphs

  4 rating—several mentions of unofficial sources; most of story includes unofficial sources

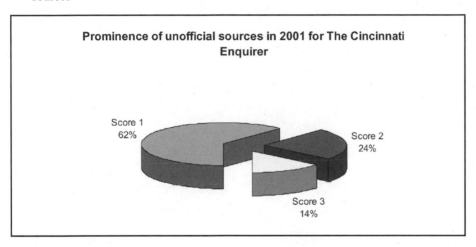

Prominence of unofficial sources in 2001 for The Cincinnati Enquirer

Score 1
62%

Score 2
24%

Score 3
14%

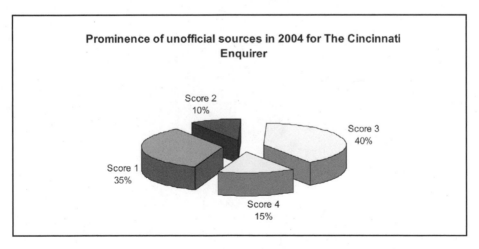

Prominence of unofficial sources in 2004 for The Cincinnati Enquirer

Score 2
10%

Score 3
40%

Score 1
35%

Score 4
15%

3. Use of Unofficial Sources

This section measures the prominence of unofficial sources in these same front page stories.
KEY:
    1 rating—up to 1 mention of unofficial source, lower in story
    2 rating—up to 2 mentions of unofficial sources, lower in story
    3 rating—up to 1 mention of unofficial source, higher in the story, with more graphs
    4 rating—several mentions of unofficial sources; most of story includes unofficial sources

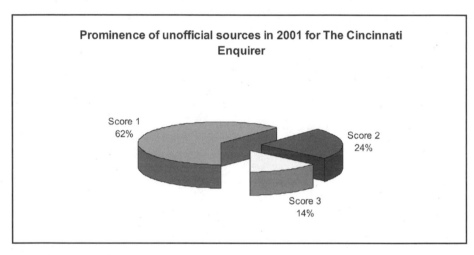

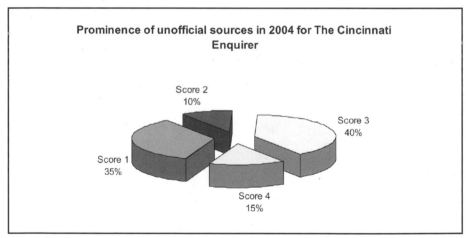

Idaho Statesman

1. Features vs. News

These pie charts show the total percentage of front page features and hard news in 2001 and 2004. There was a 51.5 percent increase in the number of features on the front page from 2001 to 2004.

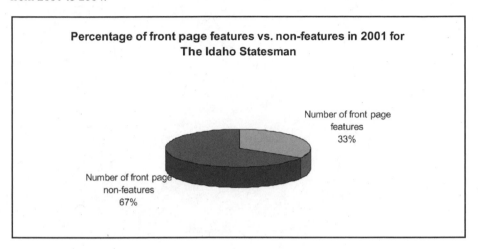

Percentage of front page features vs. non-features in 2001 for The Idaho Statesman

Number of front page features
33%

Number of front page non-features
67%

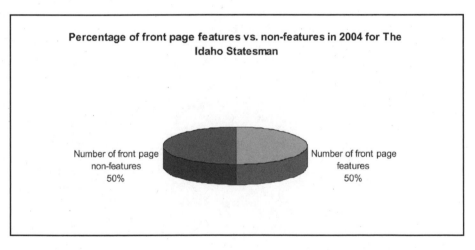

Percentage of front page features vs. non-features in 2004 for The Idaho Statesman

Number of front page non-features
50%

Number of front page features
50%

2. Feature Leads vs. Summary News Leads

This section measures all front page stories for summary news leads vs. anecdotal, descriptive, or humanistic leads on the studied dates in 2001 and 2004. There was a 31.8 percent increase in feature leads on the front page.

The Idaho Statesman in 2001 front page stories vs. feature leads

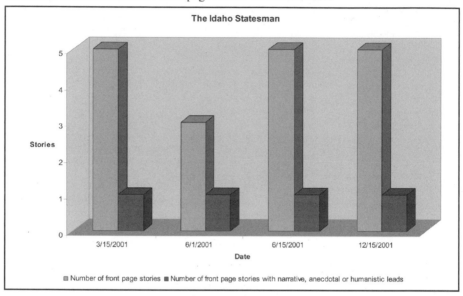

The Idaho Statesman in 2004 front page stories vs. feature leads

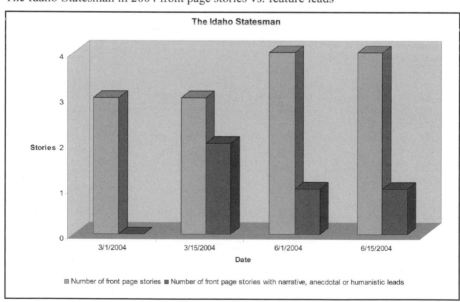

3. Use of Unofficial Sources

This section measures the prominence of unofficial sources in these same front page stories.

KEY:

    1 rating—up to 1 mention of unofficial source, lower in story

    2 rating—up to 2 mentions of unofficial sources, lower in story

    3 rating—up to 1 mention of unofficial source, higher in the story, with more graphs

    4 rating—several mentions of unofficial sources; most of story includes unofficial sources

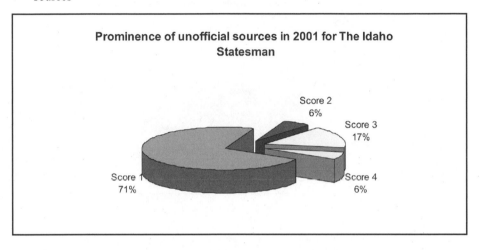

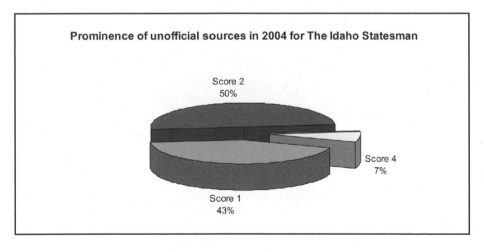

Los Angeles Times

1. Features vs. News

These pie charts show the total percentage of front page features and hard news in 2001 and 2004. There was a 10 percent increase in the number of features on the front page from 2001 to 2004.

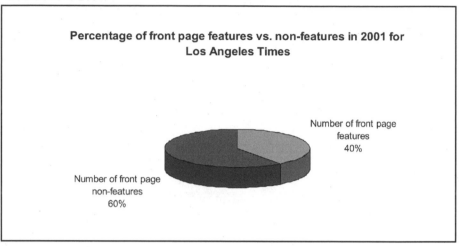

Percentage of front page features vs. non-features in 2001 for Los Angeles Times

Number of front page features 40%

Number of front page non-features 60%

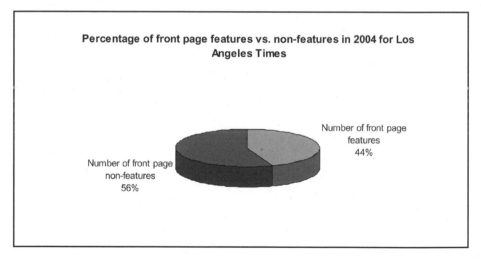

Percentage of front page features vs. non-features in 2004 for Los Angeles Times

Number of front page features 44%

Number of front page non-features 56%

2. Feature Leads vs. Summary News Leads

This section measures all front page stories for summary news leads vs. anecdotal, descriptive, or humanistic leads on the studied dates in 2001 and 2004. There was a 12 percent decrease in feature leads on the front page.

The Los Angeles Times in 2001 front page stories vs. feature leads

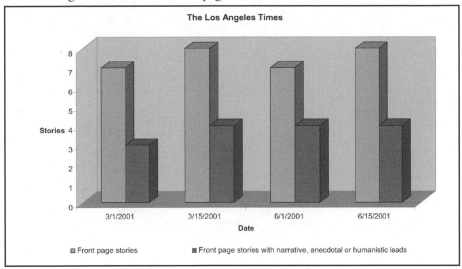

The Los Angeles Times in 2004 front page stories vs. feature leads

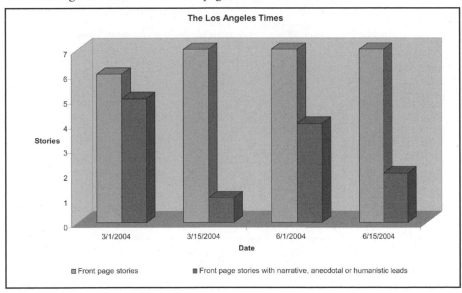

3. Use of Unofficial Sources

This section measures the prominence of unofficial sources in these same front page stories.
KEY:
    1 rating—up to 1 mention of unofficial source, lower in story
    2 rating—up to 2 mentions of unofficial sources, lower in story
    3 rating—up to 1 mention of unofficial source, higher in the story, with more graphs
    4 rating—several mentions of unofficial sources; most of story includes unofficial sources

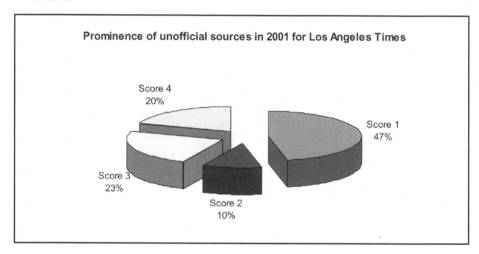

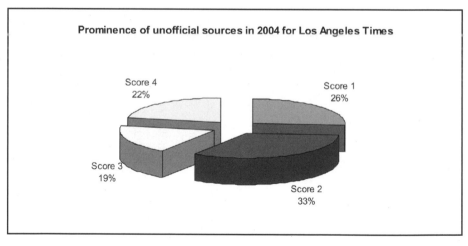

Louisville Courier-Journal

1. Features vs. News

These pie charts show the total percentage of front page features and hard news in 2001 and 2004. There was a 220 percent increase in the number of features on the front page from 2001 to 2004.

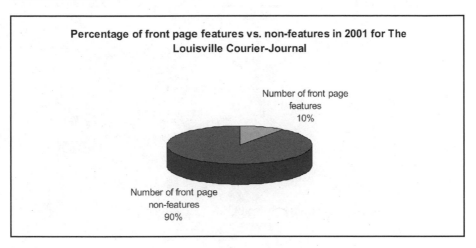

Percentage of front page features vs. non-features in 2001 for The Louisville Courier-Journal

Number of front page features
10%

Number of front page non-features
90%

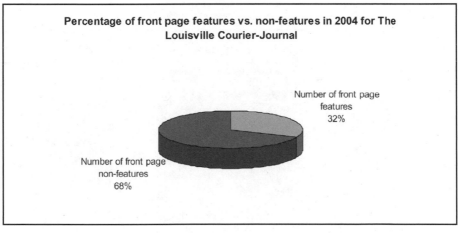

Percentage of front page features vs. non-features in 2004 for The Louisville Courier-Journal

Number of front page features
32%

Number of front page non-features
68%

2. Feature Leads vs. Summary News Leads

This section measures all front page stories for summary news leads vs. anecdotal, descriptive, or humanistic leads on the studied dates in 2001 and 2004. There was a 66.7 percent increase in feature leads on the front page.

The Louisville Courier-Journal in 2001 front page stories vs. feature leads

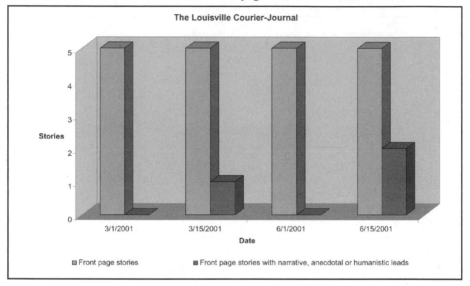

The Louisville Courier-Journal in 2004 front page stories vs. feature leads

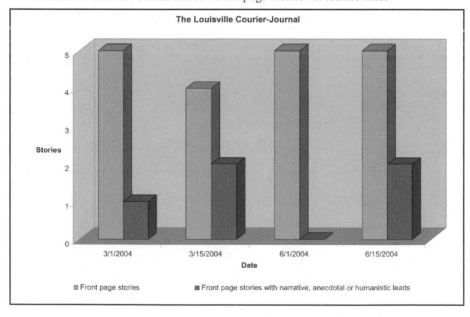

3. Use of Unofficial Sources

This section measures the prominence of unofficial sources in these same front page stories.

KEY:

    1 rating—up to 1 mention of unofficial source, lower in story

    2 rating—up to 2 mentions of unofficial sources, lower in story

    3 rating—up to 1 mention of unofficial source, higher in the story, with more graphs

    4 rating—several mentions of unofficial sources; most of story includes unofficial sources

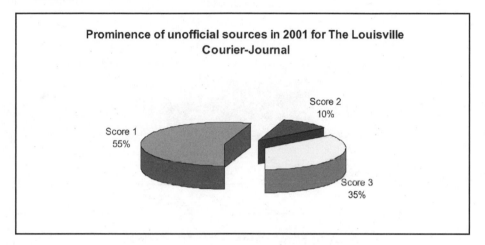

Prominence of unofficial sources in 2001 for The Louisville Courier-Journal

Score 1 55%
Score 2 10%
Score 3 35%

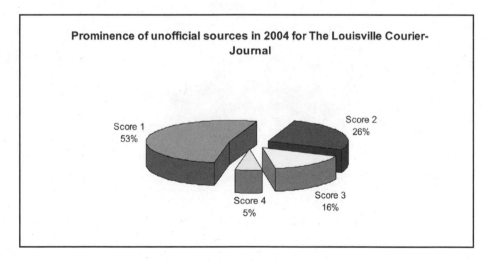

Prominence of unofficial sources in 2004 for The Louisville Courier-Journal

Score 1 53%
Score 2 26%
Score 3 16%
Score 4 5%

Miami Herald

1. Features vs. News

These pie charts show the total percentage of front page features and hard news in 2001 and 2004. There was a 126.7 percent increase in the number of features on the front page from 2001 to 2004.

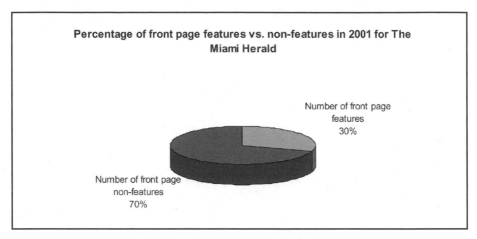

Percentage of front page features vs. non-features in 2001 for The Miami Herald

Number of front page features
30%

Number of front page non-features
70%

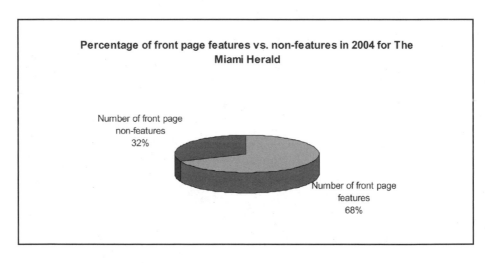

Percentage of front page features vs. non-features in 2004 for The Miami Herald

Number of front page non-features
32%

Number of front page features
68%

2. Feature Leads vs. Summary News Leads

This section measures all front page stories for summary news leads vs. anecdotal, descriptive, or humanistic leads on the studied dates in 2001 and 2004. There was a 42.9 percent increase in feature leads on the front page.

The Miami Herald in 2001 front page stories vs. feature leads

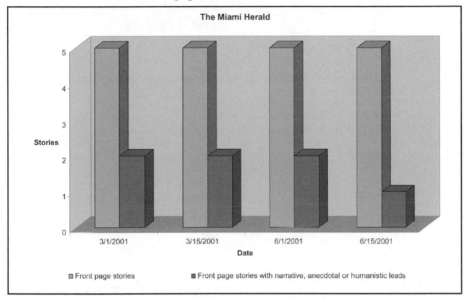

The Miami Herald in 2004 front page stories vs. feature leads

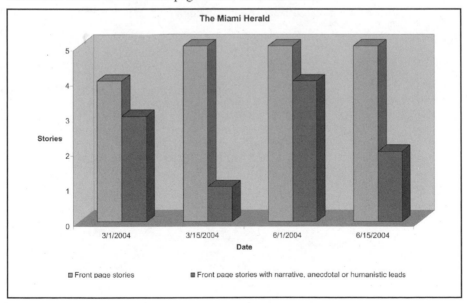

3. Use of Unofficial Sources

This section measures the prominence of unofficial sources in these same front page stories.
KEY:
    1 rating—up to 1 mention of unofficial source, lower in story
    2 rating—up to 2 mentions of unofficial sources, lower in story
    3 rating—up to 1 mention of unofficial source, higher in the story, with more graphs
    4 rating—several mentions of unofficial sources; most of story includes unofficial sources

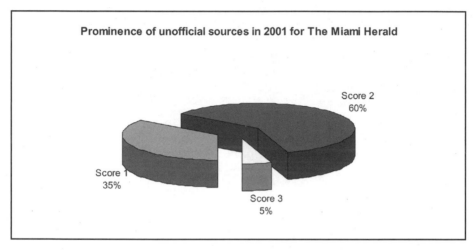

Prominence of unofficial sources in 2001 for The Miami Herald

Score 2 — 60%
Score 1 — 35%
Score 3 — 5%

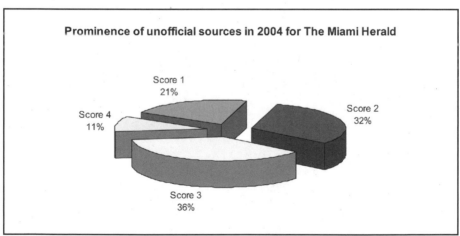

Prominence of unofficial sources in 2004 for The Miami Herald

Score 1 — 21%
Score 4 — 11%
Score 2 — 32%
Score 3 — 36%

Times-Picayune

1. Features vs. News

These pie charts show the total percentage of front page features and hard news in 2001 and 2004. There was a 39.1 percent increase in the number of features on the front page from 2001 to 2004.

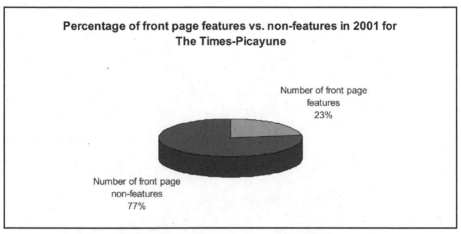

Percentage of front page features vs. non-features in 2001 for The Times-Picayune

Number of front page features
23%

Number of front page non-features
77%

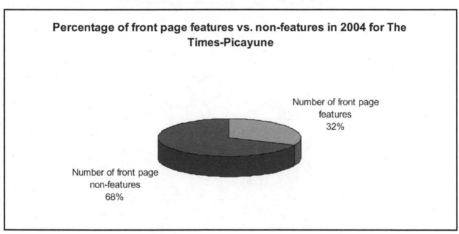

Percentage of front page features vs. non-features in 2004 for The Times-Picayune

Number of front page features
32%

Number of front page non-features
68%

2. Feature Leads vs. Summary News Leads

This section measures all front page stories for summary news leads vs. anecdotal, descriptive, or humanistic leads on the studied dates in 2001 and 2004. There was a 22.2 percent decrease in feature leads on the front page.

The Times-Picayune in 2001 front page stories vs. feature leads

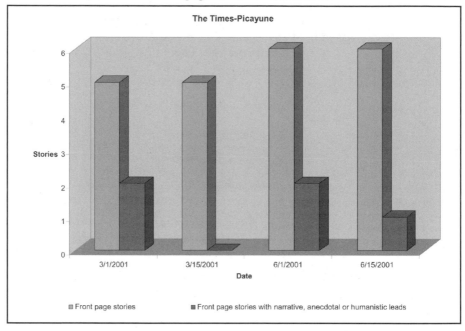

The Times-Picayune in 2004 front page stories vs. feature leads

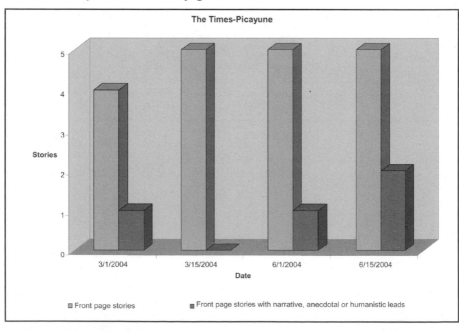

3. Use of Unofficial Sources

This section measures the prominence of unofficial sources in these same front page stories.
KEY:
    1 rating—up to 1 mention of unofficial source, lower in story
    2 rating—up to 2 mentions of unofficial sources, lower in story
    3 rating—up to 1 mention of unofficial source, higher in the story, with more graphs
    4 rating—several mentions of unofficial sources; most of story includes unofficial sources

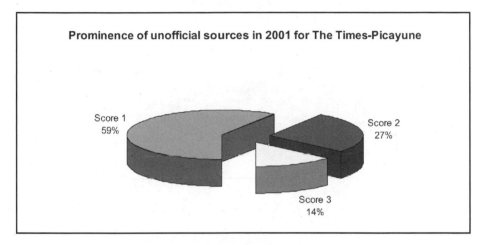

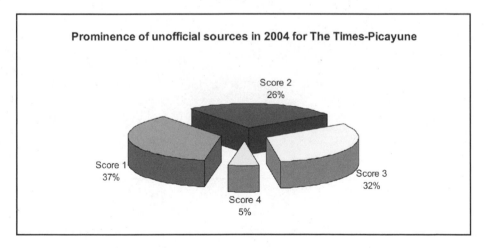

New York Times

1. Features vs. News

These pie charts show the total percentage of front page features and hard news in 2001 and 2004. There was a 42 percent increase in the number of features on the front page from 2001 to 2004.

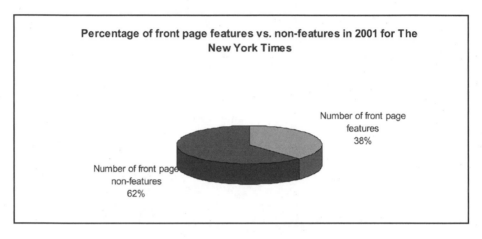

Percentage of front page features vs. non-features in 2001 for The New York Times

Number of front page features
38%

Number of front page non-features
62%

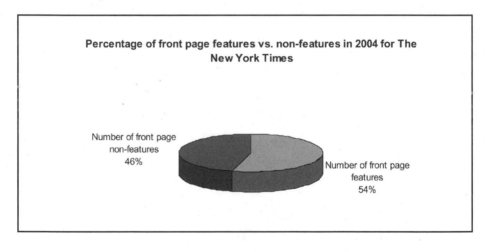

Percentage of front page features vs. non-features in 2004 for The New York Times

Number of front page non-features
46%

Number of front page features
54%

2. Feature Leads vs. Summary News Leads

This section measures all front page stories for summary news leads vs. anecdotal, descriptive, or humanistic leads on the studied dates in 2001 and 2004. There was a 13.2 percent decrease in feature leads on the front page.

The New York Times in 2001 front page stories vs. feature leads

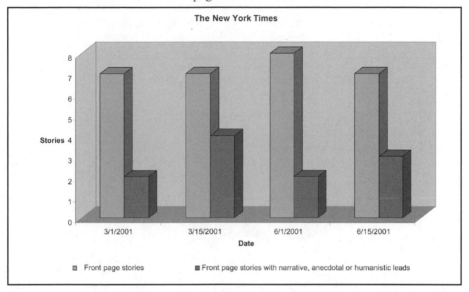

The New York Times in 2004 front page stories vs. feature leads

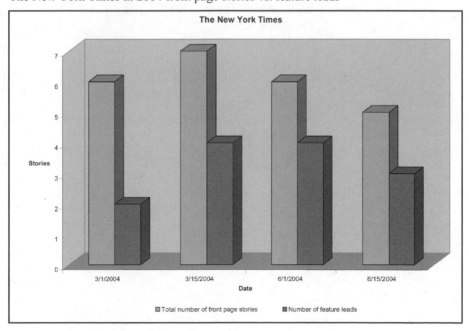

3. Use of Unofficial Sources

This section measures the prominence of unofficial sources in these same front page stories.
KEY:
   1 rating—up to 1 mention of unofficial source, lower in story
   2 rating—up to 2 mentions of unofficial sources, lower in story
   3 rating—up to 1 mention of unofficial source, higher in the story, with more graphs
   4 rating—several mentions of unofficial sources; most of story includes unofficial sources

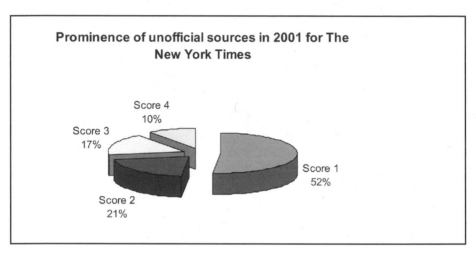

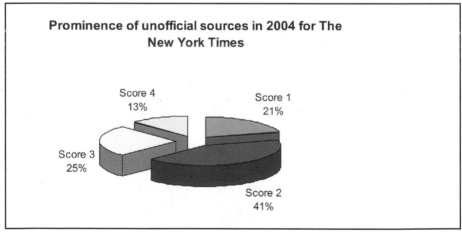

Omaha World-Herald

1. Features vs. News

These pie charts show the total percentage of front page features and hard news in 2001 and 2004. There was a 44.4 percent increase in the number of features on the front page from 2001 to 2004.

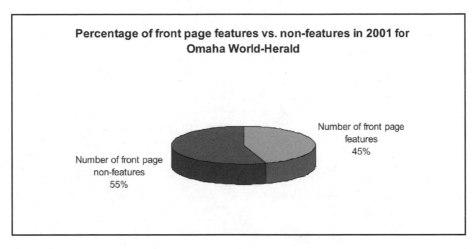

Percentage of front page features vs. non-features in 2001 for Omaha World-Herald

Number of front page features 45%

Number of front page non-features 55%

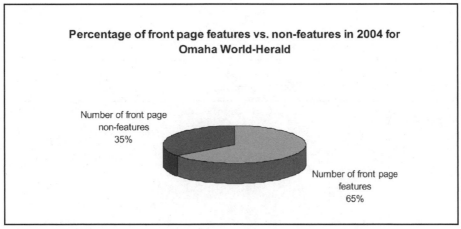

Percentage of front page features vs. non-features in 2004 for Omaha World-Herald

Number of front page non-features 35%

Number of front page features 65%

2. Feature Leads vs. Summary News Leads

This section measures all front page stories for summary news leads vs. anecdotal, descriptive, or humanistic leads on the studied dates in 2001 and 2004. There was a 2.5 percent increase in feature leads on the front page.

The Omaha World-Herald in 2001 front page stories vs. feature leads

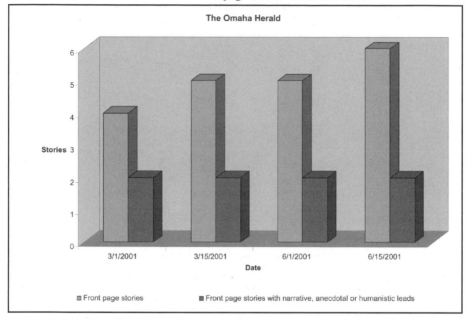

The Omaha World-Herald in 2004 front page stories vs. feature leads

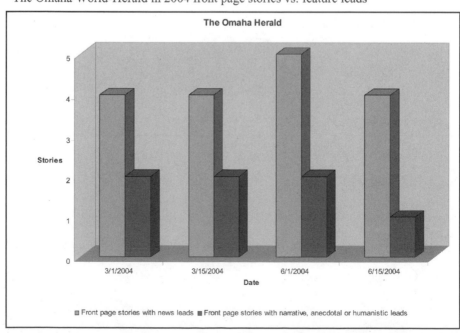

3. Use of Unofficial Sources

This section measures the prominence of unofficial sources in these same front page stories.
KEY:
    1 rating—up to 1 mention of unofficial source, lower in story
    2 rating—up to 2 mentions of unofficial sources, lower in story
    3 rating—up to 1 mention of unofficial source, higher in the story, with more graphs
    4 rating—several mentions of unofficial sources; most of story includes unofficial
    sources

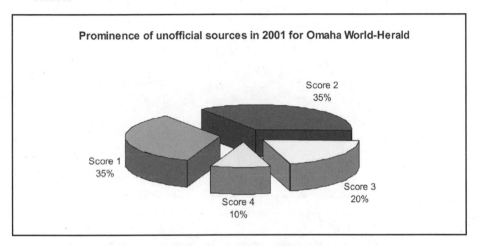

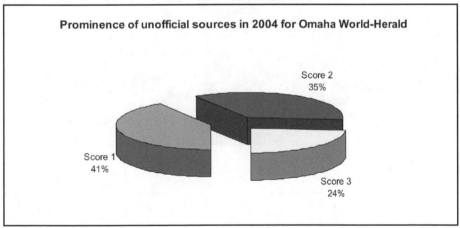

Portland Press Herald

1. Features vs. News

These pie charts show the total percentage of front page features and hard news in 2001 and 2004. There was an 80 percent increase in the number of features on the front page from 2001 to 2004.

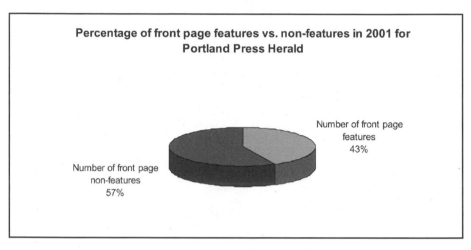

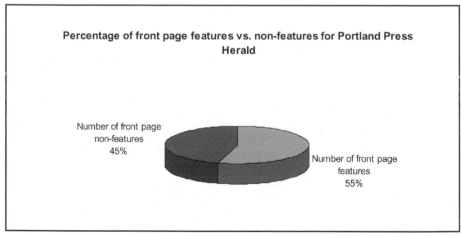

2. Feature Leads vs. Summary News Leads

This section measures all front page stories for summary news leads vs. anecdotal, descriptive, or humanistic leads on the studied dates in 2001 and 2004. There was a 16.3 percent decrease in feature leads on the front page.

The Portland Press Herald in 2001 front page stories vs. feature leads

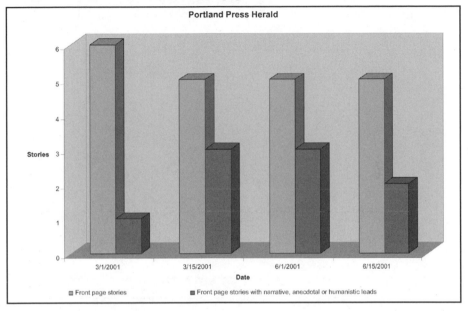

The Portland Press Herald in 2004 front page stories vs. feature leads

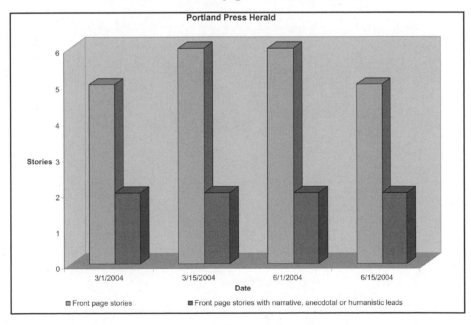

3. Use of Unofficial Sources

This section measures the prominence of unofficial sources in these same front page stories.
KEY:
    1 rating—up to 1 mention of unofficial source, lower in story
    2 rating—up to 2 mentions of unofficial sources, lower in story
    3 rating—up to 1 mention of unofficial source, higher in the story, with more graphs
    4 rating—several mentions of unofficial sources; most of story includes unofficial sources

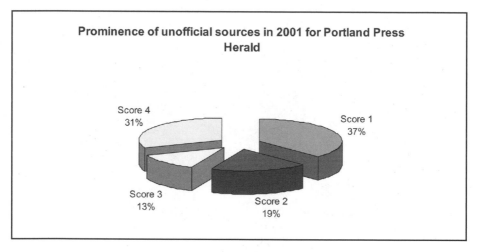

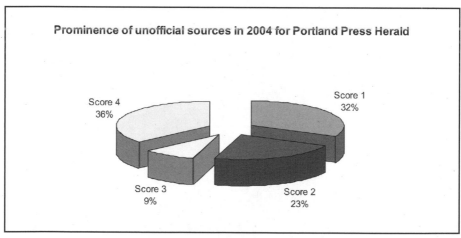

San Antonio Express-News

1. Features vs. News

These pie charts show the total percentage of front page features and hard news in 2001 and 2004. There was a 56.3 percent increase in the number of features on the front page from 2001 to 2004.

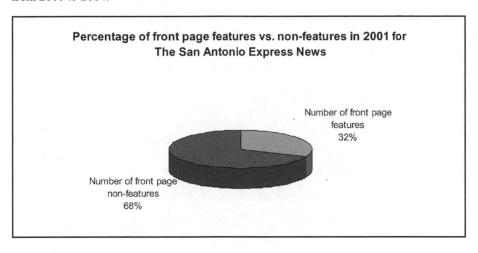

Percentage of front page features vs. non-features in 2001 for The San Antonio Express News

Number of front page features
32%

Number of front page non-features
68%

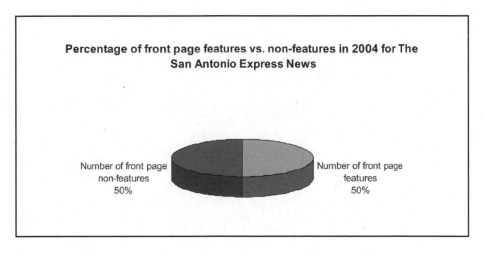

Percentage of front page features vs. non-features in 2004 for The San Antonio Express News

Number of front page non-features
50%

Number of front page features
50%

2. Feature Leads vs. Summary News Leads

This section measures all front page stories for summary news leads vs. anecdotal, descriptive, or humanistic leads on the studied dates in 2001 and 2004. There was a 190.5 percent increase in feature leads on the front page.

The San Antonio Express News in 2001 front page stories vs. feature leads

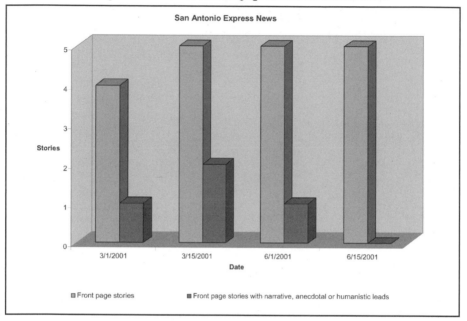

The San Antonio Express News in 2004 front page stories vs. feature leads

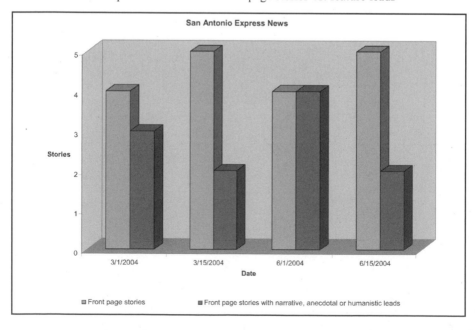

3. Use of Unofficial Sources

This section measures the prominence of unofficial sources in these same front page stories.
KEY:

    1 rating—up to 1 mention of unofficial source, lower in story
    2 rating—up to 2 mentions of unofficial sources, lower in story
    3 rating—up to 1 mention of unofficial source, higher in the story, with more graphs
    4 rating—several mentions of unofficial sources; most of story includes unofficial
    sources

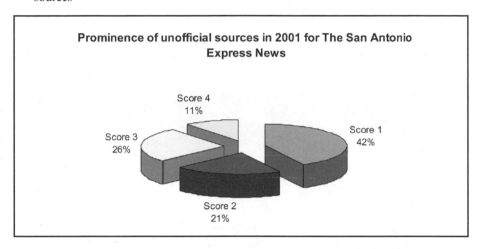

Prominence of unofficial sources in 2001 for The San Antonio Express News

Score 4 — 11%
Score 3 — 26%
Score 1 — 42%
Score 2 — 21%

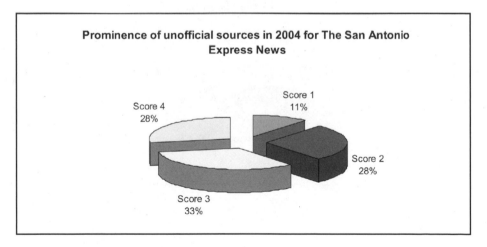

Prominence of unofficial sources in 2004 for The San Antonio Express News

Score 4 — 28%
Score 1 — 11%
Score 2 — 28%
Score 3 — 33%

San Jose Mercury News

1. Features vs. News

These pie charts show the total percentage of front page features and hard news in 2001 and 2004. There was a 3.8 percent decrease in the number of features on the front page from 2001 to 2004.

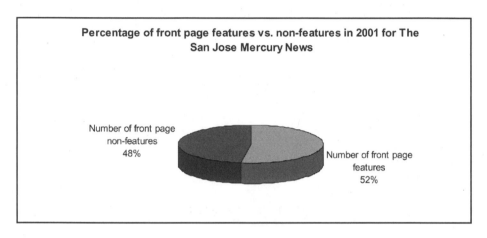

Percentage of front page features vs. non-features in 2001 for The San Jose Mercury News

Number of front page non-features
48%

Number of front page features
52%

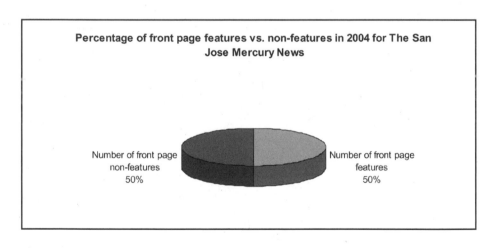

Percentage of front page features vs. non-features in 2004 for The San Jose Mercury News

Number of front page non-features
50%

Number of front page features
50%

2. Feature Leads vs. Summary News Leads

This section measures all front page stories for summary news leads vs. anecdotal, descriptive, or humanistic leads on the studied dates in 2001 and 2004. There was a 33.3 percent increase in feature leads on the front page.

The San Jose Mercury News in 2001 front page stories vs. feature leads

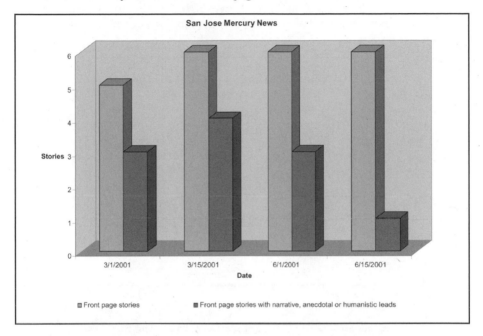

The San Jose Mercury News in 2004 front page stories vs. feature leads

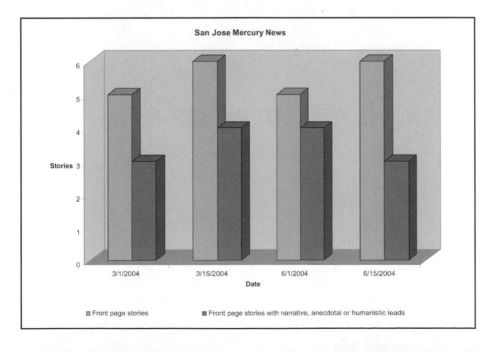

3. Use of Unofficial Sources

This section measures the prominence of unofficial sources in these same front page stories.
KEY:
    1 rating—up to 1 mention of unofficial source, lower in story
    2 rating—up to 2 mentions of unofficial sources, lower in story
    3 rating—up to 1 mention of unofficial source, higher in the story, with more graphs
    4 rating—several mentions of unofficial sources; most of story includes unofficial sources

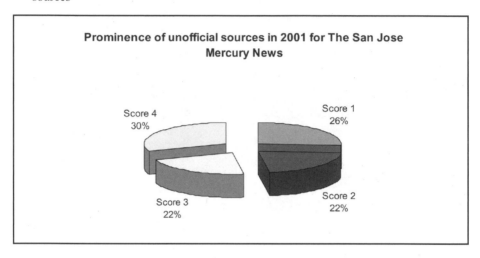

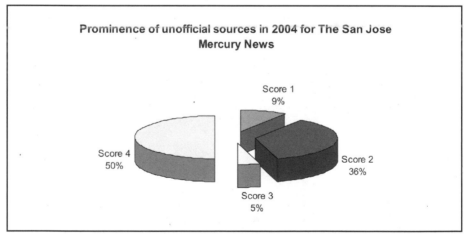

Seattle Times

1. Features vs. News

These pie charts show the total percentage of front page features and hard news in 2001 and 2004. There was a 7.3 percent increase in the number of features on the front page from 2001 to 2004.

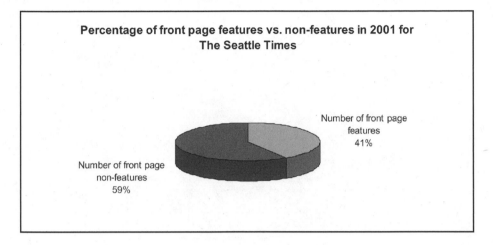

Percentage of front page features vs. non-features in 2001 for The Seattle Times

Number of front page features 41%

Number of front page non-features 59%

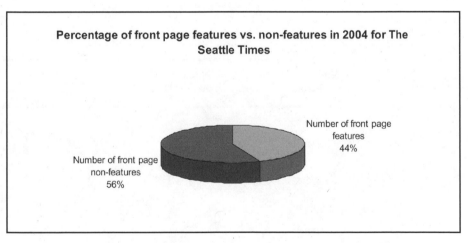

Percentage of front page features vs. non-features in 2004 for The Seattle Times

Number of front page features 44%

Number of front page non-features 56%

2. Feature Leads vs. Summary News Leads

This section measures all front page stories for summary news leads vs. anecdotal, descriptive, or humanistic leads on the studied dates in 2001 and 2004. There was a 72.4 percent increase in feature leads on the front page.

The Seattle Times in 2001 front page stories vs. feature leads

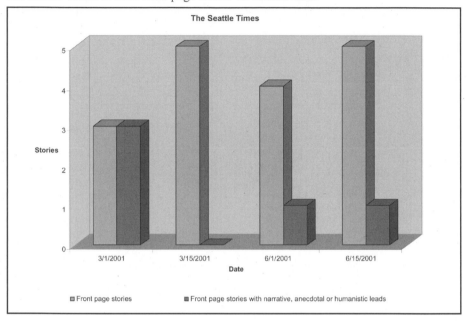

The Seattle Times in 2004 front page stories vs. feature leads

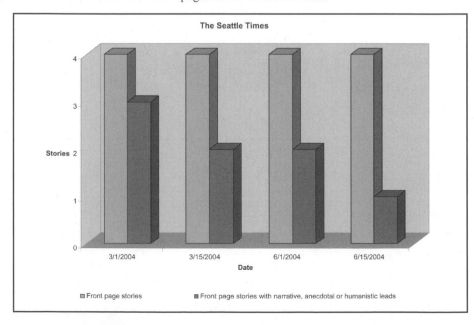

3. Use of Unofficial Sources

This section measures the prominence of unofficial sources in these same front page stories.

KEY: ˙
1 rating—up to 1 mention of unofficial source, lower in story
2 rating—up to 2 mentions of unofficial sources, lower in story
3 rating—up to 1 mention of unofficial source, higher in the story, with more graphs
4 rating—several mentions of unofficial sources; most of story includes unofficial sources

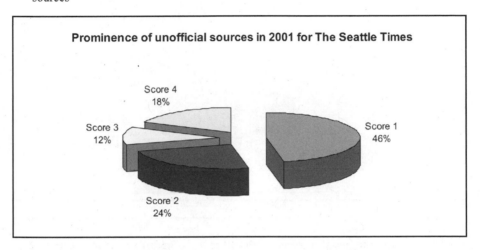

Prominence of unofficial sources in 2001 for The Seattle Times

Score 4 18%
Score 3 12%
Score 1 46%
Score 2 24%

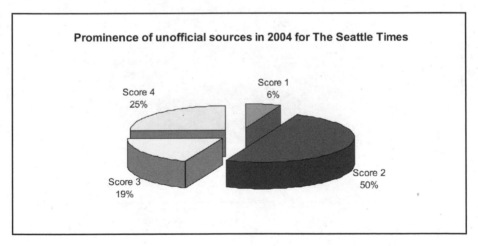

Prominence of unofficial sources in 2004 for The Seattle Times

Score 4 25%
Score 1 6%
Score 3 19%
Score 2 50%

St. Louis Post-Dispatch

1. Features vs. News

These pie charts show the total percentage of front page features and hard news in 2001 and 2004. There was a 47.4 percent increase in the number of features on the front page from 2001 to 2004.

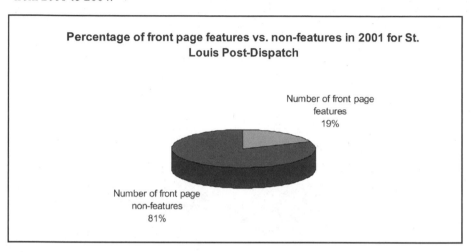

Percentage of front page features vs. non-features in 2001 for St. Louis Post-Dispatch

Number of front page features
19%

Number of front page non-features
81%

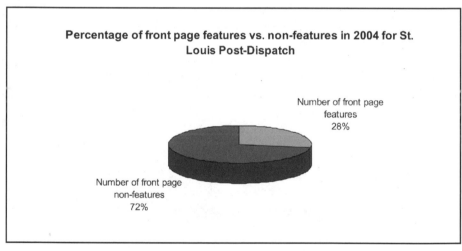

Percentage of front page features vs. non-features in 2004 for St. Louis Post-Dispatch

Number of front page features
28%

Number of front page non-features
72%

2. Feature Leads vs. Summary News Leads

This section measures all front page stories for summary news leads vs. anecdotal, descriptive, or humanistic leads on the studied dates in 2001 and 2004. There was a 33.3 percent increase in feature leads on the front page.

The St. Louis Post-Dispatch in 2001 front page stories vs. feature leads

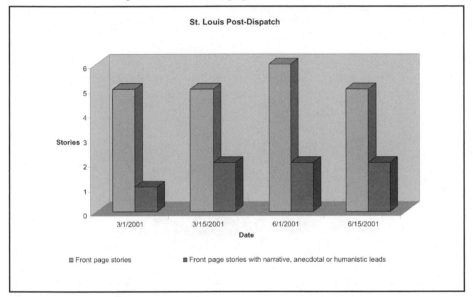

St. Louis Post-Dispatch in 2004 front page stories vs. feature leads

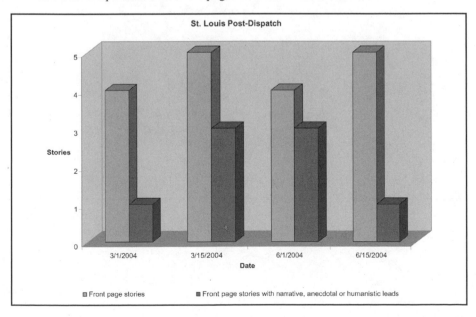

3. Use of Unofficial Sources

This section measures the prominence of unofficial sources in these same front page stories:

KEY:

    1 rating—up to 1 mention of unofficial source, lower in story

    2 rating—up to 2 mentions of unofficial sources, lower in story

    3 rating—up to 1 mention of unofficial source, higher in the story, with more graphs

    4 rating—several mentions of unofficial sources; most of story includes unofficial sources

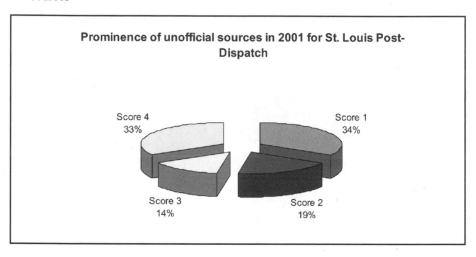

Prominence of unofficial sources in 2001 for St. Louis Post-Dispatch

Score 4 33%
Score 1 34%
Score 3 14%
Score 2 19%

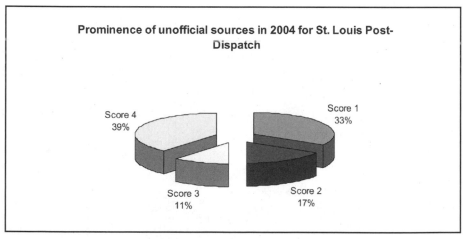

Prominence of unofficial sources in 2004 for St. Louis Post-Dispatch

Score 4 39%
Score 1 33%
Score 3 11%
Score 2 17%

Washington Post

1. Features vs. News

These pie charts show the total percentage of front page features and hard news in 2001 and 2004. There was a 44.4 percent increase in the number of features on the front page from 2001 to 2004.

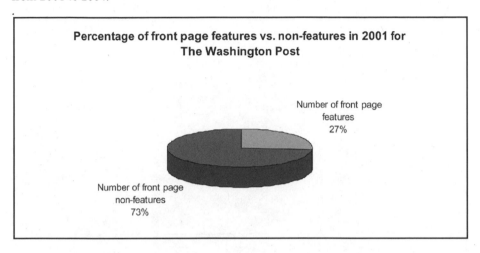

Percentage of front page features vs. non-features in 2001 for The Washington Post

Number of front page features
27%

Number of front page non-features
73%

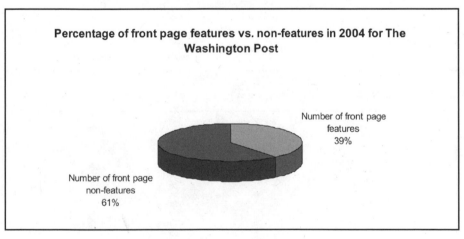

Percentage of front page features vs. non-features in 2004 for The Washington Post

Number of front page features
39%

Number of front page non-features
61%

2. Feature Leads vs. Summary News Leads

This section measures all front page stories for summary news leads vs. anecdotal, descriptive, or humanistic leads on the studied dates in 2001 and 2004. There was a 35.1 percent increase in feature leads on the front page.

The Washington Post in 2001 front page stories vs. feature leads

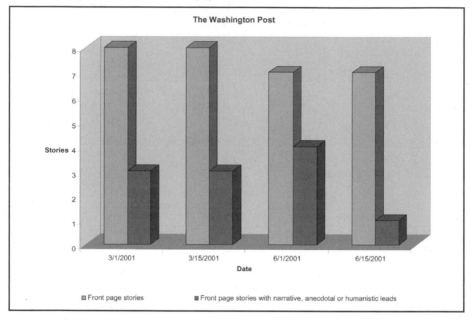

The Washington Post in 2004 front page stories vs. feature leads

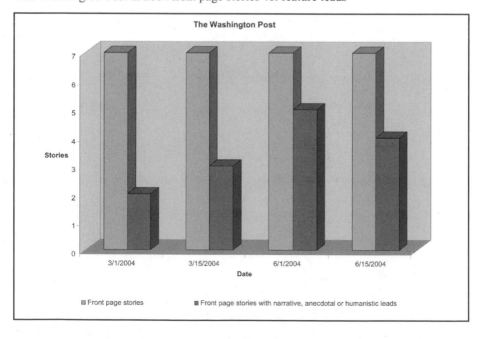

3. Use of Unofficial Sources

This section measures the prominence of unofficial sources in these same front page stories.
KEY:

1 rating—up to 1 mention of unofficial source, lower in story
2 rating—up to 2 mentions of unofficial sources, lower in story
3 rating—up to 1 mention of unofficial source, higher in the story, with more graphs
4 rating—several mentions of unofficial sources; most of story includes unofficial sources

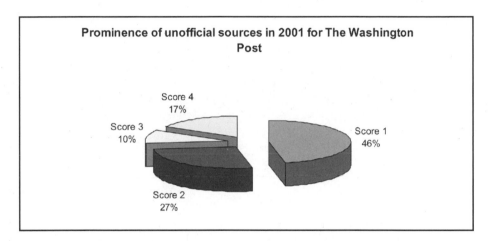

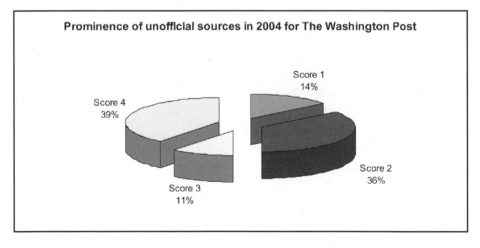

Notes

Introduction: Everyman and Everywoman on the Front Page

1. Leonard Downie Jr., introduction to *The Century: History as It Happened on the Front Page of the Capital's Newspaper,* ed. Michael Farquhar, Mary Hadar, and Robert Barkin.
2. David Croteau and William Hoynes, *The Business of Media: Corporate Media and the Public Interest,* 189, 7, 171.
3. Lev Grossman, "You—Yes, You—Are Time's Person of the Year," *Time,* Dec. 17, 2006, http://www.time.com/time/printout/0,8816,1570810,00.html#.
4. Rick Edmonds, phone interview with author, Dec. 20, 2006.
5. Ibid.
6. James T. Hamilton, *All the News That's Fit to Sell,* 10.
7. Top 10 Most Read New York Times stories, Dec. 14, 2006, http://www.nytimes.com/2006/12/03/world/middleeast/03military.html?ex=1181451600&en=41324795eaad1313&ei=5087&excamp=mkt_at1; http://www.nytimes.com/2006/12/04/us/04detain.html?ex=1181451600&en=d58e5bb93ae22a66&ei=5087&excamp=mkt_at2; http://www.nytimes.com/2006/12/08/world/middleeast/08diplo.html?ex=1181451600&en=89238c88009b4f8f&ei=5087&excamp=mkt_at3; http://www.nytimes.com/2006/11/29/science/30computecnd.html?ex=1181451600&en=b6e37ebf2f33883a&ei=5087&excamp=mkt_at4; http://www.nytimes.com/2006/12/02/us/02child.html?ex=1181451600&en=0de9c781cd024c23&ei=5087&excamp=mkt_at5; http://www.nytimes.com/2006/12/03/magazine/03arabs.html?ex=1181451600&en=c2a93022121d5a92&ei=5087&excamp=mkt_at6; http://www.nytimes.com/2006/12/08/health/08Kids.html?ex=1181451600&en=70a85891d162a834&ei=5087&excamp=mkt_at7; http://www.nytimes.com/2006/12/04/washington/04candidates.html?ex=1181451600&en=6f27c753ef7f9560&ei=5087&excamp=mkt_at8; http://www.nytimes.com/2006/12/05/movies/05apoc.html?ex=1181451600&en=719c8c8b146a7acc&ei=5087&excamp=mkt_at9; http://www.nytimes.com/2006/11/29/dining/29preg.html?ex=1181538000&en=6c6e85af699f7ed8&ei=5087&excamp=mkt_at10.
8. AMC Gremlin, http://en.wikipedia.org/wiki/AMC_Gremlin.
9. Pablo Boczkowski, *Digitizing the News: Innovation in Online Newspapers,* 7.
10. Orland Kay Armstrong, "Beginnings of the Modern Newspaper: A Comparative Study of St. Louis Dailies from 1875–1925," *University of Missouri Bulletin* 27, no. 5, Journalism Series, no. 39 (Feb. 1, 1926): 17.
11. Croteau and Hoynes, *Business of Media,* 9.
12. Geneva Overholser, "On Behalf of Journalism: A Manifesto for Change," Annenberg Public Policy Center, University of Pennsylvania, 18 http://www

.annenbergpublicpolicycenter.org/Overholser/20061011_JournStudy.pdf (accessed Mar. 15, 2007), 2.

13. Philip Meyer, *The Vanishing Newspaper: Saving Journalism in the Information Age,* 39.

14. Donna Shaw, "Remaking the Front Page," *American Journalism Review,* (June/July 2006): 1, www.ajr.org/article_printable.asp?id=4116. (accessed online May 2, 2006)

15. Hamilton, *All the News That's Fit to Sell,* 240–41.

16. Wikipedia, "Everyman Definition," www.en.wikipedia.org/wiki/Everyman (accessed May 20, 2006).

17. Norman Sims, Wikipedia comments presented at the AEJMC Conference, San Francisco, CA, Aug. 2, 2006.

18. Chris Anderson, *The Long Tail: Why The Future of Business Is Selling Less of More,* 66.

19. Philip Roth, "Everyman," *Publishers Weekly,* http://www.amazon.com/gp/product/061873516X/qid=1147122027/sr=2–1/ref=pd_bbs_b_2_1/103–0680509-6891836?s=books&v=glance&n=283155 (accessed online May 8, 2006).

20. EveryWoman Magazine, www.everywomanonline.com/index.html (accessed online May 30, 2006).

21. Everywoman Magazine in the U.K., http://www.redmagazine.co.uk/thebusiness/about_everywoman.html (accessed Jan. 11, 2007).

22. World News Media, www.wnnmedia.com and www.everyman.com (accessed Aug. 7, 2006).

23. David Meeks, "Katrina: On the Ground in New Orleans," Crain Lecture, Northwestern University, Apr. 24, 2006.

24. Frank P. Glass, "The New Journalism: News and the Newspaper," *University of Missouri Bulletin* 24, no. 15, Journalism Series, no. 28, 19.

25. Ibid., 19.

26. Rick Berke, email to *newsroom@nytimes.com,* May 5, 2006, http://www.gawke.com/news/new-york-times/how-to-improve-times-writing-a-novella-172281.php (accessed May 9, 2006).

27. Ibid.

28. Amanda Bennett, "A Shrinking Staff Propels a Newspaper's Transformation," *Nieman Reports* (spring 2006): e11.

29. Shaw, "Remaking the Front Page," 7.

30. Ibid., 8.

31. Boczkowski, *Digitizing the News,* 6–7.

32. John Hyde and Margaret Engel, mass mailing letter "To our friends in journalism," July 3, 2006.

33. The International Center for Journalists, email message, Dec. 20, 2006.

34. Leslie Cauley, "NSA Has Massive Database of Americans' Phonecalls," *USA Today,*   http://www.usatoday.com/news/washington/2006–05-10-nsa_x.htm (accessed May 12, 2006).

35. Rick Edmonds, "Letter from the Wall Street Meetings: Content Comes Center Stage," Poynteronline, www.poynter.org/content/content_print.asp?id=115082&custom (accessed Dec. 11, 2006).

36. Jody Brannon, "Our Nose for News," www.specials.msn.com/Inside MSN/default.aspx (accessed Dec. 7, 2006).

37. M. Cohn, "Google Delivers Newspaper Ads," RedHerring, www.redherring.com/printarticle.aspx?a+19572&sector=Industries (accessed Dec. 14, 2006).

38. Robert MacMillian, "Yahoo in Ad Partnership with Newspapers," Reuters, Nov. 20, 2006, http://today.reuters.com/misc/PrinterFriendlyPopup.aspx?type =internetNews&storyID=2 (accessed Nov. 28, 2006).

39. "Yahoo! Forms Strategic Partnership with Consortium of More than 150 Newspapers across the U.S.," http://www.belo.com/pressRelease.x2?release =20061120–1069.html (accessed Nov. 22, 2006).

40. MacMillian, "Yahoo in Ad Partnership."

41. Stephen Crane, www.wsu.edu/~campbelld/crane/index.html (accessed Apr. 20, 2006).

42. Ernest Hemingway, www.ernest.hemingway.com/reporter.htm (accessed Apr. 20, 2006).

Chapter 1 Should the Personal Became Universal?

1. Jack Lule, *Daily News, Eternal Stories: The Mythological Role of Journalism*, 121, 4.

2. Charles Dickens, *The Daily News,* http://www.infed.org/archives/e-texts/ dickens_ragged_schools.htm (accessed Apr. 10, 2006).

3. Charles Dana, *New York Sun,* http://www.bartleby.com/227/1308.html (accessed Apr. 10, 2006).

4. Stephen Crane, "Stephen Crane's Own Story," http://www2.sunysuffolk .edu/lewiss/CraneStory.htm (accessed June 2, 2006)

5. Graham Greene, *The Human Factor* (New York: Avon Books, 1978).

6. Quote of Karen Magnuson at *Rochester Democrat and Chronicle,* in Donna Shaw, *American Journalism Review* (June/July 2006): 3, www.ajr.org/article_printable .asp?id=4116 (accessed May 30, 2006).

7. Sara Olkron, "Buildings Redeemed by Faith," *Miami Herald,* Mar. 1, 2004, A1.

8. Lyndsey Layton, "Officer Shoves, Arrests Pregnant Woman over Loud Call," *Washington Post,* Sept. 28, 2004, A1.

9. Barbie Zelizer, interview with author, Cambridge, MA, Dec. 5, 2004.

10. Jeffrey Gettleman, "The Reach of War: The Insurgency; 21 Killed in Iraq and Dozens Hurt in Bomb Attacks," *New York Times,* June 15, 2004, A1.

11. Croteau and Hoynes, *Business of Media,* 174.

12. E. L. Doctorow, "Apprehending Reality," Crain Lecture Series speech, North-western University, Oct. 13, 2004.

13. Boczkowski, *Digitizing the News,* 189.

14. Reid Forgrave and Erica Solvig, "Sprawl Squeezes Parkland: Ball Fields, Green Space Lose to Growth, Housing," *Cincinnati Enquirer,* Mar. 15, 2004, A1.

15. David Craig, *The Ethics of the Story,* 27, 37, 38.

16. Steve James, interview with author, Oak Park, IL, July 27, 2005.

17. National Public Radio, aired promotion, Feb. 2006.

18. American Public Media, "The Story," www.thestory.org/special-features/ your-stories (accessed Jan. 5, 2007).

19. ABC-TV, "Brat Camp," http://abc.go.com/primetime/bratcamp/index .html (accessed Dec. 10, 2006).

20. Scott Peterson, http://www.cnn.com/2004/LAW/11/12/peterson.verdict/ index.html (accessed Nov. 15, 2006); Jennifer Wilbanks, http://msnbc.msn.com/ id/7692019/ (accessed July 5, 2005); Matthew Winkler, http://www.cnn.com/ 2006/US/03/24/minister.slain/ (accessed Mar. 26, 2006).

21. Ted Koppel, "The Fallen," ABC-TV *Nightline,* Apr. 30, 2004, http://abcnews.go.com/Nightline/story?id=786279&page=1.

22. Saira Khan, "Saira's Diary," msnbc.com, http://www.msnbc.msn.com/id/8511900/ (accessed June 19, 2006).

23. Michael Behr, "Eyewitnesses to Hiroshima," *Time,* Aug. 1, 2005. http://www.time.com/time/asia/mediakit/home/article/0,17540,1086721,00.html (accessed Aug. 10, 2005).

24. Associated Press, "Optional Leads Announced," http://poynter.org/forum/default.asp?id=misc&DGPCrSrt=&DGPCrPg=6; http://www.poynter.org/column.asp?id=45&aid=79847 (accessed Mar. 13, 2006).

25. Mike Dorning, "Families Endure Private War," *Chicago Tribune,* Mar. 29, 2004, A1.

26. Flynn McRoberts, "Bite-Mark Verdict Faces New Scrutiny," *Chicago Tribune,* Nov. 29, 2004, A1.

27. Bonnie Miller Rubin, "You're Accepted, but with a Catch," *Chicago Tribune,* Nov. 29, 2004, A1.

28. Michael Martinez, "Rescue of Missions Stirs Flap," *Chicago Tribune,* Nov. 29, 2004, A1.

29. Tom Hundley, "Warming Up to Language Irish Once Found Uncool," *Chicago Tribune,* Nov. 29, 2004, A1.

30. Rodney Benson and Erick Neveu, eds., *Bourdieu and the Journalistic Field,* 41.

31. Jack Hart, interview with author, Cambridge, MA, Dec. 4, 2004.

32. Ken Fuson, interview with author, Cambridge, MA, Dec. 4, 2004.

33. Laurie Hertzel, interview with author, Cambridge, MA, Dec. 4, 2004.

34. Roy Peter Clark, "Writing Tool No. 20: Narrative Opportunities," Poynter Online, http://www.poynter.org/content/content_view.asp?id=70403 (accessed Jan. 20, 2005).

35. Hart, interview, Dec. 4, 2004.

36. Blair Kamin and Thomas A. Corfman, "Tallest Tower to Twist Rivals," *Chicago Tribune,* July 26, 2005, A1.

37. Barbara Rose and Stephen Frankline, "Federation's Leaders 'Doing a New Budget,'" *Chicago Tribune,* July 26, 2005, A1.

38. Margaret Ramirez, "Mormons' New True Believers," *Chicago Tribune,* July 26, 2005, A1.

39. Ofelia Casillas, "Music Makes the Difference," *Chicago Tribune,* July 26, 2005, A1.

40. Wire story, "A Cold One's Less Cool These Days, Poll Finds," *Chicago Tribune,* July 26, 2005, A1.

41. Jack Fuller, *News Values: Ideas for an Information Age,* 227.

42. Christopher Daly, phone interview with author, Oct. 14, 2005.

43. Jack Rosenberry, interview with author, San Antonio, TX, Aug. 4, 2005.

44. Ibid.

45. Rosemary Armao, interview with author, Portland, OR, Sept. 11, 2004.

46. Daniel Okrent, "Thirteen Things I Meant to Write about but Never Did," *New York Times,* May 22, 2005, http://www.nytimes.com/2005/05/22/weekinreview/22okrent.html?ex=1274414400&en=62160b06b9929666&ei=5088&partner=rssnyt&emc=rss (accessed May 25, 2005).

47. Madeleine Blais, "Zepp's Last Stand," *Miami Herald,* http://www.pulitzer.org/cgi-bin/year.pl?1385,26.

48. Tracy Kidder, "The Temptation toward Advocacy: Reporting the Tragic," speech, Nieman Narrative Conference, Cambridge, MA, Dec. 4, 2004.

49. Julia Keller, "After the Storm's Fury: Left in Tatters by a Tornado, a Small Town Remembers, Rebuilds and Begins to Recover," *Chicago Tribune*, Dec. 7, 2004, A1.

50. Barbara Iverson, phone interview with author, July 28, 2005.

51. Robert S. Boynton, *The New Journalism: Conversations with America's Best Non-fiction Writers on Their Craft*, xxix.

52. Walt Harrington, interview with author, Cambridge, MA, Dec. 4, 2004.

53. Alex Kotlowitz, interview with author, Oak Park, IL, July 27, 2005.

54. Doctorow, "Apprehending Reality."

55. Alma Guillermoprieto, "Dancing with Your Subject: Narrative for Topics Your Readers Think Are Boring," speech, Nieman Narrative Conference, Cambridge, MA, Dec. 5, 2004.

56. Dan Gillmor, *We the Media: Grassroots Journalism by the People, for the People*, xii.

57. Dinesh C. Sharma, "Yahoo to Offer CNN/ABC Video Feeds," news.com, http://news.com.com/Yahoo+to+offer+CNN%2C+ABC+video+feeds/2100–102 5_3–5813499.html (accessed Aug. 4, 2005).

58. "Yahoo Expands News Video with CNN and ABC," AdAge.com, http://broadcastengineering.com/news/Yahoo-daily-news-feeds-20050814/ (accessed Aug. 2, 2005).

59. Rick Edmonds, "2005 State of the News Media Report," Newspapers, http://www.stateofthenewsmedia.org/2005/narrative_newspapers_intro.asp?cat =1&media=2 (accessed Jan. 5, 2006).

60. Ralph Waldo Emerson, "Goethe; or the Writer from Representative Men," http://rwe.org/works/Representative_Men_6_Goethe.html (accessed Sept. 8, 2005).

61. Anderson, *The Long Tail*, 185.

Chapter 2 The Results: An Anecdotal Companion to History

1. Shaw, "Remaking the Front Page," 8.

2. *Bacon's Newspaper/Magazine Directory*, Newspaper ownership (Chicago: Bacon's Information, Inc., 2005).

3. Days of the week determined on perpetual calendar for May 7, 1945; Jan. 4, 2006; Mar. 11, 2004; Nov. 22, 1963; Dec. 19, 1998; July 20, 1969, http://users.chariot .net.au/~gmarts/calendar (accessed Feb. 10, 2006).

4. Shaw, "Remaking the Front Page," 18.

5. Readership Institute, Northwestern University, "Newspaper Industry Content Analysis Report: Data Tables and Definitions," http://www.readership .org/content/content_analysis/data/industry_content_report.pdf (accessed Feb. 10, 2006).

6. Tom Callinan, email message to author, Oct. 28, 2005.

7. Michael Ray Smith, *Featurewriting.net: A Guide to Writing in the Electronic Age*, 75.

8. Dennis Hooey, "Stranded Seals Pose a Puzzle," *Portland Press Herald*, Mar. 1, 2001, A1.

9. Fred Fedler et al., *Reporting for the Media*, 335.

10. Brian Brooks et al., *News Reporting and Writing*, 532.

11. Carla Johnson, *Twenty-First-Century Feature Writing*, 4.

12. Barbie Zelizer, "Definitions of Journalism," in *The Press* (New York: Oxford University, 2005), 67, 71.

13. Andrew DeMillo, "Numbers of Homeless Climb during Hard Times," *Arkansas Democrat-Gazette*, Dec. 15, 2002, A1.

14. Patrick Strawbridge, "A Rousing Welcome in the Bluffs," *Omaha World-Herald*, Mar. 1, 2001, A1.

15. Edmonds, "2005 State of the Media."

16. Marc Weingarten, *The Gang That Wouldn't Write Straight: Wolfe, Thompson, Didion, and the New Journalism Revolution*, 13.

17. Charles Forelle, "Schools Score High Marks but Sink in Rankings," *Miami Herald*, June 1, 2001, A1.

18. Phil Taubman, "Who Can Be Trusted? A Seminar on Sourcing," speech, University of Southern California Annenberg School of Communication, http://ascweb.usc.edu/asc.php?pageID=110&story=344 (accessed June 5, 2006).

19. Roy Peter Clark and Christopher Scanlan, *America's Best Newspaper Writing* (New York: Bedford/St. Martin's, 2006), 165.

20. Michael Schudson, *The Power of News*, 25.

21. Callinan, email message to author, Oct. 2, 2005.

22. Andrew L. Wang and Dave Wischnowsky, "City News Becomes the News at Its Closing," *Chicago Tribune*, Jan. 1, 2006, Metro section, 1.

23. Philip L. Graham, "Rough Draft," Bartleby.com., http://www.bartleby.com/63/9/8109.html (accessed Aug. 17, 2006).

24. Thomas L. Friedman, *The World Is Flat: A Brief History of the Twenty-First Century*, 10–11.

25. Meyer, *Vanishing Newspaper*, 43.

Chapter 3 Content as Commodity: Giving Readers What They Want

1. Boczkowski, *Digitizing the News*, 6–7.

2. "New Media Keeps the Mobile Nomadic Consumer 'Connected,'" Center for Media Research, Dec. 20, 2006.

3. Newspaper Section Readership 2005, *Mediamark Research Inc.*, http://www.naa.org/artpage.cfm?AID=6426&SID=1113 (accessed Feb. 23, 2006).

4. "60 Million Americans Who File Share," http://www.eff.org/share/ (accessed Feb. 25, 2006); "American Idol May 2006 vote," http://www.msnbc.msn.com/id/12956943/ (accessed June 1, 2006).

5. John Horrigan and Lee Rainie, "The Internet's Growing Role in Life's Major Moments," Pew Internet and American Life Project, 2006.

6. "Sprint . . . Reaches 60 Million People," Dec. 12, 2006. http://www2.sprint.com/mr/news_dtl.do?id=14680 (accessed Feb. 22, 2007).

7. Patricia Whalen, "The Changing Landscape of Print and Online Media," *NewsMarket*, Aug. 25, 2006, 4.

8. Ron Martin, "Utility," *The Local News Handbook*, July 20, 1999, 1.

9. Hazel Reinhardt, email message to author, Dec. 22, 2006.

10. Charles Layton, "Market Research Is Supposed to Tell Us, but Often It's Confusing, Contradictory or Just Plain Wrong," *American Journalism Review* (Mar. 1999): 4.

11. Reinhardt, email message to author.

12. Tim Porter, "If Newspapers Are to Rise Again: Reinvent or Die. It's That Simple," *Nieman Reports* (spring 2006): e4.

13. David Levy, "A Publishing Workflow Pushes the Envelope," Apple-Pro/Design-*Atlanta Journal-Constitution*, Feb. 2006, http://www.apple.com/pro/design/atlantajournal/ (accessed May 15, 2006).

14. John B. Horrigan, "Online News," Pew Internet and American Life Project, Mar. 22, 2006. http://www.pewinternet.org/pdfs/PIP_News.and.Broadband.pdf (accessed July 10, 2006).

15. Newspaper Association of America, "Daily and Sunday Newspapers 2005 Readers per Copy," Newspaper Association of America, http://www.naa.org/artpage.cfm?AID=5137&SID=1022 (accessed Feb. 23, 2006).

16. Merrill Brown, "Abandoning the News: What's the Future of the News Business? This Report to Carnegie Corporation of New York Offers Some Provocative Ideas," *Journalism's Crisis of Confidence: A Challenge for the Next Generation, a Report of the Carnegie Corporation,* May 2006, 44.

17. Sarah Ellison and Matthew Karniteschnig, "For Tribune, a Breakup Offers No Guarantees," *Wall Street Journal,* June 9, 2006, C1.

18. Michael Stoll, "Knight Ridder Buyout Fears," Alternet.org, http://www.alternet.org/story/33571/ (accessed Mar. 15, 2006).

19. Katharine Q. Seelye, "McClatchy to Resell Twelve Papers It's Buying," *New York Times,* Mar. 14, 2006, C6.

20. Michael Stoll, "Knight Ridder breakup May Create Unprecedented Concentration of Ownership in Bay Area Newspapers," Alternet.org, http://www.gradethenews.org/2006/mcclatchy.htm (accessed Mar. 14, 2006).

21. Ira Teinowitz, "Former Ad Man and PR Maven Now True Believer in Newspapers," *Advertising Age,* www.adage.com/print?article_id=109450 (accessed May 31, 2006).

22. Newspaper Association of America, "Daily and Sunday Newspapers 2005 Readers per Copy," Newspaper Association of America, http://www.naa.org/artpage.cfm?AID=5137&SID=1022 (accessed Feb. 23, 2006).

23. Project for Excellence in Journalism, "State of the News Media 2005," http://www.stateofthenewsmedia.org/journalist_survey_commentary.asp (accessed Oct. 18, 2004).

24. Audit Bureau of Circulations Report 2005, http://www.accessabc.com/reader/top150.htm. http://www.infoplease.com/ipea/A0004420.html (accessed Feb. 25, 2006).

25. Van Essen Dirks and Murray, 2005 Year-end Report, http://www.dirksvanessen.com/article.asp?newsId=152&categoyryId=1 (accessed Jan. 19, 2006).

26. Edmonds, "2005 State of the Media."

27. Robert Coen, Universal McCann, "State of the News Media 2005."

28. Katharine Q. Seelye, "U.S. Newspaper Circulation Fell 2.5 Percent in Latest Period," *New York Times,* May 9, 2006.

29. Edward Atorino, "Wall Street Transcript: Newspaper Problems Featured in Wall Street Transcript Media Issue," http://biz.yahoo.com/twst/051213/zbc801.html (accessed Jan. 9, 2006).

30. Geraldine Fabrikant, "In a Big Bet on Newspapers, a Shy Investor Makes News," *New York Times,* Mar. 14, 2006, C1–4.

31. W. M. Corden, "The Maximisation of Profit by a Newspaper," *Review of Economic Studies* vol. 20, no. 3 (1952): 181.

32. Judith McHale, speech, Northwestern University Medill School of Journalism, Evanston, IL, Feb. 7, 2006.

33. Dana Robbins, speech, Medill faculty at Northwestern University, Evanston, IL, May 31, 2006

34. Newspaper Association of America Nielsen/Net Rating 2005 study citation, http://www.naa.org/nadbase/Top_100_Newspaper_Web_Sites.pdf.

35. Ibid., http://www.naa.org/Global/PressCenter/2006/NEWSPAPER-WEB-SITES-EXPAND-YOUNG-ADULT-AUDIENCE.aspx?lg=naaorg.

36. Kevin Craver, "Open Thread—Declining Newspaper Circulation," *Rathergate.com,* http://www.rathergate.com/?p=765 (accessed Jan. 27, 2006).

37. Bill Keller, memo to NYTimes staffers, Aug. 2, 2005, http://poynter.org/forum/view_post.asp?id=10027 (accessed May 18, 2006).

38. Katharine. Q. Seelye, "Jobs are Cut as Ads and Readers Move Online," *New York Times,* Oct. 10, 2005, C3.

39. Meeks, "Katrina."

40. Bill Kovach, "Competing with Cyberspace: The Key Is Reliability," *Nieman Reports* 53 (1) (1999): 3.

41. Hamilton, *All the News That's Fit to Sell,* 4.

42. McHale, speech.

43. Bill Kovach, "Three Keys to Newspaper Survival," *The State of the News Media 2005,* Journalism.org, http://www.stateofthemedia.org/2005/narrative_newspapers_guest.asp?cat=10&media=2 (accessed Sept. 23, 2005).

44. Dana Robbins, speech.

45. Harrington, interview.

46. Hart, interview.

47. Rachel Smolkin, "Reversing the Slide," *American Journalism Review,* http://www.ajr.org/article_printable.asp?id=3853 (accessed Jan. 23, 2006).

48. Project for Excellence in Journalism, "State of the News Media 2004," http://www.stateofthenewsmedia.org/journalist_survey_commentary.asp (accessed Oct. 18, 2004).

49. Audit Bureau of Circulations Report 2005.

50. Readership Institute, "Newspaper Content: What Makes Readers More Satisfied," Readership Institute Media Management Center at Northwestern University, 2001.

51. Ibid., "The Power to Grow Readership: Research from the Impact Study of Newspaper Readership," 9.

52. Ibid., "The Value of Feature Style Writing," Readership Institute, 2003, 10, http://www.readership.org/content/editorial/feature-style/main.htm.

53. Ibid.

54. Limor Peer, "Reader Orientation Pays Off in Higher Readership," Readership Institute, July 2003.

55. Vivian Vahlberg, "Getting Traction on Readership," Readership Institute Media Management Center at Northwestern University, http://www.readership.org/readership/surveyreport.htm (accessed Feb. 9, 2006).

56. Pew Research Center for the People and the Press, "Press Going Too Easy on Bush: Bottom-Line Pressures Now Hurting Coverage, Say Journalists," *The State of the News Media 2004,* The Project for Excellence in Journalism.

57. Ibid.

58. Ibid.

59. Ibid.

60. Ken Auletta, "Whom Do Journalists Work For?" *Red Smith Lecture in Journalism,* Kansas City, MO: Universal Press Syndicate, 12, 15.

61. Bill Kovach and Tom Rosenstiel, *The Elements of Journalism: What Newspeople Should Know and the Public Should Expect,* 155.

62. Tom Rosenstiel, "Snob Journalism: Elitism versus Ethics for a Profession in Crisis," Ruhl Symposium Speech, Journalism.org, http://www.journalism.org/resources/publications/articles/oregon.asp (accessed Feb. 7, 2006).

63. Helen MacGill Hughes, review of *The Disappearing Daily: Chapters in American Newspaper Evolution,"* by Oswald Garrison, *American Journal of Sociology* 51 (1944): 79, http://www.jstor.org/view/00029602/dm992438/99p0425v/0 (accessed May 5, 2006).

Chapter 4 Citizen Journalism and Chicken Little

1. Sen. Patrick Leahy questioning of John Roberts, http://www.c-span.org/VideoArchives.asp?CatCodePairs=Current_Event,SCourt&Archive Days=365&Page=15 (accessed June 1, 2006).

2. Robert. D. McFadden and Ralph Blumenthal, "Higher Death Toll Seen; Police Ordered to Stop Looters," http://www.nytimes.com/2005/09/01/national/nationalspecial/01storm.html (accessed Sept. 1, 2005).

3. "Share Your Hurricane Story," http://www.nytimes.com/2005/08/30/national/30readers-hurricane.html (accessed Aug. 30, 2005).

4. Dan Gillmor, phone interview with author, Sept. 16, 2005.

5. ABC-TV, *Good Morning America,* interview by Charles Gibson of *Times-Picayune* editor Jim Amoss, Sept. 28, 2005.

6. Jim Dwyer and Christopher Drew, "Fear Exceeded Crime's Reality in New Orleans," *New York Times,* Sept. 29, 2005, A1.

7. Ken Auletta, *Backstory: Inside the Business of News,* xix.

8. Norman Sims, comments during AEJMC panel, San Francisco, CA, Aug. 2, 2006.

9. Dan Gillmor, comments during AEJMC panel, San Francisco, CA, Aug. 1, 2006.

10. Jon Pareles, "2006, Brought to You by You," *New York Times,* Dec. 10, 2006, www.nytimes.com/2006/12/10/arts/music/10pare.html?-r=1&oref=slogin &pagewa (accessed Dec. 12, 2006).

11. Ron Steinman, "Babble," *Digital Journalist,* http://www.digitaljournalist.org/issue0406/steinman.html (accessed July 8, 2004).

12. Shayne Bowman and Chris Willis, "The Future Is Here, but Do News Media Companies See It?" *Nieman Reports* (winter 2005): 9.

13. Meeks, "Katrina."

14. Elizabeth Mehren, "The Messengers of Mississippi in the Wake of Hurricane Katrina," *Nieman Reports* (winter 2005): 54.

15. Rick Lyman, "In Exodus: Fleeing Town, in a Manner of Speaking," *New York Times,* Sept. 23, 2005, A13.

16. Simon Romero, "Staying Put: In Galveston, Some Await Storm with Faith and Hope," *New York Times,* Sept. 23, 2005, A13.

17. Alicia Shepard, interview with author, Sedona, AZ, Sept. 11, 2005.

18. Gwen Filosa, "At Least Ten Thousand Find Refuge at the Superdome," *Times-Picayune,* Aug. 29, 2005, A1.

19. Brian Thevenot and Manuel Torres, "Flooding Wipes Out Two Communities," *Times-Picayune,* Aug. 30, 2005, A1.

20. Thomas E. Patterson, *Doing Well and Doing Good: How Soft News and Critical Journalism Are Shrinking the News Audience and Weakening Democracy—And What News Outlets Can Do about It* (Cambridge: Joan Shorenstein Center for Press, Politics and Public Policy, John F. Kennedy School of Government, Harvard University, 2000), 3–4. http://www.ksg.harvard.edu/presspol/Research_Publications/Reports/softnews.pdf.

21. Bruce Williams, phone interview with author, Oct. 5, 2005.

22. National Radio Project, http://www.radioproject.org/ (accessed June 1, 2006).

23. John C. Merrill, *Existential Journalism,* 113.

24. Chris Lawrence, "A scene of anarchy," cnn.com, http://www.cnn.com/2005/WEATHER//09/01/scene.blog/index.html (accessed Sept. 1, 2005).

25. Jim Spellman, "A scene of anarchy," cnn.com, http://www.cnn.com/2005/WEATHER//09/01/scene.blog/index.html (accessed Sept. 1, 2005).

26. http://www.shreveporttimes.com/apps/pbes/dll/section/category=KATRINA (accessed Sept. 6, 2005).

27. Gillmor, interview.

28. Michael Siu, http://www.neworleans.metblogs.com (accessed Aug. 31, 2005).

29. Mark Tapscott, "Are You Ready for Citizen Journalism to Stop Big Government?" townhall.com, July 28, 2005, http://www.townhall.com/columnists/mtapscott/mt20050728.shtml (accessed Sept. 6, 2005).

30. David T. Z. Mindich, *Just the Facts: How "Objectivity" Came to Define American Journalism,* 4–5.

31. Mindich, phone interview with author, Aug. 31, 2005.

32. Robert Siegel, "U.S. Aid Effort Criticized in New Orleans," *All Things Considered,* National Public Radio, http://www.npr.org/templates/story/story.php?storyId=4828771 (accessed Sept. 1, 2005).

33. "The Big Disconnect on New Orleans: The Official Version; Then There's the in-the-trenches Version," *CNN,* http://www.cnn.com/2005/US/09/02/katrina.response/index.html (accessed Sept. 2, 2005).

34. Ryan Pitts, remarks made at AEJMC Conference, San Antonio, TX, Aug. 12, 2005.

35. Jan Schaffer, remarks made at AEJMC Conference, San Antonio, TX, Aug. 12, 2005.

36. Dan Gillmor, remarks made at AEJMC Conference, San Francisco, CA, Aug. 2, 2006.

37. Kristie LuStout, "Korean Bloggers Making a Difference," CNN, Mar. 31, 2005, http://www.cnn.com/2005/TECH/03/31/spark.ohmynews/index.html (accessed Sept. 4, 2005).

38. OhmyNews, http://english.ohmynews.com/ (accessed Sept. 4, 2005).

39. Wikipedia, http://en.wikinews.org/wiki/Main_Page (accessed Sept. 4, 2005).

40. Cyberjournalist info, http://www.cyberjournalist.net/news/002226.php (accessed Sept. 4, 2005).

41. Williams, interview.

42. "Minnesota Stories," www.mnstories.com/about.html (accessed June 8, 2006).

43. Paul Sullivan, "A Message from Orato's Chairman," Orato, http://www.orato.com/index.php?q=node/23 (accessed Mar. 2006).

44. Paul Sullivan, "The Power of First-Person Journalism," Orato, http://www.orato.com/contributorregistry/ (accessed Sept. 20, 2005).

45. http://stateinformer.com/content/category/1/1/30/ (accessed Sept. 20, 2005).

46. Asha Dornfest, *Front Page 2003 For Dummies,* http://www.amazon.com/gp/product/0764538829/qid=1149196491/sr=2-1/ref=pd_bbs_b_2_1/103-0680509-6891836?s=books&v=glance&n=283155 (accessed Sept. 10, 2005).

47. Adam Glenn, "Katrina Reveals Symbiosis of Journalism-Citizen Journalism," I, Reporter, http://www.ireporter.org (accessed Sept. 6, 2005).

48. Kaye D. Trammell, "Kaye's Hurricane Katrina Blog," http://hurricaneupdate.blogspot.com (accessed Sept. 22, 2005).

49. Graduate Student Presentation at the Medill School of Journalism at Northwestern University, Evanston, IL, June 2005.

50. Dan Gillmor, "What Professional and Citizen Journalists Can Learn from Each Other," Bayosphere, http://bayosphere.com/node/444 (accessed May 27, 2005).

51. Gillmor, *We the Media,* xiv.

52. "Current TV," http://www.current.tv/about/ (accessed June 1, 2006).

53. Mary Lou Fulton, "When Consumers Become Creators," presented at the Interactive Journalism Summit, AEJMC Conference, San Antonio, TX, Aug. 12, 2005.

54. Dana Robbins, presentation at Northwestern University, Evanston, IL, May 31, 2006.

55. Jay Rosen, Newassignment.net, www.journalism.nyu.edu/pubzone/weblogs/pressthink/2006/07/28/nadn_pt2.html (accessed Aug. 16, 2006).

56. http://www.participate.net/reportitnow/reportastory/audio. (accessed Apr. 12, 2006).

57. Clifford G. Christians, John P. Ferré, and P. Mark Fackler, *Good News: Social Ethics and the Press,* ix.

58. David S. Broder, *Behind the Front Page: A Candid Look at How the News Is Made,* 15.

Chapter 5 What's Blogging Got to Do with It?

1. Jeff Jarvis, remarks on panel at AEJMC Conference, Toronto, Canada, Aug. 2004; Jay Rosen, remarks on panel at AEJMC Conference, Toronto, Canada, Aug. 2004.

2. Technorati.com, http://www.technorati.com/ (accessed June 2, 2006).

3. Women, Action and the Media Conference, Mar. 2006 http://www.centerfornewwords.org/wam2005.html.

4. Nikhil Moro, interview with author following panel comments at AEJMC Conference, Toronto, Canada, Aug. 2004.

5. Amanda Lenhart and Susannah Fox, "Bloggers: A Portrait of the Internet's New Storytellers," Pew Internet and American Life Project, July 19, 2006, 3.

6. Davis Merritt, *Knightfall: Knight Ridder and How the Erosion of Newspaper Journalism Is Putting Democracy at Risk,* 101.

7. Pareles, "2006, Brought to You by You."

8. Lawrence Lessig, keynote at AEJMC Conference, San Francisco, CA, Aug. 1, 2006.

9. Technorati.com, http://www.technorati.com/blogs/.

10. Pew Internet and American Life Project, 2004.

11. Blogger, http://www.blogger.com/start.

12. Lakshmi Chaudhry, *Nation,* Jan. 29, 2007 http://www.thenation.com/doc/20070129/chaudry/2 (accessed Feb. 1, 2007).

13. Andreas Kluth, "Among the Audience: A Survey of New Media," *Economist,* Apr. 22, 2006, 4.

14. Greg Sandoval, "Newspapers Woo Bloggers with Mixed Results," news.com (accessed June 1, 2006).

15. Harrington, interview.

16. Hugh Hewitt, "Paperless News Is Doing Just Fine," *Philadelphia Inquirer,* Apr. 23, 2006, D3.

17. Mark Glaser, comments at AEJMC panel, Toronto, Canada, Aug. 2004.

18. Lenhart and Fox, "Bloggers: A Portrait," 2.

19. "Forbes.com controversy," http://abcnews.go.com/WNT/story?id=2357818&page=2 (accessed Aug. 28, 2006).

20. Stephen Quinn and Vincent F. Filak, *Convergent Journalism,* 76.

21. J. D. Lesica, *We've Got Blog: How Weblogs Are Changing Our Culture* (New York: Perseus Books Group, 2002), 171–72.

22. Keven Willey, interview with author following panel comments at AEJMC Conference, San Antonio, TX, Aug. 2005.

23. Paul Andrews, "Is Blogging Journalism? A Blogger and Journalist Finds No Easy Answer, but He Discovers Connections," Weblogs and Journalism, *Nieman Reports* (spring 2003): 63.

24. Brian Stelter, interview with author at AEJMC Conference, Toronto, Canada, Aug. 3, 2004.

25. Farnaz Fassihi, "Baghdad Diary," *Columbia Journalism Review,* Nov./Dec. 2004, http://www.cjr.org/issues/2005/1/fassihi-baghdad.asp.

26. Cyberjournalist.net, http://www.cyberjournalist.net/cyberjournalists.php.

27. Cable Neuhaus, "The Rise of the Consumer-Generated Media Machine," *MediaPost Publications,* Apr. 2005, 5.

28. Gail Collins, speech, Northwestern University, Evanston, IL, Nov. 8, 2004.

29. "Blogging," Spokesman-Review.com, http://www.spokesmanreview.com/blogs/ (accessed Jan. 12, 2007).

30. "latimes.com removes wiki," http://www.cyberjournalist.net/news/002709.php (accessed July 27, 2005).

31. *USA Today* blog, Feb. 28, 2007, http://blogs.usatoday.com/ondeadline/2007/02/new_usatodaycom.html (accessed Mar. 14, 2007).

32. Williams, interview.

33. Jeff South, panel comments at AEJMC Conference, Toronto, Canada, Aug. 2004.

34. Abraham Zapruder, http://www.jfk.org/Research/Zapruder/Zapruder_Film.htm.

35. Jason Christopher Hartley, *Just Another Soldier: A Year on the Ground in Iraq* (New York: HarperCollins, 2005) www.justanothersoldier.com (accessed Jan. 6, 2006).

36. Andrews, "Is Blogging Journalism?" 63.

37. George E. Condon Jr., "Democratic Hopefuls Debate Issues in Front of Bloggers," Aug. 5, 2007, http://www.signonsandiego.com/news/politics/20070805–9999-1n5yearlykos.html (accessed Aug. 18, 2007).

38. Meyer, *Vanishing Newspaper,* 3.

Chapter 6 Humanizing the News after 9/11

1. Lisa Finnegan, *No Questions Asked: News Coverage since 9/11,* 24.

2. Harrington, interview.

3. Lee Rainie, "One Year Later: September 11 and the Internet," Pew Internet and American Life Project, http://www.pewinternet.org/files/PIP_9–11_Report.pdf.

4. Martha Gellhorn, "Dachau," in *Tell Me No Lies: Investigative Journalism That Changed the World,* ed. John Pilger, 3.

5. Michael Schudson, *The Sociology of News,* 137.

6. Maria Hinojosa, Crain Lecture Series speech, Northwestern University, Evanston, IL, Feb. 13, 2006.

7. Rainie, "One Year Later."

8. Alex Halavais, "The Rise of Do-It-Yourself Journalism after September 11," in "One Year Later: September 11 and the Internet," Pew Research Center for People and the Press, Sept. 5, 2002, 27.

9. Williams, interview.

10. Schudson, *Sociology of News,* 150.

11. Auletta, *Backstory,* 7.

12. Jay Bookman, "Outrage: Thousands Dead, a Nation Staggered as Terrorists Strike New York, Washington," *Atlanta Journal-Constitution.* Sept. 12, 2001, 1A.

13. Paul Moses, "A Day of Infamy: Hijacked Planes Hit WTC and Pentagon," *Newsday,* Sept. 12, 2001, A1.

14. Charles Madigan, "U.S. under Attack: Hijacked Airplanes Destroy WTC Towers, Slam Pentagon; Bush and His Advisers Meet at Strategic Command Air Base," *Chicago Tribune,* Sept. 12, 2001, 1.

15. Charles Madigan, "'Our Nation Saw Evil': Hijacked Jets Destroy World Trade Center, Hit Pentagon Thousands Feared Dead in Nation's Worst Terrorist Attack," *Chicago Tribune,* Sept. 12, 2001, 1.

16. Annabelle Sreberny, "Trauma Talk," *Journalism after September 11,* ed. Barbie Zelizer and Stuart Allen, 221.

17. Rainie, "One Year Later," 6.

18. Bob Steele, "Journalism and Tragedy," Poynteronline, http://www.poynter.org/content/content_print.asp?id=5636 (accessed July 19, 1999).

19. Lisa Parks, phone interview with author, Oct. 4, 2005.

20. Cynthia Gorney, "The Business of News: A Challenge for Journalism's Next Generation," Report to the Carnegie Corporation of New York Forum on the Public Interest and the Business of News, June 2002, http://www.carnegie.org/pdf/businessofnews2.pdf.

21. Howell Raines, "Howell Raines," *New York Times,* http://www.nytimes.com/pages/national/portraits/index.html (accessed July 6, 2005).

22. "Portraits of Grief: Arcelia Castillo," *New York Times,* http://www.nytimes.com/2003/03/09/national/portraits/POG-09CASTILLO.html?ex=1145937600&en=929a2f4f37aa4407&ei=5070 (accessed July 5, 2005).

23. Raines, "Howell Raines."

24. Michael Schudson, "What's Unusual about Covering Politics as Usual," *Journalism after September 11*, ed. Barbie Zelizer and Stuart Allen, 39.

25. Fuson, interview.

26. Bruce DeSilva, interview with author, Cambridge, MA, Dec. 4, 2004.

27. Carolyn Kitch, "Mourning in America: Ritual, Redemption and Recovery in News Narrative after September 11," *Journalism Studies* 4 (2), 213–24.

28. Roy Peter Clark, "Portraits of Grief," Poynteronline, Feb. 4, 2001, http:// www.poynter.org/content/content_view.asp?id=4721 (accessed July 5, 2005).

29. John Hersey, *Hiroshima* (New York: Random House, 1989), 1.

30. Zelizer, interview.

31. Hertzel, interview.

32. Dennis D. Cali, "Journalism after September 11: Unity as Moral Imperative," *Journal of Mass Media Ethics* vol. 17, no. 4 (2002): 290–303.

33. Christine Spolar, interview with author, Evanston, IL, Jan. 2006.

34. Gregory Favre, "Forgetting Our Feelings," Poynteronline, http://www .poynter.org/content/content_print.asp?id=6047&custom (accessed June 30, 2004).

35. Anne Marie Lipinski, "When Evil Struck America," *Chicago Tribune*, CD-ROM, 2002.

36. Alex Tizon, "Crossing America: Big Empty Clears the Mind to Revisit 9/11," *Seattle Times*, http://www.seattletimes.nwsource.com/cgi-bin/PrintStory .pl?document_id=134521475&zsection (accessed Aug. 25, 2002).

37. Jacqui Banaszynski, comments at Nieman Conference panel, Cambridge, MA, Dec. 2004.

Chapter 7 The Old, the New, the Good, the Bad, and the Long and the Short of Narrative

1. Albert Merriam Smith, *United Press International*, 1963. http://www.ajr.org/ Article.asp?id=2205 (accessed Dec. 15, 2004).

2. Ibid.

3. Christopher Scanlan, phone interview with author, Aug. 23, 2005.

4. John Hohenberg, *The New Front Page*, 234.

5. Ibid., x.

6. Stephanie Shapiro, *Reinventing the Feature Story: Mythic Cycles in American Literary Journalism*, xi.

7. Gay Talese, "Writing about Ordinary Lives," *Nieman Reports* (spring 2002): 12.

8. Harrington, interview.

9. Jon Marshall, "News Gems Blog," http://www.medill.northwestern.edu/ medill/inside/news/news_gems_blog_author_and_medill_lecturer_jon_ marshall_on_chicago_tonight.html.

10. "Society of Professional Journalists Presents Jon Marshall's News Gems," www.spj.org/blog/blogs/newsgems (accessed Jan. 4, 2007).

11. Vivian Gornick, *The Situation and the Story: The Art of Personal Narrative*, 9.

12. Jon Franklin, "The Narrative Tool," in *The Journalist's Craft: A Guide to Writing Better Stories*, ed. Dennis Jackson and John Sweeney, 58.

13. Hertzel, interview.

14. Fuller, *News Values*, 136–37.

15. Norman Mailer, "Myth versus Hypothesis," keynote address, Nieman Narrative Conference, Cambridge, MA, Dec. 4, 2004.

16. Roland Schatz, phone interview with author, Nov. 7, 2005.

17. http://www.sixbillion.org/ (accessed Aug. 24, 2006).

18. Walt Harrington, *Intimate Journalism: The Art and Craft of Reporting Everyday Life*, xiii.

19. David Abrahamson, remarks at AEJMC Conference, San Antonio, TX, Aug. 2005.

20. "Doing It Daily," Society of Professional Journalists, www.spj.org/nww3.asp (accessed June 20, 2006).

21. June Nicholson and Deb Halpern Wenger, "Newsroom Strategies," Society of Professional Journalists, www.spj.org/nww6.asp (accessed June 20).

22. Malcolm Gladwell, *The Tipping Point: How Little Things Can Make a Big Difference*, 30–89.

23. Bob Batz Jr., "Starting a Narrative Cell," *Nieman Narrative Digest*, www.nieman.harvard.edu/narrative/digest/resources/start-group.html (accessed June 20, 2006).

24. Paul Pringle, "What Do You Save from a House Full of Memories?" *Los Angeles Times*, Oct. 27, 2003, A1.

25. Pulitzer Prizes 2006, http://newsbusters.org/node/4957 (accessed May 9, 2006).

26. David Finkel, "U.S. Ideals Meet Reality in Yemen," *Washington Post*, Dec. 18, 2005, http://www.washingtonpost.com/wpdyn/content/article/2005/12/17/AR2005121701237.html (accessed May 9, 2006).

27. Dana Priest, http://www.washingtonpost.com/wp-dyn/content/linkset/2006/04/17/LI2006041700530.html (accessed May 9, 2006).

28. David Carr, "The Pulitzer, Now a Badge of Controversy," *New York Times*, Apr. 24, 2006, C1.

29. Jim Sheeler, "Final Salute," *Rocky Mountain News*, http://denver.rockymountainnews.com/news/finalSalute/ (accessed May 9, 2006).

30. Nicholas Kristof, "Never Again, Again?" *New York Times*, http://www.nytimes.com/2005/11/20/opinion/20kristof.html?ex=1147320000&en=19055a623581f2a3&ei=5070 (accessed May 9, 2006).

31. Rick Attig and Doug Bates, "All the Lonely People," *Oregonian*, Jan. 9, 2005, http://www.pulitzer.org/year/2006/editorial-writing/works/oregonian01.html.

32. Paisley Dodds, "Looters Pick through Belongings in Aristide's Former Villa," *Associated Press*, Dec. 15, 2003. http://fmmac2.mm.ap.org/polk_awards_haiti_html/haiti3.html (accessed May 20, 2005).

33. Henry Louis Gates Jr., "A Republic of Letters," remarks made at 2005 Pulitzer Prize luncheon, New York, May 23, 2005.

34. Karen Rothmyer, *Winning Pulitzers: The Stories behind Some of the Best News Coverage of Our Time*, 5.

35. Jeanie McAdams Moore and Chris Lamb, *Newspaper Research Journal* (winter 2005): 50.

36. Katharine Graham quote, http://quotationspage.com/quotes/Katharine_Graham/ (accessed May 20, 2005).

37. Leonard Downie Jr. and Robert G. Kaiser, *The News about the News: American Journalism in Peril*, 75.

38. Steve Fainaru, "Taking on Sadr City in a Pickup Truck; Four Deaths Illustrate Vulnerability of Iraqi Forces," *Washington Post*, Sept. 28, 2004, A1.

39. Kelly Benham, "Trash in Home Hinders Efforts of Firefighters," *St. Petersburg Times*, Sept. 20, 2002, 3.

40. Perry Parks, *Making Important News Interesting: Reporting Public Affairs in the Twenty-First Century*, 86, 98.

41. Dawn Fallik, interview with author, Sedona, AZ, Sept. 10, 2005.

42. Linda Wertheimer, interview with author, Evanston, IL, Oct. 21, 2005.

43. Kotlowitz, interview.

44. Katherine Boo, comments made in presentation at Northwestern University, Evanston, IL, Nov. 14, 2005.

45. Fuson, interview.

46. Ken Fuson, "A Charmer Inspires a Leap of Faith," *Des Moines Register*, http://desmoinesregister.com/news/stories/c4788998/18042705.html (accessed Nov. 4, 2005).

47. Mark Masse, remarks at 2004 AEJMC Conference, Toronto, Canada, Aug. 2004.

48. Bill Reiter, "The Story of Edith: The Last Lynch Mob," *Arkansas Democrat-Gazette*, Sept. 1, 2002, A1.

49. Carl Sessions Stepp, remarks at Aug. 2004 AEJMC Conference, Toronto, Canada,.

50. Scanlan, interview.

51. Kovach and Rosenstiel, *Elements of Journalism*, 160, 149.

52. Joseph T. Hallinan, "Los Angeles Paper Bets on Softer News, Shorter Stories," *Wall Street Journal*, Oct. 3, 2005, http://pqasb.pqarchiver.com/wsj/access/905636591.html?dids=905636591:905636591&FMT=ABS&FMTS=ABS:FT&date=Oct+3%2C+2005&author=Joseph+T.+Hallinan&type=91_1996&desc=Los+Angeles+Paper+Bets+on+Softer+News%2C+Shorter+Stories (accessed Oct. 10, 2005).

53. Pamela Moreland, interview with author, Sedona, AZ, Sept. 10, 2005.

54. Stuart Wilk, APME News 2003.

55. DeSilva, interview.

56. Walt Harrington, "The Writer's Choice," *River Teeth* vol. 5, no. 2 (spring 2004), http://muse.jhu.edu/journals/river_teeth/v005/5.2harrington.html (accessed Oct. 11, 2005).

57. Norman Sims, *The Literary Journalists*, 15.

58. Fred Fedler, "Plagiarism Persists in News Despite Changing Attitudes," *Newspaper Research Journal* vol. 27, no. 2, (spring 2006): 24, 34.

59. Chris Harvey, "Tom Wolfe's Revenge," *American Journalism Review*, Oct. 1994, 40–46. http://www.ajr.org/Article.asp?id=1372 (accessed Jan. 10, 2007).

60. Ibid.

61. Hart, interview.

62. Mark Bowden, "Reliving a Firefight: Hail Mary, Then Hold On," *Philadelphia Inquirer*, Nov. 16, 1997.

63. Mary Schmich, "The Journey of Judge Joan Lefkow," *Chicago Tribune*, Nov. 20, 2005, A1.

64. Will Irwin, *Killing the Messenger: 100 Years of Media Criticism*, ed. Tom Goldstein, 138.

65. Beverly Lowry, Carolyn Forché, and Philip Gerard, eds. *Writing Creative Nonfiction: Instruction and Insights from Teachers of the Associated Writing Programs*, 97.

66. Ezra Pound quote, http://chatna.com/author/pound.htm (accessed Aug. 24, 2006).

Chapter 8 Diversity of Thought Shifts Content

1. Jenna Russell and Beth Daley, "Hope, Love, Fuel Family's Search Shrewsbury Woman, Twenty-Four, Disappeared Two Weeks Ago," *Boston Globe,* Oct. 24, 2005, B1.

2. Michael Levenson, "Teen Fatally Shot at Apartment Building Police Seeking Suspect in Hub's Fifty-Eighth Homicide," *Boston Globe,* Oct. 24, 2005, B2.

3. E. J. Graff, phone interview with author, Oct. 28, 2005.

4. Leigh Stephens Aldrich, *Covering the Community: A Diversity Handbook for Media,* 23.

5. Sally Lehrman, "News as American as America," Knight Foundation Journalism Initiatives, Oct. 11, 2005, www.knightfdn.org/diversity/index.asp.

6. Parks, *Making Important News Interesting,* 92.

7. Hertzel, interview.

8. Northwestern University Readership Institute, "New Readers: Race, Ethnicity and Readership," 2004, http://www.readership.org/new_readers/data/race_ethnicity.pdf (accessed Dec. 19, 2005).

9. Mary Arnold and Mary Nesbitt, "Women in Media 2006: Finding the Leader in You," McCormick Tribune Foundation, Media Management Center, Northwestern University, 26–28.

10. Jodi Enda, "Women Journalists See Progress, but Not Nearly Enough," *Nieman Reports* (spring 2002): 67. http://www.nieman.harvard.edu/reports/02–1NR spring/02–1NRspring.pdf (accessed Dec. 10, 2005).

11. Kovach and Rosenstiel, *Elements of Journalism,* 188, 189.

12. Christy Bulkeley, "A Pioneering Generation Marked the Path for Women Journalists," *Nieman Reports* (spring 2002): 60.

13. Lawrence T. McGill, "Newsroom Diversity: Meeting the Challenge," *Freedom Forum,* 1999.

14. American Society of Newspaper Editors, http://www.asne.org/index.cfm?id=6264 (accessed Dec. 18, 2005).

15. Cory L. Armstrong, "Story Genre Influences Whether Women Are Sources," *Newspaper Research Journal* (summer 2006): 68, 69.

16. Lehrman, "News as American as America."

17. David Manning White, "The Gate Keeper: A Case Study in the Selection of News," in *Social Meanings of News,* ed. Dan Berkowitz, 63–71.

18. Glen Bleske, "Ms. Gates Takes Over," *Social Meanings of News,* 78.

19. Kathleen A. Cairns, *Front-Page Women Journalists, 1920–1950,* 12.

20. Deborah Chambers et al., *Women and Journalism,* 81.

21. Elizabeth S. Bird and Robert Dardenne, "Myth, Chronicle and Story," in *Social Meanings of News,* ed. Dan Berkowitz, 334–35.

22. Kay Mills, *A Place in the News: From the Women's Pages to the Front Page,* 7.

23. Shesource.org, http://www.shesource.org/about_us.php (accessed Jan. 4, 2007).

24. Marie Wilson, "Who's Talking Now: A Follow-up Analysis of Guest Appearances by Women on the Sunday Morning Talk Shows," White House Project, October 2005, http://www.thewhitehouseproject.org/v2/researchandreports/whostalking/whos_talking_2005.pdf (accessed Dec. 10, 2006).

25. Maria Len-Rios, *Journal of Communication,* University of Missouri–Columbia School of Journalism, http://www.wifp.org/communicationnews.html#anchor 2015400 (accessed Dec. 11, 2006).

26. Jill Nelson, keynote address, Women, Action and the Media Conference, Cambridge, MA, Dec. 2004.

27. Project for Excellence in Journalism, "The Gender Gap: Women Are Still Missing as Sources for Journalists," Journalism.org., May 2005, http://www .journalism.org/resources/research/reports/gender/default.asp (accessed Dec. 12, 2005).

28. Jennifer Pozner, email comments, interview with author, Nov. 15, 2005.

29. Ibid.

30. Rita Henley Jensen, "An Internet News Service Reports News and Views of Women," *Nieman Reports* (spring 2002): http://www.nieman.harvard.edu/reports/02–1NRspring/02–1NRspring.pdf (accessed Nov. 10, 2005).

31. Ibid., 75

32. Eric Freedman, Frederick Fico, and Brad Love, "Male and Female Sources in Newspaper Coverage of Male and Female Candidates in U.S. Senate Races in 2004," Newspaper Division of the Association for Education in Journalism and Mass Communication, Aug. 2005.

33. Ilia Rodriguez, "Diversity Writing and the Imaginaries of Liberal Multiculturalism in the U.S. Mainstream Press," Minorities and Communication Division of AEJMC, Aug. 2005

34. Ibid.

35. Edward C. Pease, Erna Smith, and Federico Subervi, "News and Race Model of Excellence Project," Oct. 17, 2001, 4.

36. Ibid.

37. Ibid.

38. Ibid.

39. Claire Cummings, comments at WAM Conference, Cambridge, MA, March 2006.

40. Diane Lewis, comments at WAM Conference, Cambridge, MA, March 2006.

41. Pease, Smith, and Subervi, "News and Race."

42. Downie and Kaiser, *News about the News,* 9.

43. Carl Sessions Stepp, *Breach of Faith: A Crisis of Coverage in the Age of Corporate Newspapering,* ed. Gene Roberts and Thomas Kunkel, 91.

44. Ibid., 106.

45. Retha Hill, "Women in Newspapers: Still Fighting an Uphill Battle," in *Women in Newspapers Initiative,* ed. Mary Arnold Heminger and Cynthia Linton, 42.

46. Leroy Aarons and Sheila Murphy, "Lesbians and Gays in the Newsroom Ten Years Later," Annenberg School for Communication, University of Southern California, 2000.

47. Patrick Champagne, "The Double Dependency: The Journalistic Field between Politics and Markets," in *Bourdieu and the Journalistic Field,* ed. Rodney Benson and Erik Neveu, 53.

48. Beth A. Haller, "News Coverage of Disability Issues: Final Report for the Center for an Accessible Society," Center for an Accessible Society, http://www .accessiblesociety.org/topics/converage/0799haller.htm (accessed Oct. 17, 2005).

49. Davis, Joyce Davis, "Covering Muslims in America," Poynteronline, http://www.poynteronline.org/content_print.asp?id32864&custom (accessed June 30, 2004).

50. "Real Life, Real Life, Real News: Connecting with Reader's Lives," http://www.gannett.com/go/newswatch/2004/february/nw0213–1.htm (accessed Mar. 15, 2007).

51. E. J. Mitchell, comments at UNITY News Watch meeting, 2004, http://www.gannett.com/go/newswatch/2004/october/nw1008–2.htm (accessed Dec. 5, 2005).

52. Jerry Ceppos, remarks on company website, spring 2004.

53. *Post-Crescent* in Appleton, WI, http://www.postcrescent.com (accessed Mar. 15, 2007).

54. V. Raman Narayanan, "Covering Local News with International Perspective," Associated Press Managing Editors News, spring 2003.

55. Alice Tait, interview with author at AEJMC Conference, San Antonio, TX, Aug. 2005.

56. Karla Garrett Harshaw, comments to American Society of Newspaper Editors, Apr. 20, 2004. http://www.naa.org/home/presstime/2004/may/presstimecontent/naa-2004-annual-convention-report-asne-events.aspx (accessed Mar. 15, 2007).

57. Lehrman, "News as American as America."

58. Fuson, interview.

59. www.asne.org (accessed Mar. 10, 2006).

60. Tracy Everbach, "Managing Amazonia: A Cultural Case Study of Female Leadership," presentation to AEJMC Conference, San Antonio, August, 2005

61. Ibid.

62. Mindich, *Just the Facts*, 141.

63. Deepa Kumar, *Class and News*, ed. Don Heider, 20.

Chapter 9 The Therapeutic Story Flow Model

1. Stephen J. Lepore and Joshua M. Smyth, eds., *The Writing Cure: How Expressive Writing Promotes Health and Emotional Well-Being*, 3.

2. James Pennebaker, interview with author, Austin, TX, Oct. 5, 2006.

3. Craig, *Ethics of the Story*, 15–16.

4. Anna Quindlen, "Write for Your Life," *Newsweek*, Jan. 22, 2007.

5. T. J. Scheff, *Catharsis in Healing, Ritual and Drama* (Berkeley: University of California Press, 1979), 151–52.

6. Ibid.

7. Melanie Arline Greenburg, "Writing about Real vs. Imaginary Traumas: A Test of Inhibition Theory" (New York: SUNY, 1992), 152.

8. James Pennebaker, ed., *Emotion, Disclosure, and Health*, 5; James Pennebaker and Janel Segal, "Forming a Story: The Health Benefits of Narrative," *Journal of Clinical Psychology* 1999, vol. 55, no. 10, 1243, http://www3.interscience.wiley.com/cgi-bin/abstract/66000643/ABSTRACT?CRETRY=1&SRETRY=0 (accessed Mar. 15, 2007).

9. Daniel H. Pink, *A Whole New Mind: Why Right-Brainers Will Rule the Future*, 101, 103.

10. Pennebaker and Segal, "Forming a Story," 1243–54.

11. Wilma Bucci, *Emotion, Disclosure, and Health*, ed. James Pennebaker, 117.

12. Paul Auster, ed., *I Thought My Father Was God: And Other True Tales from NPR's National Story Project*, xvi, xx.

13. Tristine Rainier, *Your Life as Story*, 10.

14. Pink, *Whole New Mind*, 115.

15. Dan P. McAdams, *The Redemptive Self: Stories Americans Live By*, 272.

16. Kovach and Rosenstiel, *Elements of Journalism*, 159.

17. David Protess and Medill Innocence Project, http://www.medill.north western.edu/medill/ugrad/areas_of_study/medill_innocence_project.html (accessed Aug. 30, 2006).

18. Charlie LeDuff, *Work and Other Sins: Life in New York City and Thereabouts.*

19. Linda Joy Meyers, *Becoming Whole: Writing Your Healing Story* (San Diego: Silvercat Publications, 2003), 53.

20. Robert W. McChesney, *The Problem of the Media: U.S. Communication Politics in the Twenty-First Century*, 81.

21. Ronald Bishop, "News Media, Heal Thyselves: Sourcing Patterns in News Stories about News Media Performances," *Journal of Communication Inquiry* 25, no. 1 (2001), 22–37, http://jci.sagepub.com/cgi/content/abstract/25/1/22 (accessed Dec. 2, 2005).

22. McAdams, *Redemptive Self*, 272.

23. Pink, *Whole New Mind*, 115.

24. Stephan Lacy, "Comparative Case Study: Newspaper Source Use on the Environmental Beat," *Newspaper Research Journal* (winter 2000), http://www.find articles.com/p/articles/mi_qa3677/is_200001/ai_n8902566/print.

25. Lule, *Daily News, Eternal Stories*, 19, 21.

26. Joseph Campbell and Diane K. Osbon, *A Joseph Campbell Companion: Reflections on the Art of Living*, 271.

27. Ernest van den Haag, "Reflections on Mass Culture," in *Ideas and Patterns for Writing*, ed. Carle B. Spotts, 385.

28. Norman Mailer, comments at Nieman Narrative Conference, Cambridge, MA, Dec. 2004.

29. Rick Bragg, *All Over but the Shoutin'*, 198.

30. McAdams, interview.

31. Zelizer, interview.

32. Schudson, *Sociology of News*, 182.

33. Jerry Vannatta, Ronald Schliefer, and Sheila Crow, *Medicine and Humanistic Understanding: The Significance of Narrative in Medical Practices.*

34. Danielle Orfi, *Incidental Findings: Lessons from My Patients in the Art of Medicine.*

35. www.rushstories.org (accessed Jan. 27, 2007).

36. Jerome S. Bruner, *Making Stories: Law, Literature, Life*, 7, 8.

37. Schudson, *Sociology of News*, 12.

38. McAdams, interview.

39. Pink, *Whole New Mind*, 104.

40. Ibid., 115.

Chapter 10 Fifteen Seconds of Fame: A Cultural Reverence for Story

1. BotoxCosmetic, http://www.botoxcosmetic.com/for_me/laura.aspx (accessed July 15, 2006).

2. James Surowiecki, *The Wisdom of Crowds: Why the Many Are Smarter than the Few and How Collective Wisdom Shapes Business, Economics, Societies, and Nations*, xv.

3. Joshua Chaffin and Aline Van Duyn, "MySpace Acts to Calm Teen Safety Fears," Financialtimes.com, http://news.ft.com/cms/s/3f8a53d4-c01c-11da-939f-0000779e2340.html (accessed Jan. 10, 2007).

4. http://www.kleenex.com/home.aspx?sectionID=2&s=letitout (accessed Feb. 2, 2007).

5. S. Elizabeth Bird, *The Audience in Everyday Life: Living in a Media World,* 3, 30, 23.

6. American Express ad, www.clips.mylifemycard.com (accessed Jan. 10, 2007).

7. Verizon Wireless Broadband, www.richerdeeperbroader.com (accessed June 13, 2005) www.broadbandstories.com (accessed Aug. 15, 2005).

8. Chicago Area Volvo Retailers, "Volvo Radio Tales," http://www.chicago-volvodealers.com/RadioAd.aspx (accessed Aug. 15, 2006).

9. Woolrich ad, *National Geographic Adventurer,* Mar. 2006.

10. Nissan Pathfinder ad, http://www.iafrica.com/win/pathfinder/index.htm (accessed May 16, 2006).

11. Weber Grill ads, http://www.webernation.com/downloads/PDF/wilmw _booklet.pdf (accessed June 8, 2006).

12. White Castle ads, http://truecastlestories.com/page/home.jsp (accessed June 27, 2006).

13. Apple ad, www.apple.com/switch/stories (accessed Aug. 19, 2005).

14. Microsoft magazine ad, Sept. 2005.

15. Michele Lowe, phone interview with author, Nov. 14, 2005.

16. Dove ads, www.campaignforrealbeauty.com/flat3.asp?is=2287 (accessed Aug. 19, 2005); www.campaignforrealbeauty.com/falt3.asp?is=2091 (accessed Aug. 19, 2005).

17. Levi ads, www.us.levi.com/fal05a/levi/home/1_home.jsp (accessed Aug. 18, 2005).

18. Myra Stark, 2003, "Ideas from Trends, You, Me, Celebrity," www .saatchikevin.com/welcome-info.pinp?flash (accessed Sept. 27, 2004).

19. Ecco ad, *More,* Oct. 2005.

20. Western Union, http://www.sendmoneytransfer.com/news/75670.html (accessed June 27, 2006).

21. Gillmor, *We the Media,* 14.

22. http://www.realityshows.com/ (accessed June 27, 2006).

23. Jon Franklin, interview with author, Cambridge, MA, Dec. 2004.

24. "RU the Girl with T-Boz and Chilli," http://www.kikutv.com/shows/ English_Programs/Inactive/RU%20the%20Girl/index.html (accessed June 18, 2005).

25. Kotlowitz, interview.

26. Andrea Petersen, "The Story of My Life, Starring . . . Me!" *Wall Street Journal,* Oct. 23, 2003, 1. http://www.empoweredwealth.com/documents/WSJVideo Article.pdf; http://www.myvideostory.com/.

Chapter 11 Emergence Journalism: Where We Go from Here

1. Anthony Walters, presentation at Northwestern University, Evanston, IL, Mar. 2006.

2. Ibid.

3. Frank Ahrens, "Ink and Paper or 1s and 0s," *Washington Post,* http:// www.washingtonpost.com/wp-dyn/content/article/2005/10/14/AR2005101 402033 (accessed Oct. 21, 2005).

4. Overholser, "On Behalf of Journalism."

5. Dave Pettit, "The Perfect News Site, 2016," Wall Street Journal online, http://online.wsj.com/public/article/SB114717839352947700-Nsu_HUWPFsws M7wBQ7vJSgDhonQ_20060516.html?mod=blogs (accessed May 10, 2006).

6. Rich Gordon, "The Meanings and Implications of Convergence," in *Digital Journalism: Emerging Media and the Changing Horizons of Journalism*, ed. Kaven Kawamoto, 60.

7. David Bollier, "When Push Comes to Pull: The New Economy and Culture of Networking Technology" (Washington, DC: Aspen Institute Report, 2006), 30.

8. Boczkowski, *Digitizing the News*, 187.

9. Save Journalism Day, http://www.savejournalism.org/ (accessed Dec. 15, 2006); http://www.savejournalism.org/events/ (accessed Jan. 5, 2007).

10. IWantMedia.com. http://www.iwantmedia.com/ (accessed Jan. 15, 2007).

11. Andrew Swinand, presentation to Medill faculty at Northwestern University, Evanston, IL, May 4, 2006.

12. John Battelle, *The Search: How Google and Its Rivals Rewrote the Rules of Business and Transformed Our Culture*, 175.

13. Swinand, presentation.

14. Debra Dickerson, comments at Nieman Narrative Conference, Cambridge, MA, Dec. 4, 2004.

15. Rick Edmonds, "The State of the News Media 2006," *journalism.org*, http://www.stateofthemedia.com/2006/printable_newspapers_intro.asp?media =1&cat=1 (accessed Mar. 16, 2006).

16. Hugh Hewitt, *Blog: Understanding the Information Reformation That's Changing Your World*, xiv.

17. Nora Paul, "New News' Retrospective: Is Online News Reaching Its Potential?" 2.

18. 2006 Advertising Age Fact Pack, *Advertising Age*, Feb. 27, 2006, 33. http:// www.advertisingage.com/datacenter/article.php?article_id=48629 (accessed May 8, 2006).

19. Carolyn Marvin and Philip Meyer, "What Kind of Journalism Does the Public Need?" in *The Press*, ed. Geneva Overholser and Kathleen Hall Jamieson, 407.

20. Vikki Porter, email announcement of Knight New Media Center, May 1, 2006, http://www.knightnewmediacenter.org/ (accessed online May 9, 2006).

21. *Hero*, DVD, Columbia Pictures, 1992.

22. Richard D. Hendrickson, "Publishing E-mail Addresses Ties Readers to Writers," *Newspaper Research Journal* vol. 27, no. 2 (2006): 56.

23. David Hiller, "A Letter from the Publisher: Chicago Tribune as Citizen," http://about.chicagotribune.com/community/DavidHillerLetter.pdf (accessed May 3, 2006).

24. Email from NYTimes.com, Apr. 27, 2006.

25. Scott D. Anthony and Clark G. Gilbert, "Solving the Innovator's Dilemma," *Presstime*, Newspaper Association of America, Jan. 2006, 1.

26. Poynter Institute, "State of the News Media 2006: Skimpy Rations," *Poynteronline*. http://www.pointer.org/content/content_view.asp?id=98174 (accessed Mar. 16, 2006), 1.

27. Pew Research Center, "Public More Critical of Press, but Goodwill Persists," The Pew Research Center for the People and the Press, http://people-press.org/ reports/display.php3?ReportID=248 (accessed online May 9, 2006).

28. Marvin and Meyer, "What Kind of Journalism Does the Public Need?" 409.

29. Scott R. Meier, "Accuracy Matters: A Cross-Market Assessment of Newspaper Error and Credibility," *Journalism and Mass Communications Quarterly* 82 (autumn 2005).

30. Mitchell Charnley, "Preliminary Notes on a Study of Newspaper Accuracy," *Journalism Quarterly* 13 (1936): 394–401.

31. Meier, "Accuracy Matters."

32. David Nelson, Ellen Shearer, and Steve Rolandelli, "Newspaper Reporter Attitudes toward Credibility, Errors and Ethics," Northwestern University, Medill School of Journalism, Evanston, IL, May 2006, 9–12.

33. Larry Woiwode, "The Ethics of Writing," speech, World Journalism Institute's forum, June 27, 2003, 9.

34. Global Media Monitoring Project, "Who Makes the News?" Global Media Monitoring Project, www.whomakesthenews.org.

35. Ibid.

36. Bill Dedman and Stephen K. Doig, Newsroom Diversity Index report, Miami, FL, Knight Foundation.

37. Rev. Irene Monroe, *In Newsweekly*, http://www.innewsweekly.com/innews/?class_code=Op&article_code=1769 (accessed May 10, 2006).

38. *A Vision for Journalism Education: The Professional School for Twenty-First-Century News Leaders: A Manifesto,* Carnegie Corporation of New York and the John S. and James L. Knight Foundation, http://www.carnegie.org/sub/program/initiative-manifesto.html.

39. Linda Foley, *The Future of Media: Resistance and Reform in the Twenty-first Century,* ed. Robert W. McChesney, Russell Newman, and Ben Scott, 43.

40. Claude Jean-Betrand, in *Good News: Social Ethics and the Press,* ed. Clifford G. Christians, John P. Ferré, and P. Mark Fackler, vi.

41. Christians, Ferré, and Fackler, eds., *Good News,* 7.

42. Anders Gyllenhaal, "A Newspaper's Redesign Signals Its Renewal," *Nieman Reports* (spring 2006): e13.

43. Overholser, "On Behalf of Journalism," 6.

44. Armstrong, "Beginnings of the Modern Newspaper."

45. Ibid., 19, 17.

46. Fuson, interview.

Bibliography

Aarons, Leroy, and Sheila Murphy. "Lesbians and Gays in the Newsroom Ten Years Later." Los Angeles: University of Southern California Annenberg School for Communication, 2000.

Adams, Kathleen. *Journal to the Self: Twenty-Two Paths to Personal Growth.* New York: Warner Books, 1990.

Aldrich, Leigh Stephens. *Covering the Community: A Diversity Handbook for Media.* Thousand Oaks, CA: Pine Forge Press, 1999.

Allbritton, Christopher. "Blogging from Iraq." *Nieman Reports.* Fall 2003.

Allender, Dr. Dan B. *To Be Told: Know Your Story, Shape Your Life.* Colorado Springs: Waterbrook Press, 2005.

Alterman, Eric. "Determining the Value of Blogs." *Nieman Reports.* Fall 2003.

Alysen, Barbara, Gail Sedorkin, Mandy Oakham, and Roger Patching. *Reporting in a Multimedia World.* Sydney, Australia: Allen & Unwin, 2003.

Amos, Deborah. "Unraveling the Mystery of Vanishing Foreign News." *Nieman Reports.* Spring 1999.

Anand. "Journalistic Freedom Is Earned, Not Handed on a Platter." *http://www.prdomain.com/feature/feature_details.asp?id=122&area=J& typ=A* Nov. 11, 2005. Retrieved May 1, 2006.

Anderson, Chris. *The Long Tail: Why the Future of Business Is Selling Less of More.* New York: Hyperion, 2006.

Andrews, Paul. "Is Blogging Journalism?" *Nieman Reports.* Fall 2003.

Anthony, Scott D., and Clark G. Gilbert. "Can the Newspaper Industry Stare Disruption in the Face?" *Nieman Reports.* Spring 2006.

Arnold, Mary, and Mary Nesbitt. *Women in Media 2006: Finding the Leader in You.* Evanston, IL: Media Management Center at Northwestern University, 2006.

Auletta, Ken. *Backstory: Inside the Business of News.* New York: Penguin Press, 2003.

———. "Can the Los Angeles Times Survive Its Owners?" *New Yorker,* Oct. 10, 2005.

Auster, Paul, ed. *I Thought My Father Was God: And Other True Tales from NPR's National Story Project*. New York: Henry Holt & Co., 2001.

Balli, Cecilia. "The Unknown Soldier." *Texas Monthly* (July 2004).

Banaszynski, Jacqui. "Why We Need Stories: Without Them, the Stuff That Happens Would Float around in Some Glob and None of It Would Mean Anything." *Nieman Reports*. Spring 2002.

Battelle, John. *The Search: How Google and Its Rivals Rewrote the Rules of Business and Transformed Our Culture*. New York: Portfolio, 2005.

Beasley, Maurine, and Sheila Gibbons. *Taking Their Place: A Documentary History of Women and Journalism*. State College, PA: Strata Publishing, 2002.

Bell, Madison Smartt. *Narrative Design: Working with Imagination, Craft, and Form*. New York: W. W. Norton, 1997.

Benson, Rodney, and Erik Neveu, eds. *Bourdieu and the Journalistic Field*. Malden, MA: Polity Press, 2005.

Berkowitz, Dan, ed. *Social Meanings of News*. Thousand Oaks, CA: Sage Publications, 1997.

Bird, S. Elizabeth. *The Audience in Everyday Life: Living in a Media World*. New York: Routledge, 2003.

Blood, Rebecca. "Weblogs and Journalism: Do They Connect?" *Nieman Reports*. Fall 2003.

Boczkowski, Pablo J. *Digitizing the News: Innovation in Online Newspapers*. Cambridge: MIT Press, 2004.

Bollinger, Lee. "Sharper Focus on Media Expertise." *Australian* Apr. 23, 2003.

Bowden, Mark. *Black Hawk Down: A Story of Modern War*. New York: Penguin Books, 1999.

Boynton, Robert S. *The New Journalism: Conversations with America's Best Nonfiction Writers on Their Craft*. New York: Vintage Books, 2005.

Bradley, Patricia. *Women and the Press: The Struggle for Equality*. Evanston, IL: Northwestern University Press, 2005.

Bragg, Rick. *All Over but the Shoutin'*. New York: Pantheon Books, 1997.

Brennen, Bonnie. "Sweat Not Melodrama: Reading the Structure of Feeling in *All the President's Men*." *Journalism* vol. 4, no. 1 (2003).

Broder, David S. *Behind the Front Page*. New York: Simon & Schuster, 1987.

Brooks, Brian S., George Kennedy, Daryl R. Moen, and Don Ranly. *News Reporting and Writing*. 7th edition. Boston: Bedford/St. Martin's, 2002.

Brown Kelly, Sandra. "Advice Can Help You Avoid Pitfalls of Self-Publishing." *Roanoke Times and World News*. Jan. 14, 2003.

Brown, Teri. "The Hunt for Red-Hot Anecdotes." *Writer's Digest*. *http://www.writersdigest.com/articles/indexes/wd2004.asp*. June 2004. Retrieved Apr. 10, 2006.

Bruner, Jerome S. *Beyond the Information Given.* New York: W. W. Norton, 1973.

———. *Making Stories: Law, Literature, Life.* New York: Farrar, Straus & Giroux, 2002.

Bulkeley, Christy. "A Pioneering Generation Marked the Path for Women Journalists." *Nieman Reports.* Spring 2002.

Cairns, Kathleen A. *Front-Page Women Journalists, 1920–1950.* Lincoln: University of Nebraska Press, 2003.

Cali, Dennis D. "Journalism after September 11: Unity as Moral Imperative." *Journal of Mass Media Ethics* vol. 17, no. 4 (2002).

Campbell, Joseph, ed. *The Portable Jung.* New York: Penguin Books, 1976.

Campbell, Joseph, and Diane K. Osbon. *A Joseph Campbell Companion: Reflections on the Art of Living.* New York: Harper Perennial, 1999.

Carr, David. "The Pulitzer, Now a Badge of Controversy." *New York Times.* http://select.nytimes.com/gst/abstract.html?res=F3091EFC395B0 C778EDDAD0894DE404482&n=Top%2fReference%2fTimes%20 Topics%2fPeople%2fC%2fCarr%2c%20David. Apr. 24, 2006.

Chambers, Deborah, Linda Steiner, and Carole Fleming. *Women and Journalism.* New York: Routledge, 2004).

Chancellor, John, and Walter Mears. *The New News Business.* New York: HarperPerennial, 1995.

Christians, Clifford G., John P. Ferré, and P. Mark Fackler. *Good News: Social Ethics and the Press.* New York: Oxford University Press, 1993.

Clark, Roy Peter. "Portraits of Grief." www.poynter.org. Aug. 16, 2002. Retrieved Sept. 15, 2005.

———. "September 11 and the Curse of History." www.poynter.org. Sept. 11, 2003. Retrieved Sept. 15, 2003.

Clark, Roy Peter, and Christopher Scanlan, eds. *Newspaper Writing: A Collection of ASNE Prizewinners.* 2nd edition. New York: Bedford/St. Martin's, 2006.

Craig, David. *The Ethics of the Story.* Lanham, MD: Rowman & Littlefield, 2006.

Crockett, Roger O. "Why the Web Is Hitting a Wall," *Business Week,* Mar. 20, 2006.

Croteau, David, and William Hoynes. *The Business of Media: Corporate Media and the Public Interest.* London: Pine Forge Press, 2006.

Davis, Joyce. "The First Shock of History." www.poynter.org. May 6, 2003. Retrieved Sept. 15, 2003.

———. "Covering Muslims in America." www.poynter.org. Retrieved Nov. 15, 2003.

De Bruin, Marjan, and Karen Ross, eds. *Gender and Newsroom Cultures: Identities at Work.* Cresskill, NJ: Hampton Press, 2004.

DeSalvo, Louise. *Writing as a Way of Healing: How Telling Our Stories Transforms Our Lives.* New York: Harper, 1999.

Didion, Joan. *Slouching towards Bethlehem.* New York: Farrar, Straus & Giroux, 2002.

————. *The Year of Magical Thinking.* New York: Alfred A. Knopf, 2005.

Downie, Leonard, Jr., and Robert G. Kaiser. *The News about the News: American Journalism in Peril.* New York: Vintage Books, 2002.

Durant, Will. *The Story of Philosophy.* New York: Pocket Books, 1961.

Edwards, Julia. *Women of the World: The Great Foreign Correspondents.* Boston: Houghton Mifflin, 1988.

Emery, Edwin. *The Press and America: An Interpretative History of the Mass Media.* 3rd edition. Englewood Cliffs, NJ: Prentice-Hall, 1972.

Enda, Jodi. "Women Journalists See Progress, but Not Nearly Enough." *Nieman Reports* Spring 2002.

Ettema, James S., and Theodore L. Glasser. *Custodians of Conscience: Investigative Journalism and Public Virtue.* New York: Columbia University Press, 1998.

Fallows, Deborah, and Lee Rainie. "Millions Go Online for News and Images Not Covered in the Mainstream Press." Pew Internet and American Life Project. July 8, 2004.

Farquhar, Michael, Mary Hadar, and Robert Barkin, eds. *The Century: History as It Happened on the Front Page of the Capital's Newspaper.* Washington, DC: Washington Post Co., 1999.

Favre, Gregory. "After September 11, Newspapers Are Important Again." www.asne.org. Sept. 15, 2001. Retrieved Sept. 16, 2004.

————. "Forgetting Our Feelings." www.poynter.org. Mar. 22, 2004. Retrieved Sept. 16, 2004.

Fedler, Fred. *Reporting for the Print Media.* 3rd edition. San Diego: Harcourt Brace Jovanovich, 1984.

Fedler, Fred, John R. Bender, Lucinda Davenport, and Michael W. Drager. *Reporting for the Media.* 7th edition. Fort Worth: Harcourt College Publishers, 2001.

Fenton, Tom. *Bad News: The Decline of Reporting, the Business of News, and the Danger to Us All.* New York: Regan Books, 2005.

Fink, Conrad C. *Introduction to Professional Newswriting: Reporting for the Modern Media.* 2nd edition. New York: Longman, 1998.

————. *Introduction to Professional Newswriting: Reporting for the Modern Media.* White Plains, NY: Longman, 1992.

Finnegan, Lisa. *No Questions Asked: News Coverage since 9/11.* Westport, CT: Praeger Publishers, 2007.

Forché, Carolyn, and Philip Gerard, eds. *Writing Creative Nonfiction: Instruction and Insights from Teachers of the Associated Writing Programs.* Cincinnati: Story Press, 2001.

Franklin, Jon. *Writing for Story.* New York: Plume Books, 1986.

Freedman, Eric, Frederick Fico, and Brad Love. "Male and Female Sources in Newspaper Coverage of Male and Female Candidates in U.S. Senate Races in 2004." Newspaper Division of the Association for Education in Journalism and Mass Communication. Michigan State University study, Aug. 2005.

Freedman, Jill, and Gene Combs. *Narrative Therapy: The Social Construction of Preferred Realities.* New York: W. W. Norton, 1995.

Friedman, Thomas L. *The World Is Flat: A Brief History of the Twenty-First Century.* New York: Farrar, Straus & Giroux, 2005.

Fuller, Jack. *News Values: Ideas for an Information Age.* Chicago: University of Chicago Press, 1996.

Garner, Joe, ed. *We Interrupt This Broadcast.* Naperville, IL: Sourcebooks, 2002.

Geisler, Jill. "Leadership Lessons from September 11." www.poynter.org. Aug. 30, 2002. Retrieved Aug. 11, 2004.

Ghiglione, Loren. "The American Journalist: Fiction versus Fact." http://www.ijpc.org/ghiglione.htm. 1991. Retrieved May 11, 2006.

Gill, Peter. "The Basics of Blogging." www.oudaily.com. Apr. 22, 2004. Retrieved May 4, 2005.

Gillmor, Dan. *We the Media: Grassroots Journalism by the People, for the People.* Sebastopol, CA: O'Reilly Media, 2004.

Gladwell, Malcolm. *Blink: The Power of Thinking without Thinking.* New York: Little, Brown and Company, 2005.

———. *The Tipping Point: How Little Things Can Make a Big Difference.* Boston: Little, Brown and Company, 2002.

Goldstein, Tom, ed. *Killing the Messenger: One Hundred Years of Media Criticism.* New York: Columbia University Press, 1989.

Gornick, Vivian. *The Situation and the Story: The Art of Personal Narrative.* New York: Farrar, Straus & Giroux, 2001.

Grabowicz, Paul. "Weblogs Bring Journalists into a Larger Community." *Nieman Reports.* Fall 2003.

Greenspan, Robyn. "As the Blogs Churn." www.clickz.com. Oct. 8, 2003. Retrieved May 5, 2004.

Gubbins, Cara. *Power Stories: Everyday Women Creating Extraordinary Lives.* Mesquite, NY: Jada Press, 2004.

Haller, Beth. "News Coverage of Disability Issues: Final Report for the Center for an Accessible Society." Center for an Accessible Society. *http://www.accessiblesociety.org/topics/converage/0799haller.htm.* 1999. Retrieved Oct. 17, 2005.

Halliman, Tom. "Features Go Beyond Facts." *Quill.* July 1, 2003.

Hamilton, James T. *All The News That's Fit To Sell.* Princeton: Princeton University Press, 2004.

Harrington, Walt. *Intimate Journalism: The Art and Craft of Reporting Everyday Life.* Thousand Oaks, CA: Sage Publications, 1997.

Hartman, Steve. "Living for Moment." www.cbsnews.com. Aug. 6, 2003. Retrieved June 14, 2005.

Hartsock, John C. *A History of American Literary Journalism: The Emergence of a Modern Form.* Amherst: University of Massachusetts Press, 2000.

Hay, Vicky. *The Essential Feature: Writing for Magazines and Newspapers.* New York: Columbia University Press, 1990.

Heider, Don, ed. *Class and News.* Lanham: Rowman & Littlefield Publishers, 2004.

Hewitt, Hugh. *Blog: Understanding the Information Reformation That's Changing Your World.* Nashville, TN: Nelson Business, 2005.

Hohenberg, John. *The New Front Page.* New York: Columbia University Press, 1966.

Itule, Bruce D., and Douglas A. Anderson. *News Writing and Reporting for Today's Media.* 5th edition. Boston: McGraw-Hill Higher Education, 2000.

Jackson, Dennis, and John Sweeney, eds. *The Journalist's Craft.* New York: Allworth Press, 2002.

Jaffer, Zubeida. *Our Generation.* Cape Town, South Africa: Kwela Books, 2003.

Jensen, Rita Henley. "An Internet News Service Reports News and Views of Women." *Nieman Reports.* Spring 2002.

Johnson, Carla. *Twenty-First-Century Feature Writing.* Boston: Pearson Education, 2005.

Jung, C. G. *Memories, Dreams, Reflections.* New York: Vintage Books, 1989.

Kennedy, George, Daryl R. Moen, Don Ranly. *Beyond the Inverted Pyramid: Effective Writing for Newspapers, Magazines and Specialized Publications.* New York: Bedford/ St. Martin's, 1993,

Kerrane, Kevin, and Ben Yagoda, eds. *The Art of Fact: A Historical Anthology of Literary Journalism.* New York: Touchstone, 1997.

Kawamoto, Kevin, ed. *Digital Journalism: Emerging Media and the Changing Horizons of Journalism.* Lanham, MD: Rowman & Littlefield.

King, Stephen. *On Writing: A Memoir of the Craft.* New York: Scribner, 2003.

Kirtley, Jane E. "Bloggers and Their First Amendment Rights." *Nieman Reports.* Fall 2003.

Knudson, Jerry W. *In the News: American Journalists View Their Craft.* Wilmington, DE: Scholarly Resources, 2000.

Kovach, Bill, and Tom Rosenstiel. *The Elements of Journalism: What Newspeople Should Know and the Public Should Expect.* New York: Crown Publishers, 2001.

Kramer, Mark. "Reporting Differently: How to Come Back with a Notebook Full of Narrative. *Nieman Reports.* 2002

Kumar, Deepa. *Class and News.* Lanham, MD: Rowman & Littlefield, 2004.

Kural, Phil. "Reality TV: Why the Hype, and Why the Slump since 9/11?" www.realitynewsonline.com. July 10, 2005. Retrieved July 14, 2005.

Lapham, Chris. "The Evolution of the Newspaper of the Future." http://www.december.com/cmc/mag/1995/jul/lapham.html *CMC Magazine.* July 1, 1995. Retrieved June 8, 2004.

Lauber, Lynn. *Listen to Me: Writing Life into Meaning.* New York: W. W. Norton, 2004.

Lauterer, Jock. "The State of Community Journalism." Huck Boyd National Center for Community Media, July 1999.

LeDuff, Charlie, *Work and Other Sins: Life in New York City and Thereabouts.* New York: Penguin Press, 2004.

Lehrman, Sally. "News as American as America." Knight Foundation Journalism Initiatives. www.knightfdn.org/diversity/index.asp. Oct. 11, 2005. Retrieved Nov. 7, 2005.

Lennon, Sheila. "Blogging Journalisms Invite Outsiders' Reporting" *Nieman Reports.* Fall 2003.

Lepore, Stephen J., and Joshua M. Smyth, eds. *The Writing Cure: How Expressive Writing Promotes Health and Emotional Well-Being.* Washington, DC: American Psychological Association, 2002.

Lesica, J. D. "Blogs and Journalism Need Each Other." *Nieman Reports.* Fall 2003.

Levenson, Michael. "Teen Fatally Shot at Apartment Building Police Seeking Suspect in Hub's Fifty-Eighth Homicide." *Boston Globe.* Oct. 24, 2005.

Levy, Steven. "Bloggers' Delight." www.poynter.org. Apr. 25, 2003. Retrieved May 4, 2004.

Lewis, Jon E., ed. *The Mammoth Book of Journalism.* New York: Carroll & Graf Publishers, 2003.

Lileks, James. "Blog On: Every Laptop Is a Truth Squad." www.nola.com. Jan. 28, 2004. Retrieved Jan. 29, 2004.

Little, John, ed. *The Greatest Minds and Ideas of All Time, Will Durant.* New York: Simon & Schuster, 2002.

Lule, Jack. *Daily News, Eternal Stories: The Mythological Role of Journalism.* New York: Guildford Press, 2001.

Mailer, Norman. *The Spooky Art: Thoughts on Writing.* New York: Random House, 2003.

Maisel, Eric. *Living the Writer's Life: A Complete Self-Help Guide.* New York: Waston-Guptill Publications, 1999.

Mann, Robert S., ed. "Beginnings of the Modern Newspaper: A Comparative Study of St. Louis Dailies from 1875 to 1925." Journalism Series, no. 39. *University of Missouri Bulletin* vol. 27, no. 15 (Feb. 1, 1926).

Marcano, Tony. "Flogging by Blogging: Sorry, Editing Isn't Censorship." www.sacbee.com. Sept. 28, 2003. Retrieved May 11, 2004.

Marovich, Peter. "Everyday Heroes." *Harrisonburg [VA] Daily News Record.* Aug. 1, 2005

Martin, Eric, and Christi Ravenberg. "Students Spring into Action for Final Project." www.medill.northwestern.edu. Retrieved June 18, 2004.

McAdams, Dan, P. *The Redemptive Self: Stories Americans Live By.* New York: Oxford University Press, 2006.

McChesney, Robert W. *The Problem of the Media: U.S. Communication Politics in the Twenty-First Century.* New York: Monthly Review Press, 2004.

McChesney, Robert W., Russell Newman, and Ben Scott, eds. *The Future of the Media: Resistance and Reform in the Twenty-First Century.* New York: Seven Stories Press, 2005.

McCollum, Douglas. "A Way Out: How Newspapers Might Escape Wall Street and Redeem Their Future." *Columbia Journalism Review.* Jan./Feb. 2006.

McGuire, Tim. "I Prayed for Wisdom." Asne.org http://www.asne.org/index.cfm?ID=632. Sept. 25, 2001. Retrieved June 17, 2004.

Merrill, John C. *Existential Journalism.* New York: Hastings House Publishers, 1977.

————. *Twilight of Press Freedom: The Rise of People's Journalism.* Mahweh, NJ: Lawrence Erlbaum Associates, 2001.

Merritt, Davis. *Knightfall: Knight Ridder and How the Erosion of Newspaper Journalism is Putting Democracy at Risk.* New York: AMACOM, 2005.

Meyer, Philip. *The Vanishing Newspaper: Saving Journalism in the Information Age.* Columbia: University of Missouri Press, 2004.

Miller, Michael J. "The Democratization of Content." *PC Magazine.* http://www.pcmag.com/article2/0,1895,1862161,00.asp. Sept. 28, 2005. Retrieved Oct. 1, 2005.

Mills, Eleanor, and Kira Cochrane. *Journalistas.* New York: Carroll & Graf, 2005.

Mills, Kay. *A Place in the News: From the Women's Pages to the Front Page.* New York: Dodd, Mead & Company, 1988.

Mindich, David T. Z. *Just the Facts: How "Objectivity" Came to Define American Journalism.* New York: New York University Press, 1998.

———. *Tuned Out: Why Americans under Forty Don't Follow the News.* New York: Oxford University Press, 2005.

Mitchell, Bill. "Weblogs: A Road Back to Basics." *Nieman Review.* Fall 2003.

———. "September 11, 2002: Chronicling the Coverage." www.poynter .org. Jan. 9, 2003. Retrieved June 9, 2004.

Mnookin, Seth. *Hard News: The Scandals at the New York Times and the Future of American Media.* New York: Random House, 2004.

Mooney, Chris. Forum. "How Blogging Changed Journalism—Almost." www.postgazette.com. Feb. 2, 2003. Retrieved Dec. 10, 2005.

Moors, Julie, M. "Journalism Continues to Be a Risky Occupation." www.poynter.org. Sept. 10, 2003. Retrieved June 9, 2004.

Napoli, Philip. *Audience Economics: Media Institutions and the Audience Marketplace.* New York: Columbia University Press, 2003.

Narayanan, V. Raman. "Covering Local News with International Perspective." *Associated Press Managing Editors News.* Spring 2003.

Nord, David Paul. *Communities of Journalism: A History of American Newspapers and Their Readers.* Urbana: University of Illinois Press, 2001.

O'Connell, Vanessa. "U.S. Suspends TV Ad Campaign Aimed at Winning Over Muslims." *Wall Street Journal.* Jan. 16, 2003.

Olafson, Steve. "Reporter Is Fired for Writing a Weblog." *Nieman Reports.* Fall 2003.

Orfi, Danielle. *Incidental Findings: Lessons from My Patients in the Art of Medicine.* Boston: Beacon Press, 2005.

Outing, Steve. "News Weblogs: To Edit or Not to Edit." www.poynter.org. July 18, 2002. Retrieved June 9, 2004.

———. "Weblogs: Put Them to Work in Your Newsroom." www .poynter.org. July 18, 2002. Retrieved June 9, 2004.

———. "9/11: Outside U.S., It Doesn't Mean the Same Thing." www.poynter.org. Nov. 15, 2001. Retrieved June 9, 2004.

———. "The First Shock of History." www.poynter.org. Nov. 15, 2001. Retrieved June 9, 2004.

Overholser, Geneva, and Kathleen Hall Jamieson, eds. *The Press.* New York: Oxford University Press, 2005.

Parks, Perry. *Making Important News Interesting: Reporting Public Affairs in the Twenty-First Century.* Oak Park, IL: Marion Street Press, 2006.

Patterson, Thomas E. *Out of Order.* New York: Vintage Books, 1994.

Paul, Nora. "'New News' Retrospective: Is Online News Reaching Its Potential?" *Online Journalism Review.* Mar. 25, 2005.

Pennebaker, James, ed. *Emotion, Disclosure, and Health.* Washington, DC: American Psychological Association, 2002.

————. *Opening Up: The Healing Power of Expressing Emotions.* New York: Guilford Press, 1997.

Picard, Robert G. "Commercialism and Newspaper Quality." *Newspaper Research Journal.* Jan. 1, 2004.

Pilger, John, ed. *Tell Me No Lies: Investigative Journalism That Changed the World.* New York: Avalon, 2005.

Pink, Daniel H. *A Whole New Mind: Why Right-Brainers Will Rule the Future.* New York: Penguin, 2005.

Pryor, Larry. "A Weblog Sharpens Journalism Students' Skills." *Nieman Reports.* Fall 2003.

Quinn, Stephen, and Vincent F. Filak. *Convergent Journalism: An Introduction.* Amsterdam: Focal Press, 2005.

Rainie, Lee. "How Americans Used the Internet after the Terror Attack." Pew Internet and American Life Project. Sept. 15, 2001.

Rainie, Lee, Susannah Fox, and Mary Madden et al. "One Year Later: September 11 and the Internet." Pew Internet and American Life Project. Sept. 5, 2002.

Rainier, Tristine. *Your Life as Story.* New York: J. P. Tarcher, 1997.

Regan, Tom. "Weblogs Threaten and Inform Traditional Journalism." *Nieman Reports.* Fall 2003.

Reynolds, Glenn Harlan. "Weblogs and Journalism: Back to the Future." *Nieman Reports.* Fall 2003.

Roberts, Gene, editor-in-chief, and Thomas Kunkel, general editor. *Breach of Faith: A Crisis of Coverage in the Age of Corporate Newspapering.* Fayetteville: University of Arkansas Press, 2002.

Robertson, Nan. *The Girls in the Balcony: Women, Men, and the New York Times.* New York: Random House, 1992.

Rodriguez, Ilia. "Diversity Writing and the Imaginaries of Liberal Multiculturalism in the U.S. Mainstream Press." Minorities and Communication Division of Association for Education in Journalism and Mass Communication. Aug. 2005.

Roeper, Richard. "Today's Reality Shows Would Make Even Allen Funt Blush." *Chicago Sun-Times.* www.suntimes.com. June 10, 2004. Retrieved July 8, 2005.

Rosenstiel, Tom. "Snob Journalism: Elitism versus Ethics for a Profession in Crisis." Ruhl Symposium Speech. Journalism.org. http://www .journalism.org/resources/publications/articles/oregon.asp. May 22, 2003. Retrieved Feb. 7, 2006.

Rosenstiel, Tom, and Amy S. Mitchell, eds. *Thinking Clearly: Cases in Journalistic Decision-Making.* New York: Columbia University Press, 2003.

Rothmyer, Karen. *Winning Pulitzers: The Stories behind Some of the Best News Coverage of Our Time.* New York: Columbia University Press, 1991.

Rountree, Cathleen. *The Writer's Mentor: A Guide to Putting Passion on Paper.* Berkeley, CA: Conari Press, 2002.

Rush, Ramona R., Carol E. Oukrop, and Pamela J. Creedon, eds. *Seeking Equity for Women in Journalism and Mass Communication Education: A Thirty-Year Update.* Mahwah, NJ: Lawrence Erlbaum Associates, 2004.

Russell, Jenna, and Beth Daley. "Hope, Love, Fuel Family's Search Shrewsbury Woman, Twenty-four, Disappeared Two Weeks Ago." *Boston Globe.* Oct. 24.

Ryan, Michael, and James W. Tankard Jr. *Writing for Print and Digital Media.* Boston: McGraw-Hill, 2005.

Scanlan, Christopher. *Reporting and Writing: Basics for the Twenty-First Century.* Fort Worth: Harcourt College Publishers, 2000.

Schneider, Myra, and John Killick. *Writing for Self-Discovery.* Boston: Element Books, 1998.

Schudson, Michael. *The Power of News.* Cambridge: Harvard University Press, 1995.

———. *The Sociology of News.* New York: W. W. Norton & Company, 2003.

Seaton, Edward. "September 11: A Wake-Up Call for Foreign News." www.poynter.org. Nov. 15, 2001. Retrieved June 9, 2004.

Shafer, Jack. "Not Just Another Column about Blogging." Slate.com http://www.slate.com/toolbar.aspx?action=print&id=2134918. Jan. 30, 2006. Retrieved Feb. 5, 2006.

Shapiro, Stephanie. *Reinventing the Feature Story: Mythic Cycles in American Literary Journalism.* Baltimore, MD: Apprentice House, 2005.

Shaw, Donald L., Maxwell McCombs, and Gerry Keir. *Advanced Reporting: Discovering Patterns in News Events.* 2nd edition. Prospect Heights, IL: Waveland Press, 1997.

Sims, Norman, ed. *The Literary Journalists.* New York: Ballantine Books, 1984.

Slade, David. "Service in Retrospect." *Quill.* July 1, 2003.

Smith, Jay R. "My Twenty Wishes for 2006." Presstime. http://www.naa .org/presstime/PTArtPage.cfm?AID=7376 Jan. 9, 2006. Retrieved Feb. 5, 2006.

Smith, Michael Ray. *Featurewriting.net: A Guide to Writing in the Electronic Age.* Bloomington, IL: Epistelogic, 2005.

Spotts, Carle B. *Ideas and Patterns for Writing.* New York: Holt, Rinehart & Winston, 1967.

Stanek, Lou Willett. *Writing Your Life: Putting Your Past on Paper.* New York: Avon Books, 1996.

Steinman, Rob. "Babble." www.digitaljournalist.com. June 2004. Retrieved July 16, 2005.

Stepp, Carl Sessions. "I'll Be Brief." *American Journalism Review.* Aug./Sept. 2005.

Stewart, James B. *Follow the Story: How to Write Successful Nonfiction.* New York: Touchstone, 1998.

Stovall, James. *Journalism: Who, What, When, Where, Why and How.* New York: Pearson, 2004.

Surowiecki, James. *The Wisdom of Crowds: Why the Many Are Smarter than the Few and How Collective Wisdom Shapes Business, Economies, Societies, and Nations.* New York: Doubleday, 2004.

Talese, Gay. "Writing about Ordinary Lives." *Nieman Reports.* Spring 2002.

Toolan, Brian. "An Editor Acts to Limit a Staffer's Weblog." *Nieman Reports.* Fall 2003.

Tuggles, C. A., Forest Carr, and Suzanne Huffman, eds. *Broadcast News Handbook: Writing, Reporting and Producing in a Converging Media World.* Boston: McGraw-Hill, 2000.

Vannatta, Jerry, Ronald Schliefer, and Sheila Crow. *Medicine and Humanistic Understanding: The Significance of Narrative in Medical Practices* (CD-ROM). Philadelphia: University of Pennsylvania Press, 2005.

Watson, Warren. Using Narrative Style. *www.asne.org.* Retrieved Aug. 18, 2004. (Jan. 9, 2003)

Weingarten, Marc. *The Gang That Wouldn't Write Straight: Wolfe, Thompson, Didion, and the New Journalism Revolution.* New York: Crown Publishers, 2006.

Weisstuch, Liza. "Talking Stories: Nieman Hosts 'Narrative Journalism' Luminaries at Conference." *Harvard University Gazette* (Dec. 3, 2001).

Wendland, Mike. "Blogging Connects a Columnist to New Story Ideas." *Nieman Reports.* Fall 2003.

Whalen, Patricia T. *The Changing Landscape of Print and Online Media*. New York: NewsMarket, 2006.

White, Theodore H. *In Search of History: A Personal Adventure*. New York: Harper & Row, 1978.

Wicker, Tom. *On The Record: An Insider's Guide to Journalism*. Boston: Bedford/St. Martin's, 2002.

Wilber, Rick, and Randy Miller. *Modern Media Writing*. Belmont, CA: Wadsworth, 2003.

Wilgoren, Jodi. "Tender Stories from Family Position Kerry in a Soft Light." *www.nytimes.com* Retrieved Aug. 10, 2004. (July 30, 2003)

Willey, Keven Ann. "Readers Glimpse an Editorial Board's Thinking." *Nieman Reports*. Fall 2003.

Wilson, Marie. "Who's Talking Now: A Follow-up Analysis of Guest Appearances by Women on the Sunday Morning Talk Shows." White House Project. *http://www.thewhitehouseproject .org/v2/researchandreports/whostalking/whos_talking_2005.pdf* Retrieved Nov. 9, 2005 (Oct. 2005).

Winfield, Betty Houchin, and Janice Hume. "The American Hero and the Evolution of the Human Interest Story." *American Journalism*. Spring 1998.

Wood, Monica. *Description*. Cincinnati: Writer's Digest Books, 1995.

Woods, Keith M. "What Journalism Needs Now: Independence and Courage." www.poynter.org. (Sept. 28, 2001) Retrieved June 9, 2004.

Zelizer, Barbie, and Stuart Allan, eds. *Journalism after September 11*. New York: Routledge, 2002.

———. *Taking Journalism Seriously*. Thousand Oaks, CA: Sage Publications, 2004.

Index

ABC News, 27
Abrahamson, David, 104
Accuracy, 159
Advertising, 144
Advertising Age, 27, 156–57
Advocate, The, 133
ADWEEK, 5
Ahrens, Frank, 152
ALANA, 130
Alicia Patterson Foundation, 13
All the President's Men, 75
American Express, 146
American Public Media, 20
American Society of Newspaper Editors (ASNE), 130
Amoss, Jim, 61
Anchorage Daily News, 181–83
Anderson, Chris, 8, 29
Approaches: anecdotal, 17–18, 63–64, 101–4; democratic, 19–20, 44, 117, 138; feature approaches to hard news, 35–40; humanistic, 39; summary, 111. *See also* Inverted pyramid; Narrative
Arizona Republic, 184–86
Arkansas Democrat-Gazette, 37, 38, 110, 187–89
Armao, Rosemary, 24
Armstrong, Orlando Kay, 6, 162
Aspen Institute, The, 153
Associated Press, The (AP), 21, 27
Atlanta Journal-Constitution, 47, 91, 129, 190–92
Audience, 153, 155
Audit Bureau of Circulations, 55
Auletta, Ken, 45, 58, 62, 90
Auster, Paul, 136
Austin American-Statesman, 79, 82
Authenticity, 29

Bacon's Newspaper/Magazine Directory, 32
Baker, Bob, 151
Banaszynski, Jacqui, 97–98
Baquet, Dean, 112
Barnicle, Mike, 113
Battelle, John, 155
Benham, Kelly, 108
Bennett, Amanda, 12
Berke, Rick, 12
Bernstein, Carl, 75
Blais, Madeleine, 25
Blethen Maine Newspapers, 32
Blevens, Frederick R., 16
BlogBurst, 79
Blogs, 10–12, 42, 68, 77–78, 81, 85–86; bloguage, 82; gender in, 78; and professional journalists, 92; vs. citizen journalism, 78
Boczkowski, Pablo, 6, 13, 45, 153
Boo, Katherine, 110
Boston Globe, 116, 193–95
Botox Cosmetic, 145
Bottom-line pressures, 57
Bowden, Mark, 100, 114
Boynton, Robert S., 26
Bragg, Rick, 139
Breuer, Josef, 133
Briski, Zana, 13
Broder, David S., 75–76
Bruner, Jerome S., 141–42
Bucci, Wilma, 135
Bulkeley, Christy, 119
Burnham, David, 13
Buzzmachine.com, 77

Callinan, Tom, 34, 42–43
Campbell, Joseph, 139
Capote, Truman, 100